ECONOMIC AND SOCIAL HISTORY OF ANCIENT INDIA

Encyclopaedic History of India Series

ECONOMIC AND SOCIAL HISTORY OF ANCIENT INDIA

Dr. Mahesh Vikram Singh
Professor, Deptt. of History
Mahatma Gandhi Kashi Vidyapeeth
Varanasi (UP)

Dr. Brij Bhushan Shrivastava
Head of Deptt., Ancient History, Archeology & Culture
SMMTPG College, Ballia (UP)

CENTRUM PRESS
NEW DELHI-110002 (INDIA)

CENTRUM PRESS
H.O.: 4360/4, Ansari Road, Daryaganj,
New Delhi-110002 (India)
Tel: 23278000, 23261597, 23255577, 23286875
B.O.: No. 1015, Ist Main Road, BSK IIIrd Stage,
IIIrd Phase, IIIrd Block, Bangalore-560085 (INDIA)
Tel: 080-41723429
Email: centrumpress@gmail.com
Visit us at: www.centrumpress.com

Economic and Social History of Ancient India

First Edition, 2011

ISBN 978-93-80836-65-2

PRINTED IN INDIA

Printed at Mehra Offset Press, Delhi

प्रो. विपिन चंद्रा
अध्यक्ष
Prof. Bipan Chandra
Chairman

नेशनल बुक ट्रस्ट, इंडिया
नेहरू भवन
5 इंस्टीट्यूशनल एरिया, फेज़-II, वसंत कुंज, नई दिल्ली-110 070
फोन/ Phone: 011-26121880 फैक्स/ Fax: 011-26121883

NATIONAL BOOK TRUST, INDIA
Nehru Bhawan
5 Institutional Area, Phase II, Vasant Kunj, New Delhi-110 070
ई-मेल / E-mail: chairman@nbtindia.org.in
वेबसाइट / Website: www.nbtindia.org.in

FOREWORD

The term 'history' is derived from the Greek word 'historia' that means knowledge acquired through investigation. Obviously, this knowledge can be correct if the method of investigation is objective and not vitiated by any kind of bias. In other words, if the study of human past is comprehensive and obtained through scientific inquiry, it can provide perspective on the present day problems and help one plan for the future.

A true historian has to identify the sources that can be most useful in a given context. Documents, coins, archaeology, anthropology, geography, travel accounts, oral traditions, mythology and so on can be useful but they can be used only after their veracity is tested and they are critically examined. They should be checked and counter-checked.

Over the centuries, one finds the study and writing of history vitiated by biases. There are numerous instances in which historical data have been distorted to support or oppose certain preconceived ideas and purposes. Strictly speaking such history is just like fiction to accord with preconceived notions and serve some ulterior purposes.

The study of the past has never been static. Conclusions go on changing because of the discovery of new materials and tools of investigation. To give a concrete example, the carbon 14 or radiocarbon dating test has revolutionized the study of civilizations and settlements, especially of prehistoric times, for which written documents, coins, etc. are seldom available. This method has enabled historians to determine more accurately than before the time period of a particular civilization or settlement. This method was discovered only 70 years ago by American scientists.

In our country, excavations brought to light the Indus Valley Civilization and its various features, hitherto unknown. Similarly, no complete text of Kautilya's Arthashastra was available before it was discovered by Shamasastry, the chief of the Mysore Government Oriental Library in the first decade of the last century. Likewise, people's knowledge of the history of the Buddhist period got extended after excavations at Sarnath and the ruins of the Asokan period at Patna. In the future, if the Harappan inscriptions are deciphered, our knowledge of the Indus Valley Civilization will increase enormously. All these instances underline the fact that our knowledge of history is never static and its frontiers go on extending.

In the light of what has been said above the encyclopedic history is going to be of great help to students interested in Indian history. It is comprehensive and as far as possible free from biases. It includes the latest materials, and objective conclusions.

Prof . Bipan Chandra

Professor Emeritus, JNU

Chairman, National Book Trust, India

Contents

Preface

The people of India have had a continuous civilization since 2500 B.C., when the inhabitants of the Indus River valley developed an urban culture based on commerce and sustained by agricultural trade. This civilization declined around 1500 B.C., probably due to ecological changes. During the second millennium B.C., pastoral, Aryan-speaking tribes migrated from the northwest into the subcontinent. As they settled in the middle Ganges River valley, they adapted to antecedent cultures.

The political map of ancient and medieval India was made up of myriad kingdoms with fluctuating boundaries. In the 4th and 5th centuries A.D., northern India was unified under the Gupta Dynasty. During this period, known as India's Golden Age, Hindu culture and political administration reached new heights. Islam spread across the Indian subcontinent over a period of 500 years. In the 10th and 11th centuries, Turks and Afghans invaded India and established sultanates in Delhi. In the early 16th century, descendants of Genghis Khan swept across the Khyber Pass and established the Mughal (Mogul) Dynasty, which lasted for 200 years. From the 11th to the 15th centuries, southern India was dominated by Hindu Chola and Vijayanagar Dynasties. During this time, the two systems—the prevailing Hindu and Muslim—mingled, leaving lasting cultural influences on each other.

The first British outpost in South Asia was established in 1619 at Surat on the northwestern coast. Later in the century, the East India Company opened permanent trading stations at Madras, Bombay, and Calcutta, each under the protection of native rulers. The British expanded their influence from these footholds until, by the 1850s, they controlled most of present-day India, Pakistan, and Bangladesh. In 1857, a rebellion in north India led by mutinous Indian soldiers caused the British Parliament to transfer all political power from the East India Company to the Crown. Great Britain began administering most of India directly while controlling the rest through treaties with local rulers.

In the late 1800s, the first steps were taken toward self-government in British India with the appointment of Indian councillors to advise the British viceroy and the establishment of provincial councils with Indian members; the British subsequently widened participation in legislative councils. Beginning in 1920, Indian leader Mohandas K. Gandhi transformed the Indian National Congress political party into a mass movement to campaign against British colonial rule.

—Authors

1

Kautilya on the Scope and Methodology of Economy

The Duties of Government Superintendents

Formation of Villages

Either by inducing foreigners to immigrate (*paradesapravahanena*) or by causing the thickly-populated centres of his own kingdom to send forth the excessive population (*svadesabhishyandavamanena va*), the king may construct villages either on new sites or on old ruins (*bhutapurvama va*). Villages consisting each of not less than a hundred families and of not more than five-hundred families of agricultural people of *sudra* caste, with boundaries extending as far as a *krosa* (2250 yds.) or two, and capable of protecting each other shall be formed. Boundaries shall be denoted by a river, a mountain, forests, bulbous plants (*grishti*), caves, artificial buildings (*setubandha*), or by trees such as *salmali* (silk cotton tree), sami (*Acacia Suma*), and kshiravriksha (milky trees).

There shall be set up a *sthaniya* (a fortress of that name) in the centre of eight-hundred villages, a dronamukha in the centre of four-hundred villages, a kharvatika in the centre of two-hundred villages and sangrahana in the midst of a collection of ten villages. There shall be constructed in the extremities of the kingdom forts manned by boundary-guards (*antapala*) whose duty shall be to guard the entrances into the kingdom. The interior of the kingdom shall be watched by trap-keepers (*vagurika*), archers (*sabara*), hunters (*pulinda*), chandalas, and wild tribes (*aranyachara*). Those who perform sacrifices (*ritvik*), spiritual guides, priests, and those learned in the Vedas shall be granted Brahmadaya lands yielding sufficient produce and exempted from taxes and fines (*adandkarani*).

Superintendents, Accountants, Gopas, Sthanikas, Veterinary Surgeons (*Anikastha*), physicians, horse-trainers, and messengers shall also be endowed with lands which they shall have no right to alienate by sale or mortgage. Lands prepared for cultivation shall be given to tax-payers (*karada*) only for life (*ekapurushikani*). Unprepared lands shall not be taken away from those who are preparing them for cultivation.

Lands may be confiscated from those who do not cultivate them; and given to others; or they may be cultivated by village labourers (*gramabhritaka*) and traders (*vaidehaka*), lest those owners who do not properly cultivate them might pay less (to the government). If cultivators pay their taxes easily, they may be favourably supplied with grains, cattle, and money.

The king shall bestow on cultivators only such favour and remission (*anugrahapariharau*) as will tend to swell the treasury, and shall avoid such as will deplete it. A king with depleted treasury will eat into the very vitality of both citizens and country people. Either on the occasion of opening new settlements or on any other emergent occasions, remission of taxes shall be made. He shall regard with fatherly kindness those who have passed the period of remission of taxes.

He shall carry on mining operations and manufactures, exploit timber and elephant forests, offer facilities for cattlebreeding and commerce, construct roads for traffic both by land and water, and set up market towns (*panyapattana*).

He shall also construct reservoirs (*setu*) filled with water either perennial or drawn from some other source. Or he may provide with sites, roads, timber, and other necessary things those who construct reservoirs of their own accord. Likewise in the construction of places of pilgrimage (*punyasthana*) and of groves.

Whoever stays away from any kind of cooperative construction (*sambhuya setubhandhat*) shall send his servants and bullocks to carry on his work, shall have a share in the expenditure, but shall have no claim to the profit.

The king shall exercise his right of ownership (*swamyam*) with regard to fishing, ferrying and trading in vegetables (*haritapanya*) in reservoirs or lakes (*setushu*).

Those who do not heed the claims of their slaves (*dasa*), hirelings (*ahitaka*), and relatives shall be taught their duty. The king shall provide the orphans, (*bala*), the aged, the infirm, the afflicted, and the helpless with maintenance. He shall also provide subsistence to helpless women when they are carrying and also to the children they give birth to. Elders among the villagers shall improve the property of bereaved minors till the latter attain their age; so also the property of Gods.

When a capable person other than an apostate (*patita*) or mother neglects to maintain his or her child, wife, mother, father, minor brothers, sisters, or widowed girls (*kanya vidhavascha*), he or she shall be punished with a fine of twelve panas. When, without making provision for the maintenance of his wife and sons, any person embraces ascetism, he shall be punished with the first amercement; likewise any person who converts a woman to ascetism (*pravrajayatah*).

Whoever has passed the age of copulation may become an ascetic after distributing the properties of his own acquisition (among his sons); otherwise, he will be punished.

No ascetic other than a *vanaprastha* (forest-hermit), no company other than the one of local birth (*sajatadanyas-sanghah*), and no guilds of any kind other than local cooperative guilds (*samutthayika-danyassamayanubandhah*) shall find entrance into the villages of the kingdom. Nor shall there be in villages buildings (*salah*) intended for sports and plays. Nor, in view of procuring money, free labour, commodities, grains, and liquids in plenty, shall actors, dancers, singers, drummers, buffoons (*vagjivana*), and bards (*kusilava*) make any disturbance to the work of the villagers; for helpless villagers are always dependent and bent upon their fields.

The king shall avoid taking possession of any country which is liable to the inroads of enemies and wild tribes and which is harassed by frequent visitations of famine and pestilence. He shall also keep away from expensive sports.

He shall protect agriculture from the molestation of oppressive fines, free labour, and taxes (*dandavishtikara-badhaih*); herds of cattle from thieves, tigers, poisonous creatures and cattle-disease. He shall not only clear roads of traffic from the molestations of courtiers (*vallabha*), of workmen (*karmika*), of robbers, and of boundary-guards, but also keep them from being destroyed by herds of cattle.

Thus the king shall not only keep in good repair timber and elephant forests, buildings, and mines created in the past, but also set up new ones.

Division of Land

The King shall make provision for pasture grounds on uncultivable tracts. Brahmans shall be provided with forests for soma plantation, for religious learning, and for the performance of penance, such forests being rendered safe from the dangers from animate or inanimate objects, and being named after the tribal name (*gotra*) of the Brahmans resident therein.

A forest as extensive as the above, provided with only one entrance rendered inaccessible by the construction of ditches all round, with plantations of delicious fruit trees, bushes, bowers, and thornless trees, with an expansive lake of water full of harmless animals, and with tigers (*vyala*), beasts of prey (*margayuka*), male and female elephants, young elephants, and bisons—all deprived of their claws and teeth—shall be formed for the king's sports.

On the extreme limit of the country or in any other suitable locality, another game-forest with game-beasts; open to all, shall also be made. In view of procuring all kinds of forest-produce described elsewhere, one or several forests shall be specially reserved.

Manufactories to prepare commodities from forest produce shall also be set up.

Wild tracts shall be separated from timber-forests. In the extreme limit of the country, elephant forests, separated from wild tracts, shall be formed. The superintendent of forests with his retinue of forest guards shall not only maintain the upkeep of the forests, but also acquaint himself with all passages for entrance into, or exit from such of them as are mountainous or boggy or contain rivers or lakes.

Whoever kills an elephant shall be put to death.

Whoever brings in the pair of tusks of an elephant, dead from natural causes, shall receive a reward of four-and-a-half panas.

Guards of elephant forests, assisted by those who rear elephants, those who enchain the legs of elephants, those who guard the boundaries, those who live in forests, as well as by those who nurse elephants, shall, with the help of five or seven female elephants to help in tethering wild ones, trace the whereabouts of herds of elephants by following the course of urine and dungs left by elephants and along forest-tracts covered over with branches of Bhallataki (*Semicarpus Anacardium*), and by observing the spots where elephants slept or sat before or left dungs, or where they had just destroyed the banks of rivers or lakes. They shall also precisely ascertain whether any mark is due to the movements of elephants in herds, of an elephant roaming single, of a stray elephant, of a leader of herds, of a tusker, of a rogue elephant, of an elephant in rut, of a young elephant, or of an elephant that has escaped from the cage.

Experts in catching elephants shall follow the instructions given to them by the elephant doctor (*anikastha*) and catch such elephants as are possessed of auspicious characteristics and good character. The victory of kings (in battles) depends mainly upon elephants; for elephants, being of large bodily frame, are capable not only to destroy the arrayed army of an enemy, his fortifications, and encampments, but also to undertake works that are dangerous to life.

Elephants bred in countries, such as Kalinga, Anga, Karusa, and the East are the best; those of the Dasarna and western countries are of middle quality; and those of Saurashtra and Panchajana countries are of low quality. The might and energy of all can, however, be improved by suitable training.

The Business of Collection of Revenue by the Collector-general

The Collector-General shall attend to (the collection of revenue from) forts (*durga*), country-parts (*rashtra*), mines (*khani*), buildings and gardens (*setu*), forests (*vana*), herds of cattle (*vraja*), and roads of traffic (*vanikpatha*).

Tolls, fines, weights and measures, the town-clerk (*nagaraka*), the superintendent of coinage (*lakshanadhyakshah*), the superintendent of seals and passports, liquor, slaughter of animals, threads, oils, ghee, sugar (*kshara*), the state-goldsmith (*sauvarnika*), the warehouse of merchandise, the prostitute, gambling, building sites (*vastuka*), the corporation of artisans and handicrafts-men (*karusilpiganah*), the superintendent of gods, and taxes collected at the gates and from the people (known as) *Bahirikas* come under the head of forts.

Produce from crown-lands (*sita*), portion of produce payable to the government (*bhaga*), religious taxes (*bali*), taxes paid in money (*kara*), merchants, the superintendent of rivers, ferries, boats, and ships, towns, pasture grounds, road-cess (*vartani*), ropes (*rajju*) and ropes to bind thieves (*chorarajju*) come under the head of country parts.

Gold, silver, diamonds, gems, pearls, corals, conch-shells, metals (*loha*), salt, and other minerals extracted from plains and mountain slopes come under the head of mines.

Flower-gardens, fruit-gardens, vegetable-gardens, wet fields, and fields where crops are grown by sowing roots for seeds (*mulavapah, i.e.*, sugar-cane crops, etc.) come under *setu*.

Game-forests, timber-forests, and elephant-forests are forests. Cows, buffaloes, goats, sheep, asses, camels, horses, and mules come under the head of herds. Land and water ways are the roads of traffic. All these form the body of income (*ayasariram*).

Capital (*mula*), share (*bhaga*), premia (*vyaji*), *parigha* fixed taxes (*klripta*), premia on coins (*rupika*), and fixed fines (*atyaya*) are the several forms of revenue (*ayamukha, i.e.*, the mouth from which income is to issue).

The chanting of auspicious hymns during the worship of gods and ancestors, and on the occasion of giving gifts, the harem, the kitchen, the establishment of messengers, the storehouse, the armoury, the warehouse, the storehouse of raw materials, manufactories (*karmanta*), free labourers (*vishti*), maintenance of infantry, cavalry, chariots, and elephants, herds of cows, the museum of beasts, deer, birds, and snakes, and storage of firewood and fodder constitute the body of expenditure (*vyayasariram*).

The royal year, the month, the *paksha*, the day, the dawn (*vyushta*), the third and seventh *pakshas* of (the seasons such as) the rainy season, the winter season, and the summer short of their days, the rest complete, and a separate intercalary month are (the divisions of time). He shall also pay attention to the work in hand (*karaniya*), the work accomplished (*siddham*), part of a work in hand (*sesha*), receipts, expenditure, and net balance.

The business of upkeeping the government (*samsthanam*), the routine work (*pracharah*), the collection of necessaries of life, the collection and audit of all kinds of revenue,—these constitute the work in hand. That which has been credited to the treasury; that which has been taken by the king; that which has been spent in connection with the capital city not entered (into the register) or continued from year before last, the royal command dictated or orally intimated to be entered (into the register),—all these constitute the work accomplished.

Preparation of plans for profitable works, balance of fines due, demand for arrears of revenue kept in abeyance, and examination of accounts,—these constitute what is called part of a work in hand which may be of little or no value.

Receipts may be (1) current, (2) last balance, and (3) accidental (*anyajatah*= received from external source).

What is received day after day is termed current (*vartamana*).

Whatever has been brought forward from year before last, whatever is in the hands of others, and whatever has changed hands is termed last balance (*puryushita*).

Whatever has been lost and forgotten (by others), fines levied from government servants, marginal revenue (*parsva*), compensation levied for any damage (*parihinikam*), presentations to the king, the property of those who have fallen victims to epidemics (*damaragatakasvam*) leaving no sons, and treasure-troves— all these constitute accidental receipts.

Investment of capital (*vikshepa*), the relics of a wrecked undertaking, and the savings from an estimated outlay are the means to check expenditure (*vyayapratyayah*).

The rise in price of merchandise due to the use of different weights and measures in selling is termed *vyaji*; the enhancement of price due to bidding among buyers is also another source of profit. Expenditure is of two kinds—daily expenditure and profitable expenditure. What is continued every day is daily.

Whatever is earned once in a *paksha*, a month, or a year is termed profit.

Whatever is spent on these two heads is termed as daily expenditure and profitable expenditure respectively.

That which remains after deducting all the expenditure already incurred and excluding all revenue to be realised is net balance (*nivi*) which may have been either just realised or brought forward.

Thus a wise collector-general shall conduct the work of revenue-collection, increasing the income and decreasing the expenditure.

The Business of Keeping up Accounts in the Office of Accountants

The superintendent of accounts shall have the accountant's office constructed with its door facing either the north or the east, with seats (for clerks) kept apart and with shelves of account-books well arranged.

Therein the number of several departments; the description of the work carried on and of the results realised in several manufactories (*Karmanta*); the amount of profit, loss, expenditure, delayed earnings, the amount of *vyaji* (premia in kind or cash) realised,—the status of government agency employed, the amount of wages paid, the number of free labourers engaged (*vishti*) pertaining to the investment of capital on any work; likewise in the case of gems and commodities of superior or inferior value, the rate of their price, the rate of their barter, the counterweights (*pratimana*) used in weighing them, their number, their weight, and their cubical measure; the history of customs, professions, and transactions of countries, villages, families, and corporations; the gains in the form of gifts to the king's courtiers, their title to possess and enjoy lands, remission of taxes allowed to them, and payment of provisions and salaries to them; the gains to the wives and sons of the king in gems, lands, prerogatives, and provisions made to remedy evil portents; the treaties with, issues of ultimatum to, and payments of tribute from or to, friendly or inimical kings,—all these shall be regularly entered in prescribed registers.

From these books the superintendent shall furnish the accounts as to the forms of work in hand, of works accomplished, of part of works in hand, of receipts, of expenditure, of net balance, and of tasks to be undertaken in each of the several departments. To supervise works of high, middling and low description, superintendents with corresponding qualifications shall be employed. The king will have to suffer in the end if he curtails the fixed amount of expenditure on profitable works.

(When a man engaged by Government for any work absents himself), his sureties who conjointly received (wages) from the government, or his sons, brothers, wives, daughters or servants living upon his work shall bear the loss caused to the Government.

The work of 354 days and nights is a year. Such a work shall be paid for more or less in proportion to its quantity at the end of the month, *Ashadha* (about the middle of July). (The work during) the intercalary month shall be (separately) calculated.

A government officer, not caring to know the information gathered by espionage and neglecting to supervise the despatch of work in his own department as regulated, may occasion loss of revenue to the government owing to his ignorance, or owing to his idleness when he is too weak to endure the trouble of activity, or due to inadvertence in perceiving sound and other objects of sense, or by being timid when he is afraid of clamour, unrighteousness, and untoward results, or owing to selfish desire when he is favourably disposed towards those who are desirous to achieve their own selfish ends, or by cruelty due to anger, or by lack of dignity when he is surrounded by a host of learned and needy sycophants, or by making use of false balance, false measures, and false calculation owing to greediness.

The school of Manu hold that a fine equal to the loss of revenue and multiplied by the serial number of the circumstances of the guilt just narrated in order shall be imposed upon him.

The school of *Parasara* hold that the fine in all the cases shall be eight times the amount lost. The school of *Brihaspathi* say that it shall be ten times the amount. The school of *Usanas* say that it shall be twenty times the amount. But Kautilya says that it shall be proportional to the guilt.

Accounts shall be submitted in the month of *Ashadha*.

When they (the accountants of different districts) present themselves with sealed books, commodities and net revenue, they shall all be kept apart in one place so that they cannot carry on conversation with each other. Having heard from them the totals of receipts, expenditure, and net revenue, the net amount shall be received.

By how much the superintendent of a department augments the net total of its revenue either by increasing any one of the items of its receipts or by decreasing anyone of the items of expenditure, he shall be rewarded eight times that amount. But when it is reversed (*i.e.*, when the net total is decreased), the award shall also be reversed (*i.e.*, he shall be made to pay eight times the decrease).

Those accountants who do not present themselves in time or do not produce their account books along with the net revenue shall be fined ten times the amount due from them.

When a superintendent of accounts (*karanika*) does not at once proceed to receive and check the accounts when the clerks (*karmika*) are ready, he shall be punished with the first amercement. In the reverse case (*i.e.*, when the clerks are not ready), the clerks shall be punished with double the first amercement.

All the ministers (*mahamaras*) shall together narrate the whole of the actual accounts pertaining to each department.

Whoever of these (ministers or clerks) is of undivided counsel or keeps himself aloof, or utters falsehood shall be punished with the highest amercement.

When an accountant has not prepared the table of daily accounts (*akritahorupaharam*), he may be given a month more (for its preparation). After the lapse of one month he shall be fined at the rate of 200 *panas* for each month (during which he delays the accounts).

If an accountant has to write only a small portion of the accounts pertaining to net revenue, he may be allowed five nights to prepare it.

Then the table of daily accounts submitted by him along with the net revenue shall be checked with reference to the regulated forms of righteous transactions and precedents and by applying such arithmetical processes as addition, subtraction, inference and by espionage. It shall also be verified with reference to (such divisions of time as) days, five nights, *pakshas*, months, four-months, and the year.

The receipt shall be verified with reference to the place and time pertaining to them, the form of their collection (*i.e.*, capital, share), the amount of the present and past produce, the person who has paid it, the person who caused its payment, the officer who fixed the amount payable, and the officer who received it. The expenditure shall be verified with reference to the cause of the profit from any source in the place and time pertaining to each item, the amount payable, the amount paid, the person who ordered the collection, the person who remitted the same, the person who delivered it, and the person who finally received it.

Likewise the net revenue shall be verified with reference to the place, time, and source pertaining to it, its standard of fineness and quantity, and the persons who are employed to guard the deposits and magazines (of grains, etc.).

When an officer (*karanika*) does not facilitate or prevents the execution of the king's order, or renders the receipts and expenditure otherwise than prescribed, he shall be punished with the first amercement.

Any clerk who violates or deviates from the prescribed form of writing accounts, enters what is unknown to him, or makes double or treble entries (*punaruktam*) shall be fined 12 *panas.*

He who scrapes off the net total shall be doubly punished.

He who eats it up shall be fined eight times.

He who causes loss of revenue shall not only pay a fine equal to five times the amount lost (*panchabandha*), but also make good the loss. In case of uttering a lie, the punishment levied for theft shall be imposed. (When an entry lost or omitted) is made later or is made to appear as forgotten, but added later on recollection, the punishment shall be double the above. The king shall forgive an offence when it is trifling, have satisfaction even when the revenue is scanty, and honour with rewards (*pragraha*) such of his superintendents as are of immense benefit to him.

Detection of What is Embezzled by Government Servants Out of State Revenue

All undertakings depend upon finance. Hence foremost attention shall be paid to the treasury.

Public prosperity (*pracharasamriddhih*), rewards for good conduct (*charitranugrahah*), capture of thieves, dispensing with (the service of too many) government servants, abundance of harvest, prosperity of commerce, absence of troubles and calamities (*upasargapramokshah*), diminution of remission of taxes, and income in gold (*hiranyopayanam*) are all conducive to financial prosperity.

Obstruction (*pratibandha*), loan (*prayoga*), trading (*vyavahara*), fabrication of accounts (*avastara*), causing the loss of revenue (*parihapana*), self-enjoyment (*upabhoga*), barter (*parivartana*), and defalcation (*apahara*) are the causes that tend to deplete the treasury.

Failure to start an undertaking or to realise its results, or to credit its profits (to the treasury) is known as obstruction. Herein a fine of ten times the amount in question shall be imposed.

Lending the money of the treasury on periodical interest is a loan. Carrying on trade by making use of government money is trading. These two acts shall be punished with a fine of twice the profit earned.

Whoever makes as unripe the ripe time or as ripe the unripe time (of revenue collection) is guilty of fabrication. Herein a fine of ten times the amount (*panchabandha*) shall be imposed.

Whoever lessens a fixed amount of income or enhances the expenditure is guilty of causing the loss of revenue. Herein a fine of four times the loss shall be imposed.

Whoever enjoys himself or causes others to enjoy whatever belongs to the king is guilty of self-enjoyment. Herein death-sentence shall be passed for enjoying gems, middlemost amercement for enjoying valuable articles, and restoration of the articles together with a fine equal to their value shall be the punishment for enjoying articles of inferior value.

The act of exchanging government articles for (similar) articles of others is barter. This offence is explained by self-enjoyment.

Whoever does not take into the treasury the fixed amount of revenue collected, or does not spend what is ordered to be spent, or misrepresents the net revenue collected is guilty of defalcation of government money. Herein a fine of twelve times the amount shall be imposed.

There are about forty ways of embezzlement: what is realised earlier is entered later on; what is realised later is entered earlier; what ought to be realised is not realised; what is hard to realise is shown as realised; what is collected is shown as not collected; what has not been collected is shown as collected; what is collected in part is entered as collected in full; what is collected in full is entered as collected in part; what is collected is of one sort, while what is entered is of another sort; what is realised from one source is shown as realised from another; what is payable is not paid; what is not payable is paid; not paid in time; paid untimely; small gifts made large gifts; large gifts made small gifts; what is gifted is of one sort while what is entered is of another; the real donee is one while the person entered (in the register) as donee is another; what has been taken into (the treasury) is removed while what has not been credited to it is shown as credited; raw materials that are not paid for are entered, while those that are paid for are not entered; an aggregate is scattered in pieces; scattered items are converted into an aggregate; commodities of greater value are bartered for those of small value; what is of smaller value is bartered for one of greater value; price of commodities enhanced; price of commodities lowered; number of nights increased; number of nights decreased; the year not in harmony with its months; the month not in harmony with its days; inconsistency in the transactions carried on with personal supervision (*samagamavishanah*); misrepresentation of the source of income; inconsistency in giving charities; incongruity in representing the work turned out; inconsistency in dealing with fixed items; misrepresentation of test marks or the standard of fineness (of gold and silver); misrepresentation of prices of commodities; making use of false weight and measures; deception in counting articles; and making use of false cubic measures such as *bhajan*—these are the several ways of embezzlement.

Under the above circumstances, the persons concerned such as the treasurer (*nidhayaka*), the prescriber (*nibandhaka*), the receiver (*pratigrahaka*), the payer (*dayaka*), the person who caused the payment (dapaka), the ministerial servants of the officer (*mantri-vaiyavrityakara*) shall each be separately examined. If any one of these tells a lie, he shall receive the same punishment as the chief-officer, (*yukta*) who committed the offence. A proclamation in public (*prachara*) shall be made to the effect "whoever has suffered at the hands of this offender may make their grievances known to the king."

Those who respond to the call shall receive such compensation as is equal to the loss they have sustained.

When there are a number of offences in which a single officer is involved, and when his being guilty of *parokta* in any one of those charges has been established, he shall be answerable for all those offences. Otherwise (*i.e.,* when it is not established), he shall be tried for each of the charges.

When a government servant has been proved to be guilty of having misappropriated part of a large sum in question, he shall be answerable for the whole.

Any informant (*suchaka*) who supplies information about embezzlement just under perpetration shall, if he succeeds in proving it, get as reward one-sixth of the amount in question; if he happens to be a government servant (*bhritaka*), he shall get for the same act one-twelfth of the amount.

If an informant succeeds in proving only a part of a big embezzlement, he shall, nevertheless, get the prescribed share of the part of the embezzled amount proved. An informant who fails to prove (his assertion) shall be liable to monetary or corporal punishment, and shall never be acquitted.

When the charge is proved, the informant may impute the talebearing to someone else or clear himself in any other way from the blame. Any informant who withdraws his assertion prevailed upon by the insinuations of the accused shall be condemned to death.

Examination of the Conduct of Government Servants

Those who are possessed of ministerial qualifications shall, in accordance with their individual capacity, be appointed as superintendents of government departments. While engaged in work, they shall be daily examined; for men are naturally fickle-minded and like horses at work exhibit constant change in their temper. Hence the agency and tools which they make use of, the place and time of the work they are engaged in, as well as the precise form of the work, the outlay, and the results shall always be ascertained.

Without dissension and without any concert among themselves, they shall carry on their work as ordered. When in concert, they eat up (the revenue). When in disunion, they mar the work.

Without bringing to the knowledge of their master (*bhartri*, the king), they shall undertake nothing except remedial measures against imminent dangers.

A fine of twice the amount of their daily pay and of the expenditure (incurred by them) shall be fixed for any inadvertence on their part. Whoever of the superintendents makes as much as, or more than, the amount of fixed revenue shall be honoured with promotion and rewards.

My teacher holds that, that officer who spends too much and

brings in little revenue eats it up; while he who proves the revenue (*i.e.*, brings in more than he spends) as well as the officer who brings inasmuch as he spends does not eat up the revenue.

But Kautilya holds that cases of embezzlement or no embezzlement can be ascertained through spies alone.

Whoever lessens the revenue eats the king's wealth. If owing to inadvertence he causes diminution in revenue, he shall be compelled to make good the loss.

Whoever doubles the revenue eats into the vitality of the country. If he brings in double the amount to the king, he shall, if the offence is small, be warned not to repeat the same; but if the offence be grave he should proportionally be punished.

Whoever spends the revenue (without bringing in any profit) eats up the labour of workmen. Such an officer shall be punished in proportion to the value of the work done, the number of days taken, the amount of capital spent, and the amount of daily wages paid.

Hence the chief officer of each department (*adhikarana*) shall thoroughly scrutinise the real amount of the work done, the receipts realised from, and the expenditure incurred in that departmental work both in detail and in the aggregate.

He shall also check (*pratishedhayet*) prodigal, spendthrift and niggardly persons.

Whoever unjustly eats up the property left by his father and grandfather is a prodigal person (*mulahara*).

Whoever eats all that he earns is a spendthrift (*tadatvika*).

Whoever hordes money, entailing hardship both on himself and his servants is niggardly.

Whoever of these three kinds of persons has the support of a strong party shall not be disturbed; but he who has no such support shall be caught hold of (*paryadatavyah*).

Whoever is niggardly in spite of his immense property, hordes, deposits, or sends out—hordes in his own house, deposits with citizens or country people or sends out to foreign countries;—a spy shall find out the advisers, friends, servants, relations, partisans, as well as the income and expenditure of such a niggardly person. Whoever in a foreign country carries out the work of such a niggardly person shall be prevailed upon to give out the secret. When the secret is known, the niggardly person shall be murdered apparently under the orders of (his) avowed enemy.

Hence the superintendents of all the departments shall carry on their respective works in company with accountants, writers, coin-examiners, the treasurers, and military officers (*uttaradhyaksha*).

Those who attend upon military officers and are noted for their honesty and good conduct shall be spies to watch the conduct of accountants and other clerks. Each department shall be officered by several temporary heads.

Just as it is impossible not to taste the honey or the poison that finds itself at the tip of the tongue, so it is impossible for a government servant not to eat up, at least, a bit of the king's revenue. Just as fish moving under water cannot possibly be found out either as drinking or not drinking water, so government servants employed in the government work cannot be found out (while) taking money (for themselves).

It is possible to mark the movements of birds flying high up in the sky; but not so is it possible to ascertain the movement of government servants of hidden purpose.

Government servants shall not only be confiscated of their ill-earned hordes, but also be transferred from one work to another, so that they cannot either misappropriate Government money or vomit what they have eaten up. Those who increase the king's revenue instead of eating it up and are loyally devoted to him shall be made permanent in service.

Examination of Gems That are to be Entered into the Treasury

The Superintendent of the treasury shall, in the presence of qualified persons, admit into the treasury whatever he ought to, gems (*ratna*) and articles of superior or inferior value.

Tamraparnika, that which is produced in the *tamraparni; Pandyakavataka,* that which is obtained in *Pandyakavata; Pasikya,* that which is produced in the *Pasa; Kauleya,* that which is produced in the *kula; Chaurneya,* that which is produced in the *Churna; Mahendra,* that which is obtained near the mountain of *Mahendra; Kardamika,* that which is produced in the *Kardama; Srautasiya,* that which is produced in the *Srotasi; Hradiya,* that which is produced in (a deep pool of water known as) *Hrada;* and *Haimavata,* that which is obtained in the vicinity of the Himalayas are the several varieties of pearls.

Oyster-shells, conch-shells, and other miscellaneous things are the wombs of pearls.

That which is like *masura* (*ervum hirsutam*), that which consists of three joints (*triputaka*), that which is like a tortoise (*kurmaka*), that which is semi-circular, that which consists of several coatings, that which is double (*yamaka*), that which is scratched, that which is of rough surface, that which is possessed of spots (*siktakam*), that which is like the water-pot used by an ascetic, that which is of dark-brown or blue colour, and that which is badly perforated are inauspicious.

That which is big, circular, without bottom (*nistalam*), brilliant, white, heavy, soft to the touch, and properly perforated is the best. *Sirshaka, upasirshaka, prakandaka, avaghataka,* and *taralapratibandha* are several varieties of pearl necklaces.

One thousand and eight strings of pearls form the necklace, *Indrachchhanda.*

Half of the above is *Vijayachchhanda.*

Sixty-four strings make up *Ardhahara.*

Fifty-four strings make up *Rasmikalapa.*

Thirty-two strings make up *Guchchha.*

Twenty-seven strings make up *Nakshatramala.*

Twenty-four strings make up *Ardhaguchchha.*

Twenty strings make up *Manavaka.*

Half of the above is *Ardhamanavaka.*

The same necklaces with a gem at the centre are called by the same names with the words '*Manavaka*' suffixed to their respective names.

When all the strings making up a necklace are of *sirshaka* pattern, it is called pure necklace (*suddhahara*); likewise with strings of other pattern. That which contains a gem in the centre is (also) called *Ardhamanavaka*. That which contains three slab-like gems (*triphalaka*) or five slab-like gems (*panchaphalaka*) in the centre is termed *Phalakahara*. An only string of pearls is called pure *Ekavali*; the same with a gem in the centre is called *Yashti*; the same variegated with gold globules is termed *Ratnavali*.

A string made of pearls and gold globules alternately put is called *Apavartaka*.

Strings of pearls with a gold wire between two strings is called *Sopanaka*.

The same with a gem in the centre is called *Manisopanaka*. The above will explain the formation of head-strings, bracelets, anklets, waistbands, and other varieties.

Kauta, that which is obtained in the *Kuta*; *Mauleyaka*, that which is found in the *Muleya*; and *Parasamudraka*, that which is found beyond the ocean are several varieties of gems.

That which possesses such pleasant colour as that of the red lotus flower, or that of the flower of *Parijata* (*Erithrina Indica*), or that of the rising sun is the *Saugandhika* gem.

That which is of the colour of blue lotus flower, or of *sirisha* (*Acacia Sirisa*), or of water, or of fresh bamboo, or of the colour of the feathers of a parrot is the *Vaidurya* gem *Pushyaraga*, *Gomutraka*, and *Gomedika* are other varieties of the same.

That which is characterised with blue lines, that which is of the colour of the flower of *Kalaya* (a kind of *phraseolus*), or which is intensely blue, which possesses the colour of *Jambu* fruit (rose apple), or which is as blue as the clouds is the *Indranila* gem; *Nandaka* (pleasing gem), *Sravanmadhya* (that which appears to pour water from its centre), *Sitavrishti* (that which appears to pour cold shower), and *Suryakanta* (sunstone) are other forms of gems.

Gems are hexagonal, quadrangular, or circular possessed of dazzling glow, pure, smooth, heavy, brilliant, transparent (*antargataprabha*) and illuminating; such are the qualities of gems. Faint colour, sandy layer, spots, holes, bad perforation, and scratches are the defects of gems.

Vimalaka (pure), *sasyaka* (plant-like), *Anjanamulaka* (deep-dark), *Pittaka* (like the bile of a cow) *Sulabhaka* (easily procurable), *Lohitaka* (red), *Amritamsuka* (of white rays), *Jyotirasaka* (glowing), *Maileyaka, Ahichchhatraka,* (procured in the country of *Ahichchhatra*), *Kurpa, Putikurpa,* and *Sugandhikurpa, Kshirapaka, Suktichurnaka* (like the powder of an oystershell), *Silapravalaka* (like coral), *Pulaka, Sukrapulaka* are varieties of inferior gems.

•The rest are metalic beads (*kachamani*).

Sabharashtraka, that which is found in the country of *Sabharashtra; Madhyamarashtraka,* that which is found in the Central Province; *Kasmaka,* that which is found in the country of *Kasmaka; Srikatanaka,* that which is found in the vicinity of the mountain, *Vedotkata; Manimantaka,* that which is found near the mountain *Maniman* or *Manimanta;* and *Indravanaka* are diamonds. Mines, streams, and other miscellaneous places are their sources.

The colour of a diamond may be like that of a cat's eye, that of the flower of *Sirisha* (*Acacia Sirisa*), the urine of a cow, the bile of a cow, like alum (*sphatika*), the flower of *Malati,* or like that of any of the gems (described above).

That which is big, heavy, hard (*praharasaham,* tolerant of hitting), regular (*samakona*), capable of scratching on the surface of vessels (*bhajanalekhi*), refractive of light (*kubrami*), and brilliant is the best.

That which is devoid of angles, uneven (*nirasrikam*), and bent on one side (*parsvapavrittam*) is inauspicious.

Alakandaka, and *Vaivarnaka* are the two varieties of coral which is possessed of ruby-like colour, which is very hard, and which is free from the contamination of other substances inside.

Satana is red and smells like the earth; *Gosirshaka* is dark red and smells like fish; *Harichandana* is of the colour of the feathers of a parrot and smells like tamarind or mango fruit; likewise *Tarnasa; Grameruka* is red or dark red and smells like the urine of a goat; *Daivasabheya* is red and smells like a lotus flower; likewise *Aupaka* (*Japaka*); *Jongaka* and *Taurupa* are red or dark red and soft; *Maleyaka* is reddish white; *Kuchandana* is as black as *Agaru* (resin of the aloe) or red or dark red and very rough; *Kala-parvataka* is of pleasant appearance; *Kosakaraparvataka* (that which is the product of that mountain which is of the shape of a bud) is black or variegated black; *Sitodakiya* is black and soft, and smells like a lotus-flower; *Nagaparvataka* (that which is the product of Naga mountain) is rough and is possessed of the colour of *Saivala* (*Vallisneria*); and *Sakala* is brown.

Light, soft, moist (*asyana*, not dry), as greasy as ghee, of pleasant smell, adhesive to the skin, of mild smell, retentive of colour and smell, tolerant of heat, absorptive of heat, and comfortable to the skin—these are the characteristics of sandal (*chandana*).

(As to) *Agaru* (*Agallochum*, resin of aloe):

Jongaka is black or variegated black and is possessed of variegated spots; *Dongaka* is black; and *Parasamudraka* is of variegated colour and smells like cascus or like *Navamalika* (*jasminum*).

(*Agaru* is) heavy, soft, greasy, smells far and long, burns slowly, gives out continuous smoke while burning, is of uniform smell, absorbs heat, and is so adhesive to the skin as not to be removable by rubbing;—these are the characteristics of *Agaru*.

(As to) *Tailaparnika*:

Asokagramika, the product of *Asokagrama*, is of the colour of meat and smells like a lotus flower; *Jongaka* is reddish yellow and smells like a blue lotus flower or like the urine of a cow; *Grameruka* is greasy and smells like a cow's urine; *Sauvarnakudyaka*, product of the country of *Suvarnakudya*, is reddish yellow and smells like *Matulunga* (the fruit of citron tree or sweet lime); *Purnadvipaka*, the product of the island, *Purnadviipa*, smells like a lotus flower or like butter; *Bhadrasriya* and *Paralauhityaka* are of the colour of nutmeg; *Antarvatya* is of the colour of cascus—the last two smell like *Kushtha* (*Costus Speciosus*); *Kaleyaka* which is a product of *Svarna-bhumi*, gold-producing land, is yellow and greasy; and *Auttaraparvataka* (a product of, the north mountain) is reddish yellow. The above (fragrant substances) are commodities of superior value (*Sara*).

The smell of the *Tailaparnika* substances is lasting, no matter whether they are made into a paste or boiled or burnt; also it is neither changed nor affected even when mixed with other substances; and these substances resemble sandal and *Agallochum* in their qualities.

Kantanavaka, Praiyaka, and *Auttara-parvataka* are the varieties of skins.

Kantanavaka is of the colour of the neck of the peacock; *Praiyaka* is variegated with blue, yellow, and white spots; these two are eight *angulas* (inches) long.

Also *Bisi* and *Mahabisi* are the products of *Dvadasagrama,* twelve villages. That which is of indistinct colour, hairy, and variegated (with spots) is (called) *Bisi.*

That which is rough and almost white is *Mahabisi* (great *Bisi*); These two are twelve angulas long.

Syamika, Kalika, Kadali, Chandrottara, and *Sakula* are (other kinds of skins) procured from *Aroha* (*Arohaja*).

Syamika is brown and contains variegated spots; *Kalika* is brown or of the colour of a pigeon; these two are eight angulas long. *Kadali* is rough and two feet long; when *Kadali* bears variegated moonlike spots, it is called *Chandrottarakadali* and is one-third of its length; *Sakula* is variegated with large round spots similar to those that manifest themselves in a kind of leprosy (*kushtha*), or is furnished with tendrils and spotted like a deer's skin.

Samura, Chinasi, and *Samuli* are (skins procured from *Bahlava,* (*Bahlaveya*).

Samura is thirty-six angulas long and black; *Chinasi* is reddish black or blackish white; *Samuli* is of the colour of wheat.

Satina, Nalatula, and *Vrittapuchchha* are the skins of aquatic animals (*Audra*).

Satina is black; *Nalatula* is of the colour of the fibre of *Nala,* a kind of grass; and *Vrittapuchchha* (that which possesses a round tail) is brown.The above are the varieties of skins. Of skins, that which is soft, smooth and hairy is the best.

Blankets made of sheep's wool may be white, purely red, or as red as a lotus flower. They may be made of worsted threads by sewing (*khachita*); or may be woven of woollen threads of various colour (*vanachitra*); or may be made of different pieces (*khandasanghatya*); or may be woven of uniform woollen threads (*tantuvichchhinna*).

Woollen blankets are (of ten kinds):—*Kambala, Kauchapaka, Kulamiṭika, Saumitika, Turagastarana, Varnaka, Talichchhaka, Varavana, Paristoma,* and *Samantabhadraka.*

Of these, that which is slippery (*pichchhila*) as a wet surface, possessed of fine hair, and soft, is the best. That (blanket) which is made up of eight pieces and black in colour is called *Bhingisi* used as rain-proof; likewise is *Apasaraka;* both are the products of Nepal.

Samputika, Chaturasrika, Lambara, Katavanaka, Pravaraka, and *Sattalika* are (blankets made of) the wool of wild animals.

That which is manufactured in the country, *Vanga* (*vangaka*) is a white and soft fabric (*dukula*); that of *Pandya* manufacture (*Paundraka*) is black and as soft as the surface of a gem; and that which is the product of the country, *Suvarnakudya,* is as red as the sun, as soft as the surface of the gem, woven while the threads are very wet, and of uniform (*chaturasra*) or mixed texture (*vyamisravana*). Single, half, double, treble and quadruple garments are varieties of the same.

The above will explain other kinds of fabrics such as *Kasika, Benarese* products, and *Kshauma* which is manufactured in *Pandya* (*Paundraka*).

Magadhika (product of the *Magadha* country), *Paundraka,* and *Sauvarnakudyaka* are fibrous garments.

Nagavriksha (a species of a tree), *Likucha* (*Artocarpus Lakucha*), and *Vakula* (*Mimusops Elengi*), and *Vata* (*Ficus Indica*) are the sources (of their fibres).

That of *Nagavriksha* is yellow (*pita*); that of *Likucha* is of the colour of wheat; that of *Vakula* is white; and the rest is of the colour of butter.

Of these, that which is produced in the country of *Suvarnakudya* is the best.

The above will explain the fabrics known as *kauseya*, silk-cloth, and *chinapatta*, fabrics of China manufacture.

Of cotton fabrics, those of *Madhura*, of *Aparanta*, western parts, of *Kalinga*, of *Kasi*, of *Vanga*, of *Vatsa*, and of *Mahisha* are the best.

As to other kinds of gems (which are not treated of here), the superintendent shall ascertain their size, their value, species, form, utility, their treatment, the repair of old ones, any adulteration that is not easily detected, their wear and tear due to lapse of time and place, as well as remedies against those which are inauspicious (*himsra*).

Conducting Mining Operations and Manufacture

Possessed of the knowledge of the science dealing with copper and other minerals (*Sulbadhatusastra*), experienced in the art of distillation and condensation of mercury (*rasapaka*) and of testing gems, aided by experts in mineralogy and equipped with mining labourers and necessary instruments, the superintendent of mines shall examine mines which, on account of their containing mineral excrement (*kitta*), crucibles, charcoal, and ashes, may appear to have been once exploited or which may be newly discovered on plains or mountain-slopes possessing mineral ores, the richness of which can be ascertained by weight, depth of colour, piercing smell, and taste.

Liquids which ooze out from pits, eaves, slopes, or deep excavations of well-known mountains; which have the colour of the fruit of rose-apple (*jambu*), of mango, and of *fanpalm*; which are as yellow as ripe turmeric, sulphurate of arsenic (*haritala*), honey-comb, and vermilion; which are as resplendent as the petals of a lotus, or the feathers of a parrot or a peacock; which are adjacent to (any mass of) water or shrubs of similar colour; and which are greasy (*chikkana*), transparent (*visada*), and very heavy are ores of gold (*kanchanika*). Likewise liquids which, when dropped on water, spread like oil to which dirt and filth adhere, and which amalgamate themselves more than cent per cent (*satadupari veddharah*) with copper or silver.

Of similar appearance as the above (*tatpratirupakam*), but of piercing smell and taste is Bitumen.

Those ores which are obtained from plains or slopes of mountains; which are either yellow or as red as copper or reddish yellow; which are disjoined and marked with blue lines; which have the colour of black beans (*masha, Phraseolus Radiatus*), green beans (*mudga, Phraseolus Mungo*), and sesamum; which are marked with spots like a drop of curd and resplendent as turmeric, yellow myrobalan, petals of a lotus, acquatic plant, the liver or the spleen; which possess a sandy layer within them and are marked with figures of a circle or a *svastika*; which contain globular masses (*sagulika*); and which, when roasted do not split, but emit much foam and smoke are the ores of gold (*suvarnadhatavah*), and are used to form amalgams with copper or silver (*prativaparthaste stamrarupyavedharah*).

Those ores which have the colour of a conch-shell, camphor, alum, butter, a pigeon, turtle-dove, *Vimalaka* (a kind of precious stone), or the neck of a peacock; which are as resplendent as opal (*sasyaka*), agate (*gomedaka*), cane-sugar (*guda*), and granulated sugar (*matsyandika*) which has the colour of the flower of *kovidara* (*Bauhinia Variegata*), of lotus, of *patali* (*Bignonia Suaveolens*), of *kalaya* (a kind of *phraseolus*), of *kshauma* (flax), and of *atasi* (*Dinuin Usitatissimum*); which may be in combination with lead or iron (*anjana*); which smell like raw meat, are disjoined gray or blackish white, and are marked with lines or spots; and which, when roasted, do not split, but emit much foam and smoke are silver ores.

The heavier the ores, the greater will be the quantity of metal in them (*satvavriddhih*).

The impurities of ores, whether superficial or inseparably combined with them can be got rid of and the metal melted when the ores are (chemically) treated with Tikshna urine (*mutra*) and alkalies (*kshara*), and are mixed or smeared over with the mixture of (the powder of) *Rajavriksha* (*Clitoria Ternatea*), *Vata* (*Ficus Indica*), and *Pelu* (*Carnea Arborea*), together with cow's bile and the urine and dung of a buffalo, an ass and an elephant. Metals are rendered soft when they are treated with (the powder of) *kandali* (mushroom), and *vajrakanda,* (Antiquorum) together with the ashes of barley, black beans, *palasa* (*Butea Frondosa*), and *pelu* (*Carnea Arborea*), or with the milk of both the cow and the sheep. Whatever metal is split into a hundred thousand parts is rendered soft when it is thrice soaked in the mixture made up of honey (*madhu*), *madhuka* (*Bassia Latifolia*), sheep's milk, sesamum oil, clarified butter, jaggery, *kinva* (ferment) and mushroom.

Permanent softness (*mridustambhana*) is also attained when the metal is treated with the powder of cow's teeth and horn.

Those ores which are obtained from plains or slopes of mountains; and which are heavy, greasy, soft, tawny, green, dark, bluish-yellow (*harita*), pale-red, or red are ores of copper.

Those ores which have the colour of *kakamechaka* (*Solanum Indica*), pigeon, or cow's bile, and which are marked with white lines and smell like raw meat are the ores of lead. Those ores which are as variegated in colour as saline soil or which have the colour of a burnt lump of earth are the ores of tin.

Those ores which are of orange colour (*kurumba*), or pale-red (*pandurohita*), or of the colour of the flower of *sinduvara* (*Vitex Trifolia*) are the ores of *tikshna*.

Those ores which are of the colour of the leaf of *kanda* (*Artemisia Indica*) or of the leaf of birch are the ores of *vaikrintaka*.

Pure, smooth, efflugent, sounding (when struck), very hard (*satativrah*), and of little colour (*tanuraga*) are precious stones.

The yield of mines may be put to such uses as are in vogue.

Commerce in commodities manufactured from mineral products shall be centralized and punishment for manufacturers, sellers, and purchasers of such commodities outside the prescribed locality shall also be laid down.

A mine-labourer who steals mineral products except precious stones shall be punished with a fine of eight times their value.

Any person who steals mineral products or carries on mining operations without license shall be bound (with chains) and caused to work (as a prisoner). Mines which yield such minerals as are made use of in preparing vessels (*bhanda*) as well as those mines which require large outlay to work out may be leased out for a fixed number of the shares of the output or for a fixed rent (*bhagena prakrayena va*) Such mines as can be worked out without much outlay shall be directly exploited (by Government agency).

The superintendent of metals (*lohadhyakshah*) shall carry on the manufacture of copper, lead, tin, *vaikrintaka* (mercury), *arakuta* (brass), *vritta; kamsa* (bronze or bell-metal), *tala* (sulphurate of arsenic), and *lodhra,* and also of commodities (*bhanda*) from them.

The superintendent of mint (*lakshnadhyakshah*), shall carry on the manufacture of silver coins (*rupyarupa*) made up of four parts of copper and one-sixteenth part (*masha*) of any one of the metals, *tikshna, trapu, sisa,* and *anjana.* There shall be a *pana,* half a *pana,* a quarter and one-eighth. Copper coins (*tamrarupa*) made up of four parts of an alloy (*padajivam*), shall be a *mashaka,* half a *mashaka, kakani* and half a *kakani.*

The examiner of coins (*rupadarsaka*) shall regulate currency both as a medium of exchange (*vyavaharikim*) and as legal tender admissible into the treasury (*kosapravesyam*): The premia levied on coins paid into the treasury shall be) 8 per cent, known as *rupika,* 5 per cent known as *vyaji,* one-eighth *pana* per cent as *parikshika* (testing charge), besides (cha) a fine of 25 *pana* to be imposed on offenders other than the manufacturer, the seller, the purchaser and the examiner. The superintendent of ocean-mines (*khanyadhyakshah*) shall attend to the collection of conch-shells, diamonds, precious stones, pearls, corals, and salt (*kshara*) and also regulate the commerce in the above commodities.

Soon after crystalisation of salt is over, the superintendent of salt shall in time collect both the money-rent (*prakraya*) and the quantity of the shares of salt due to the government; and by the sale of salt (thus collected as shares) he shall realise not only its value (*mulyam*), but also the premium of five per cent (*vyajim*), both in cash (*rupa*).

Imported salt (*agantulavanam*) shall pay one-sixth portion (*shadbhaga*) to the king. The sale of this portion (*bhagavibhaga*) shall fetch the premia of five per cent (*vyaji*), of eight per cent (*rupika*) in cash (*rupa*). The purchasers shall pay not only the toll (*sulka*), but also the compensation (*vaidharana*) equivalent to the loss entailed on the king's commerce. In default of the above payment, he shall be compelled to pay a fine of 600 *panas*.

Adulteration of salt shall be punished with the highest amercement; likewise persons other than hermits (*vanaprastha*) manufacturing salt without license.

Men learned in the Vedas, persons engaged in penance, as well as labourers may take with them salt for food; salt and alkalies for purposes other than this shall be subject to the payment of toll.

Thus; besides collecting from mines the ten kinds of revenue, such as (1) value of the output (*mulya*), (2) the share of the output (*vibhaga*), (3) the premium of five per cent (*vyaji*), (4) the testing charge of coins (*parigha*), (5) fine previously announced (*atyaya*), (6) toll (*sulka*), (7) compensation for loss entailed on the king's commerce (*vaidharana*), (8) fines to be determined in proportion to the gravity of crimes (*danda*), (9) coinage (*rupa*), (10) the premium of eight per cent (*rupika*), the government shall keep as a state monopoly both mining and commerce (in minerals).

Thus taxes (*mukhasangraha*) on all commodities intended for sale shall be prescribed once for all.

The Superintendent of Storehouse

The superintendent of storehouse (*Koshthagara*) shall supervise the accounts of agricultural produce (*sita*); taxes coming under *Rashtra*, country-parts; commerce (*krayima*); barter (*parivartna*); begging for grains (*pramityaka*); grains borrowed with promise to repay (*apamityaka*); manufacture of rice, oils, etc. (*simhanika*); accidental revenue (*anyajata*); statements to check expenditure (*vyayapratyaya*); and recovery of past arrears (*upasthanam*).

Whatever in the shape of agricultural produce is brought in by the superintendent of agriculture, (of crown-lands) is termed *sita*.

The taxes that are fixed (*pindakara*), taxes that are paid in the form of one-sixth of produce (*shadbhaga*), provision paid (by the people) for the army (*senabhakta*), taxes that are levied for religious purposes (*bali*), taxes or subsidies that are paid by vassal kings and others (*kara*), taxes that are specially collected on the occasion of the birth of a prince (*utsanga*), taxes that are collected when there is some margin left for such collection (*parsva*), compensation levied in the shape of grains for any damage done by cattle to crops (*parihinaka*), presentation made to the king, (*aupayanika*), and taxes that are levied on lands below tanks, lakes, etc., built by the king (*Kaushtheyaka*),—all these come under the head '*Rashtra*.'

Sale proceeds of grains, grains purchased and the collection of interest in kind or grain debts (*prayogapratyadana*) are termed commerce.

Profitable exchange of grains for grains is termed barter (*parivarthana*).

Grains collected by begging is termed *pramityaka*.

Grains borrowed with promise to repay the same is termed *apamityaka*.

Pounding (rice, etc.), dividing (pulses, etc.), frying (corns and beans), manufacture of beverages (*suktakarma*), manufacture of flour by employing those persons who live upon such works, extracting oil by employing shepherds and oil-makers, and manufacture of sugar from the juice of sugar-cane are termed *simhanika*.

Whatever is lost and forgotten (by others) and the like form accidental revenue (*anyajata*).

Investment, the relic of a wrecked undertaking, and savings from an estimated outlay are the means to check expenditure (*vyayapratyaya*).

That amount or quantity of compensation which is claimed for making use of a different balance or for any error in taking a handful is termed *vyaji*.

Collection of arrears is termed '*upasthana*,' 'recovery of past arrears.'

Of grains, oils, sugar, and salt, all that concerns grains will be treated of in connection with the duties of the 'Superintendent of

Agriculture.' Clarified butter, oil, serum of flesh, and pith or sap (of plants, etc.)., are termed oils (*sneha*).

Decoction (*phanita*), jaggory, granulated sugar, and sugar-candy are termed *kshara*.

Saindhava, that which is the product of the country of *Sindhu*; *Samudra*, that which is produced from seawater; *Bida*; *Yavakshara*, *nitre*, *Sauvarchala*, that which is the product of the country of *suvarchala*; and *udbhedaja*, that which is extracted from saline soil are termed *lavana*, salt.

The honey of the bee as well as the juice extracted from grapes are called *madhu*.

Mixture made by combining any one of the substances, such as the juice of sugar-cane, jaggory, honey, the, juice of grapes, the essence of the fruits of *jambu* (*Euginia Jambolana*) and of *jaka* tree—with the essence of *meshasringa* (a kind of plant) and long pepper, with or without the addition of the essence of *chirbhita* (a kind of gourd), cucumber, sugar-cane, mango-fruit and the fruit of *myrobalam*, the mixture being prepared so as to last for a month, or six months, or a year, constitute the group of astringents (*sukta-varga*).

The fruits of those trees which bear acid fruits, those of *karamarda* (*Carissa Carandas*), those of *vidalamalka* (*myrobalam*), those of *matulanga* (citron tree), those of kola (small jujuba), those of *badara* (*Flacourtia Cataphracta*), those of *sauvira* (big jujuba), and those of *parushaka* (*Grewia Asiatica*) and the like come under the group of acid fruits. Curds, acid prepared from grains and the like are acids in liquid form.

Long pepper, black pepper, ginger, cumin seed, *kiratatikta* (*Agathotes Chirayta*), white mustard, coriander, *choraka* (a plant), *damanaka* (*Artemisia Indica*), *maruvaka* (*Vangueria Spinosa*), *sigru* (*Hyperanthera Moringa*), and the like together with their roots (*kanda*) come under the group of pungent substances (*tiktavarga*).

Dried fish, bulbous roots (*kandamula*), fruits and vegetables form the group of edibles (*sakavarga*).

Of the store, thus, collected, half shall be kept in reserve to ward off the calamities of the people and only the other half shall be used. Old collection shall be replaced by new supply. The superintendent shall also personally supervise the increase or diminution sustained in grains when they are pounded (*kshunna*), or frayed (*ghrishta*), or reduced to flour (*pishta*), or fried (*bhrashta*), or dried after soaking in water.

The essential part (*sara, i.e.*, that which is fit for food) of *kodrava* (*Paspalam Scrobiculatum*) and of *vrihi* (rice) is one-half; that of *sali* (a kind of rice) is (half) less by one-eighth part; that of *varaka* (*Phraseolus Trilobus*) is (half) less by one-third part; that of *priyangu* (panic seed or millet) is one-half; that of *chamasi* (barley), of *mudga* (*Phraseolus Mungo*) and of *masha* (*Phraseolus Radiatus*) is (half) less by one-eighth part; that of *saibya* (*simbi*) is one-half; that of *masura* (*Ervum Hirsutum*) is (half) less by one-third part (than the raw material or grains from which it is prepared).

Raw flour and *kulmasha* (boiled and forced rice) will be as much as one and a half of the original quantity of the grains.

Barley gruel as well as its flour baked will be twice the original quantity.

Kodrava (*Paspalam Scrobiculatum*), *varaka* (*Phraseolus Trilobus*), *udaraka* (*Panicum*), and *priyangu* (millet) will increase three times the original quantity when cooked. *Vrihi* (rice) will increase four times when cooked. *Sali* (a kind of rice) will increase five times when cooked.

Grains will increase twice the original quantity when moistened; and two and a half times when soaked to sprouting condition. Grains fried will increase by one-fifth the original quantity; leguminous seeds (*kalaya*), when fried, will increase twice the original; likewise rice when fried.

Oil extracted from *atasi* (linseed) will be one-sixth (of the quantity of the seed); that extracted from the seeds, *nimba* (*Azadirachta Indica*), *kusamra*, and *Kapittha* (*Feronia Elephantum*) will be one-fifth; and that extracted from *tila* (seasumum), *kusumba* (a sort of kidney bean), *madhuka* (*Bassia Latifolia*), and *ingudi* (*Terminalia Catappa*) will be one-fourth.

Five *palas* of *karpasa* (cotton) and of *kshauma* (flax) will yield one *pala* of threads.

Rice prepared in such a way that five *drona* of *sali* yield ten *adhakas* of rice will be fit to be the food of young elephants; eleven *adhakas* from five *dronas* for elephants of bad temper (*vyala*); ten *adhakas* from the same quantity for elephants trained for riding; nine *adhakas* from the same quantity for elephants used in war; eight *adhakas* from the same for infantry; eleven *adhakas* from the same for chiefs of the army; six *adhakas* from the same for queens and princes and five *adhakas* from the same quantity for kings.

One *prastha* of rice, pure and unsplit, one-fourth *prastha* of *supa*, and clarified butter or oil equal to one-fourth part of (*supa*) will suffice to form one meal of an Arya.

One-sixth *prastha* of *supa* for a man; and half the above quantity of oil will form one meal for low castes (*avara*).

The same rations less by one-fourth the above quantities will form one meal for a woman; and half the above rations for children.

For dressing twenty *palas* of flesh, half a *kutumba* of oil, one *pala* of salt, one *pala* of sugar (*kshara*), two *dharanas* of pungent substances (*katuka*, spices), and half a *prastha* of curd (will be necessary). For dressing greater quantities of flesh, the same ingredients can be proportionally increased.

For cooking *sakas* (dried fish and vegetables), the above substances are to be added one and a half times as much.

For dressing dried fish, the above ingredients are to be added twice as much. Measures of rations for elephants and horses will be described in connection with the "Duties of Their Respective Superintendents."

For bullocks, one *drona* of *masha* (*Phraseolus Radiatus*) or one *drona* of barley cooked with other things, as prescribed for horses, is the requisite quantity of food, besides the special and additional provision of one *tula* of oilcakes (*ghanapinyaka*) or ten *adhakas* of bran (*kanakuttana-kundaka*).

Twice the above quantity for buffaloes and camels.

Half a *drona* for asses, red spotted deer and deer with white stripes.

One *adhaka* for an antelope and big red deer.

Half an *adhaka* or one *adhaka* of grain together with bran for a goat, a ram and a boar.

One *prastha* of cooked rice for dogs.

Half a *prastha* for a *hamsa* (goose), a *krauncha* (heron) and a peacock.

From the above, the quantity of rations enough for one meal for other beasts, cattle, birds, and rogue elephants (*vyala*) may be inferred.

Charcoal and chaff may be given over for iron smelting and lime-kiln (*bhittilepya*).

Bran and flour (*kanika*) may be given to slaves, labourers, and cooks. The surplus of the above may be given to those who prepare cooked rice, and rice-cakes.

The weighing balance, weights, measures, mill-stone (*rochani*), pestle, mortar, wooden contrivances for pounding rice, etc., (*kuttakayantra*), contrivances for splitting seeds into pieces (*rochakayantra*), winnowing fans, sieves (*chalani*) grain-baskets (*kandoli*), boxes, and brooms are the necessary instruments.

Sweepers; preservers; those who weigh things (*dharaka*); those who measure grains, etc.; those who supervise the work of measuring grains (*mapaka*); those who supervise the supply of commodities to the storehouse (*dapaka*); those who supply commodities (*dayaka*); those who are employed to receive compensation for any real or supposed error in measuring grains, etc. (*salakaipratigrahaka*); slaves; and labourers;—all these are called *vishti*.

Grains are heaped up on the floor; jaggory (*kshara*) is bound round in grass-rope (*muta*); oils are kept in earthenware or wooden vessels; and salt is heaped up on the surface of the ground.

The Superintendent of Commerce

The Superintendent of Commerce shall ascertain demand or absence of demand for, and rise or fall in the price of, various kinds of merchandise which may be the products either of land or of water and which may have been brought in either by land or by water path. He shall also ascertain the time suitable for their distribution, centralisation, purchase, and sale.

That merchandise which is widely distributed shall be centralised and its price enhanced. When the enhanced rate becomes popular, another rate shall be declared.

That merchandise of the king which is of local manufacture shall be centralised; imported merchandise shall be distributed in several markets for sale. Both kinds of merchandise shall be favourably sold to the people.

He shall avoid such large profits as will harm the people.

There shall be no restriction to the time of sale of those commodities for which there is frequent demand; nor shall they be subject to the evils of centralisation (*sankuladosha*).

Or pedlars may sell the merchandise of the king at a fixed price in many markets and pay necessary compensation (*vaidharana*) proportional to the loss entailed upon it (*chhedanurupam*).

The amount of *vyaji* due on commodities sold by cubical measure is one-sixteenth of the quantity (*shodasabhago manavyaji*); that on commodities sold by weighing balance is one-twentieth of the quantity; and that on commodities sold in numbers is one-eleventh of the whole.

The superintendent shall show favour to those who import foreign merchandise: mariners (*navika*) and merchants who import foreign merchandise shall be favoured with remission of the trade-taxes, so that they may derive some profit (*ayatikshamam pariharam dadyat*).

Foreigners importing merchandise shall be exempted from being sued for debts unless they are (local) associations and partners (*anabhiyoga-scharthesshva-gantunamanya-tassabh-yopakari bhyah*).

Those who sell the merchandise of the king shall invariably put their sale proceeds in a wooden box kept in a fixed place and provided with a single aperture on the top.

During the eighth part of the day, they shall submit to the superintendent the sale report, saying "this much has been sold and this much remains;" they shall also hand over the weights and measures. Such are the rules applicable to local traffic. As regards the sale of the king's merchandise in foreign countries:—

Having ascertained the value of local produce as compared with that of foreign produce that can be obtained in barter, the superintendent will find out (by calculation) whether there is any margin left for profit after meeting the payments (to the foreign king) such as the toll (*sulka*), road-cess (*vartani*), conveyance-cess (*ativahika*), tax payable at military stations (*gulmadeya*), ferry-charges (*taradeya*), subsistence to the merchant and his followers (*bhakta*), and the portion of merchandise payable to the foreign king (*bhaga*).

If no profit can be realised by selling the local produce in foreign countries, he has to consider whether any local produce can be profitably bartered for any foreign produce. Then he may send one quarter of his valuable merchandise through safe roads to different markets on land. In view of large profits, he (the deputed merchant) may make friendship with the forest-guards, boundary-guards, and officers in charge of cities and of country-parts (of the foreign king). He shall take care to secure his treasure (*sara*) and life from danger. If he cannot reach the intended market, he may sell the merchandise (at any market) free from all dues (*sarvadeyavisuddham*).

Or he may take his merchandise to other countries through rivers (*nadipatha*).

He shall also gather information as to conveyance-charges (*yanabhagaka*), subsistence on the way (*pathyadana*), value of foreign merchandise that can be obtained in barter for local merchandise, occasions of pilgrimages (*yatrakala*), means that can be employed to ward off dangers (of the journey), and the history of commercial towns (*panyapattanacharitra*).

Having gathered information as to the transaction in commercial towns along the banks of rivers, he shall transport his merchandise to profitable markets and avoid unprofitable ones.

The Superintendent of Forest Produce

The Superintendent of Forest Produce shall collect timber and other products of forests by employing those who guard productive forests. He shall not only start productive works in forests, but also fix adequate fines and compensations to be levied from those who cause any damage to productive forests except in calamities.

The following are forest products.

Saka (teak), *tinisa* (Dalbergia Ougeinensis), *dhanvana, arjuna* (Terminalia Arjuna), *madhuka* (Bassia Latifolia), *tilaka* (Barleria Cristata), *tala* (palmyra), *simsupa* (Dalbergia Sissu), *arimeda* (Fetid Mimosa), *rajadana* (Mimosops Kauki), *sirisha* (Mimosa Sirisha), *khadira* (Mimosa Catechu), *sarala* (Pinus Longifolia), *talasarja* (*sal* tree or Shorea Robesta), *asvakarna* (Vatica Robesta), *somavalka* (a kind of white *khadira*), *kasamra, priyaka* (yellow *sal* tree), *dhava* (Mimosa Hexandra), etc., are the trees of strong timber (*sarada.uvarga*).

Utaja, Chimiya, Chava, Venu, Vamsa, Satina, Kantaka, and *Bhalluka,* etc., form the group of bamboo.

Vetra (cane), *sokavalli, vasi* (Justicia Ganderussa), *syamalata* (Ichnocarpus), *nagalata* (betel), etc., form the group of creepers.

Malati (Jasminum Grandiflorum), *durva* (panic grass), *arka* (Calotropis Gigantea), *sana* (hemp), *gavedhuka* (Coix Barbata), *atasi* (Linum Usitatis simum), etc., form the group of fibrous plants (*valkavarga*).

Munja (Saccharum Munja), *balbaja* (Eleusine Indica), etc., are plants which yield rope-making material (*rajjubhanda*).

Tali (Corypha Taliera), *tala* (palmyra or Borassus Flabelliformis), and *bhurja* (birch) yield leaves (*patram*).

Kimsuka (Butea Frondosa), *kusumbha* (Carthamus Tinctorius), and *kumkuma* (Crocus Sativus) yield flowers.

Bulbous roots and fruits are the group of medicines.

Kalakuta, Vatsanabha, Halahala, Meshasringa, Musta, (Cyperus Rotundus), *kushtha, mahavisha, vellitaka, gaurardra, balaka, markata, haimavata, kalingaka, daradaka, kolasaraka, ushtraka,* etc., are poisons.

Likewise snakes and worms kept in pots are the group of poisons. Skins are those of *godha* (alligator), *seraka, dvipi* (leopard), *simsumara* (porpoise), *simha* (lion), *vyaghra* (tiger), *hasti,* (elephant.), *mahisha* (buffalo), *chamara* (bos grunniens), *gomriga* (bos gavaeus), and *gavaya* (the *gayal*). Bones, bile (*pittha*), *snayu*, teeth, horn, hoofs, and tails of the above animals as well as of other beasts, cattle, birds and snakes (*vyala*).

Kalayasa (iron), *tamra* (copper), *vritta*, *kamsya* (bronze), *sisa* (lead), *trapu* (tin), *vaikrintaka* (mercury), and *arakuata* (brass), are metals.

Utensils (*bhanda*), are those made of cane, bark (*vidala*), and clay (*mrittika*).

Charcoal, bran, and ashes are other things.

Menageries of beasts, cattle, and birds.

Collection of firewood and fodder.

The superintendent of forest produce shall carry on either inside or outside (the capital city) the manufacture of all kinds of articles which are necessary for life or for the defence of forts.

The Superintendent of Weights and Measures

The Superintendent of Weights and Measures shall have the same manufactured.

10 seeds of *masha* (*Phraseolus Radiatus*) or 5 *gunja* (*Cabrus Precatorius*) = 1 *suvarna-masha*.

16 *mashas* = 1 *suvarna* or *karsha*.

4 *karshas* = 1 *pala*.

88 white mustard seeds = 1 silver-*masha*.

16 silver *mashas* or 20 *saibya* seeds = 1 *dharana*.

Ardha-masha (half a masha), one masha, two mashas, four mashas, eight mashas, one suvarna, two suvarnas, four suvarnas, eight suvarnas, ten suvarnas, twenty suvarnas, thirty suvarnas, forty suvarnas and one hundred suvarnas are different units of weights.

Similar series of weights shall also be made in dharanas.

Weights (pratimanani) shall be made of iron or of stones available in the countries of Magadha and Mekala; or of such things as will neither contract when wetted, nor expand under the influence of heat. Beginning with a lever of six angulas in length and of one pala in the weight of its metallic mass, there shall be made ten (different) balances with levers successively increasing by one pala in the weight of their metallic masses, and by eight angulas in their length. A scale-pan shall be attached to each of them on one or both sides.

A balance called samavritta, with its lever 72-angulas long and weighing 53 palas in its metallic mass shall also be made. A scalepan of 5 palas in the weight of its metallic mass being attached to its edge, the horizontal position of the lever (samakarana) when weighing a karsha shall be marked (on that part of the lever where, held by a thread, it stands horizontal).

To the left of that mark, symbols such as 1 pala, 12, 15 and 20 palas shall be marked. After that, each place of tens up to 100 shall be marked. In the place of Akshas, the sign of Nandi shall be marked.

Likewise a balance called parimani of twice as much metallic mass as that of samavritta and of 96 angulas in length shall be made. On its lever, marks such as 20, 50 and 100 above its initial weight of 100 shall be carved.

20 tulas = 1 bhara.

10 dharanas = 1 pala.

100 such palas = 1 ayamani (measure of royal income).

Public balance (vyavaharika), servants' balance (bhajini), and harem balance (antahpurabhajini) successively decrease by five palas (compared with ayamani).

A pala in each of the above successively falls short of the same in ayamani by half a dharana.

The metallic mass of the levers of each of the above successively decreases in weight by two ordinary palas and in length by six angulas.

Excepting flesh, metals, salt, and precious stones, an excess of five palas (prayama) of all other commodities (shall be given to the king) when they are weighed in the two first-named balances. A wooden balance with a lever 8 hands long, with measuring marks and counterpoise weights shall be erected on a pedestal like that of a peacock. Twenty-five palas of firewood will cook one prastha of rice. This is the unit (for the calculation) of any greater or less quantity (of firewood).

Thus weighing balance and weights are commented upon.

Then,

200 palas in the grains of masha	1 drona which is an ayamana, a measure of royal income.
187½ palas in the grains of masha	1 public drona.
175 palas in the grains of masha	1 bhajaniya, servants' measure
162½ palas in the grains of masha	1 antahpurabhajaniya, harem measure.

Adhaka, prastha, and kudumba, are each ¼ of the one previously mentioned.

16 dronas == 1 vari.

20,, == 1 kumbha.

10 kumbhas == 1 vaha.

Cubic measures shall be so made of dry and strong wood that when filled with grains, the conically heaped-up portion of the grains standing on the mouth of the measure is equal to ¼th of the quantity of the grains (so measured); or the measures may also be so made that a quantity equal to the heaped-up portion can be contained within (the measure).

But liquids shall always be measured level to the mouth of the measure.

With regard to wine, flowers, fruits, bran, charcoal and slaked lime, twice the quantity of the heaped-up portion (*i.e.*, ¼th of the measure) shall be given in excess.

1¼ panas is the price of	a drona.
¾ pana,,	an adhaka.
6 mashas,,	a prastha.
1 masha,,	a kudumba.

The price of similar liquid-measures is double the above.

20 panas is the price of a set of counter-weights.

6 panas „ of a tula (balance).

The Superintendent shall charge 4 mashas for stamping weights or measures. A fine of 27¼ panas shall be imposed for using unstamped weights or measures.

Traders shall every day pay one kakani to the Superintendent towards the charge of stamping the weights and measures.

Those who trade in clarified butter, shall give, (to purchasers) 1/32 part more as taptavyaji (*i.e.*, compensation for decrease in the quantity of ghi owing to its liquid condition).

Those who trade in oil shall give 1/64 part more as taptavyaji.

(While selling liquids, traders) shall give 1/50 part more as manasrava (*i.e.*, compensation for diminution in the quantity owing to its overflow or adhesion to the measuring can).

Half, one-fourth, and one-eighth parts of the measure, kumbha, shall also be manufactured.

84 kudumbas of clarified butter are held to be equal to

a waraka of the same;

64 kudumbas of clarified butter are held to be equal to

make one waraka of oil (taila); and¼ of a waraka is called ghatika, either of ghi or of oil.

The Superintendent of Tolls

The Superintendent of Tolls shall erect near the large gate of the city both the toll-house and its flag facing either the north or the south. When merchants with their merchandise arrive at the toll-gate, four or five collectors shall take down who the merchants are, whence they come, what amount of merchandise they have brought and where for the first time the sealmark (abhijnanamudra) has been made (on the merchandise).

Those whose merchandise has not been stamped with sealmark shall pay twice the amount of toll. For counterfeit seal they shall pay eight times the toll. If the sealmark is effaced or torn, (the merchants in question) shall be compelled to stand in ghatikasthana. When one kind of seal is used for another or when one kind of merchandise has been otherwise named (namakrite), the merchants shall pay a fine of 1¼ panas for each load (sapadapanikam vahanam dapayet).

The merchandise being placed near the flag of the toll-house, the merchants shall declare its quantity and price, cry out thrice "who will purchase this quantity of merchandise for this amount of price," and hand over the same to those who demand it (for that price). When purchasers happen to bid for it, the enhanced amount of the price together with the toll on the merchandise shall be paid into the king's treasury. When under the fear of having to pay a heavy toll, the quantity or the price of merchandise is lowered, the excess shall be taken by the king or the merchants shall be made to pay eight times the toll. The same punishment shall be imposed when the price of the merchandise packed in bags is lowered by showing an inferior sort as its sample or when valuable merchandise is covered over with a layer of an inferior one.

When under the fear of bidders (enhancing the price), the price of any merchandise is increased beyond its proper value, the king shall receive the enhanced amount or twice the amount of toll on it. The same punishment or eight times the amount of toll shall be imposed on the Superintendent of tolls if he conceals (merchandise).

Hence commodities shall be sold only after they are precisely weighed, measured, or numbered.

With regard to inferior commodities as well as those which are to be let off free of toll, the amount of toll due shall be determined after careful consideration.

Those merchants who pass beyond the flag of the toll-house without paying the toll shall be fined eight times the amount of the toll due from them.

Those who pass by to and from (the city) shall ascertain (whether or not toll has been paid on any merchandise going along the road.)

Commodities intended for marriages, or taken by a bride from her parents' house to her husband's (anvayanam), or intended for presentation, or taken for the purpose of sacrificial performance, confinement of women, worship of gods, ceremony of tonsure, investiture of sacred thread, gift of cows (godana, made before marriage), any religious rite, consecration ceremony (diksha), and other special ceremonials shall be let off free of toll.

Those who utter a lie shall be punished as thieves.

Those who smuggle a part of merchandise on which toll has not been paid with that on which toll has been paid as well as those who, with a view to smuggle with one pass a second portion of merchandise, put it along with the stamped merchandise after breaking open the bag shall forfeit the smuggled quantity and pay as much fine as is equal to the quantity so smuggled.

He who, falsely swearing by cow-dung, smuggles merchandise, shall be punished with the highest amercement.

When a person imports such forbidden articles as weapons (Shastra), mail armour, metals, chariots, precious stones, grains and cattle, he shall not only be punished as laid down elsewhere, but also be made to forfeit his merchandise. When any of such commodities has been brought in for sale, they shall be sold, free of toll far outside (the fort).

The officer in charge of boundaries (antapala) shall receive a pana-and-a-quarter as roadcess (vartani) on each load of merchandise (panyavahanasya).

He shall levy a pana on a single-hoofed animal, half a pana on each head of cattle, and a quarter on a minor quadruped.

He shall also receive a masha on a head-load of merchandise. He shall also make good whatever has been lost by merchants (in the part of the country under his charge).

After carefully examining foreign commodities as to their superior or inferior quality and stamping them with his seal, he shall send the same to the superintendent of tolls.

Or he may send to the king a spy in the guise of a trader with information as to the quantity and quality of the merchandise.

(Having received this information,) the king shall in turn send it to the superintendent of tolls in view of exhibiting the king's omniscient power. The superintendent shall tell the merchants (in question) that such and such a merchant has brought such and such amount of superior or inferior merchandise, which none can possibly hide, and that information is due to the omniscient power of the king.

For hiding inferior commodities, eight times the amount of toll shall be imposed; and for hiding or concealing superior commodities, they shall be wholly confiscated.

Whatever causes harm or is useless to the country shall be shut out; and whatever is of immense good as well as seeds not easily available shall be let in free of toll.

Regulation of Toll-dues

Merchandise, external (bahyam, *i.e.*, arriving from country parts), internal (abhyantaram, *i.e.*, manufactured inside forts), or foreign (atithyani, *i.e.*, imported from foreign countries) shall all be liable to the payment of toll alike when exported (nishkramya) and imported (pravesyam).

Imported commodities shall pay 1/5th of their value as toll.

Of flower, fruit, vegetables (saka), roots (mula), bulbous roots (kanda), pallikya, seeds, dried fish, and dried meat, the superintendent shall receive 1/6th as toll.

As regards conch-shells, diamonds, precious stones, pearls, corals, and necklaces, experts acquainted with the time, cost, and finish of the production of such articles shall fix the amount of toll.

Of fibrous garments (kshauma), cotton cloths (dukula), silk (krimitana), mail armour (kankata), sulphuret of arsenic (haritala), red arsenic (manassila), vermilion (hingulaka), metals (loha), and colouring ingredients (varnadhatu); of sandal, brown sandal (agaru), pungents (katuka), ferments (kinva), dress (avarana), and the like; of wine, ivory, skins, raw materials used in making fibrous or cotton garments, carpets, curtains (pravarana), and products yielded by worms (krimijata); and of wool and other products yielded by goats and sheep, he shall receive 1/10th or 1/15th as toll. Of cloths (vastra), quadrupeds, bipeds, threads, cotton, scents, medicines, wood, bamboo, fibres (valkala), skins, and clay-pots; of grains, oils, sugar (kshara), salt, liquor (madya) cooked rice and the like, he shall receive 1/20th or 1/25th as toll.

Gate-dues (dvaradeya) shall be 1/5th of toll dues; this tax may be remitted if circumstances necessitate such favour. Commodities shall never be sold where they are grown or manufactured.

When minerals and other commodities are purchased from mines, a fine of 600 panas shall be imposed.

When flower or fruits are purchased from flower or fruit gardens, a fine of 54 panas shall be imposed.

When vegetables, roots, bulbous roots are purchased from vegetable gardens, a fine 51¾ panas shall be imposed.

When any kind of grass or grain is purchased from field, a fine of 53 panas shall be imposed.

(Permanent) fines of 1 pana and 1½ panas shall be levied on agricultural produce (sitatyayah).

Hence in accordance with the customs of countries or of communities, the rate of toll shall be fixed on commodities, either old or new; and fines shall be fixed in proportion to the gravity of offences.

The Superintendent of Agriculture

Possessed of the knowledge of the science of agriculture dealing with the plantation of bushes and trees (krishitantragulmavrikshshayurvedajnah), or assisted by those who are trained in such sciences, the superintendent of agriculture shall in time collect the seeds of all kinds of grains, flowers, fruits, vegetables, bulbous roots, roots, pallikya, fibre-producing plants, and cotton.

He shall employ slaves, labourers, and prisoners (dandapratikartri) to sow the seeds on crown-lands which have been often and satisfactorily ploughed.

The work of the above men shall not suffer on account of any want in ploughs (karshanayantra) and other necessary instruments or of bullocks. Nor shall there be any delay in procuring to them the assistence of blacksmiths, carpenters, borers (medaka), ropemakers, as well as those who catch snakes, and similar persons.

Any loss due to the above persons shall be punished with a fine equal to the loss.

The quantity of rain that falls in the country of jangala is 16 dronas; half as much more in moist countries (anupanam); as to the countries which are fit for agriculture (desavapanam);—13½ dronas in the country of asmakas; 23 dronas in avanti; and an immense quantity in western countries (aparantanam), the borders of the Himalayas, and the countries where water channels are made use of in agriculture (kulyavapanam).

When one-third of the requisite quantity of rain falls both during the commencement and closing months of the rainy season and two-thirds in the middle, then the rainfall is (considered) very even (sushumarupam).

A forecast of such rainfall can be made by observing the position, motion, and pregnancy (garbhadana) of the Jupiter (Brihaspati), the rise and set and motion of the Venus, and the natural or unnatural aspect of the sun.

From the sun, the sprouting of the seeds can be inferred; from (the position of) the Jupiter, the formation of grains (stambakarita) can be inferred; and from the movements of the Venus, rainfall can be inferred.

Three are the clouds that continuously rain for seven days; eighty are they that pour minute drops; and sixty are they that appear with the sunshine—this is termed rainfall. Where rain, free from wind and unmingled with sunshine, falls so as to render three turns of ploughing possible, there the reaping of good harvest is certain.

Hence, *i.e.*, according as the rainfall is more or less, the superintendent shall sow the seeds which require either more or less water.

Sali (a kind of rice), vrihi (rice), kodrava (Paspalum Scrobiculatum), tila (sesamum), priyangu (panic seeds), daraka, and varaka (Phraseolus Trilobus) are to be sown at the commencement (purvavapah) of the rainy season. Mudga (Phraseolus Mungo), masha (Phraseolus Radiatus), and saibya are to be sown in the middle of the season.

Kusumbha (safflower), masura (Ervum Hirsutum), kuluttha (Dolichos Uniflorus), yava (barley), godhuma (wheat), kalaya (leguminus seeds), atasi (linseed), and sarshapa (mustard) are to be sown last. Or seeds may be sown according to the changes of the season.

Fields that are left unsown (vapatiriktam, *i.e.*, owing to the inadequacy of hands) may be brought under cultivation by employing those who cultivate for half the share in the produce (ardhasitika); or those who live by their own physical exertion (svaviryopajivinah) may cultivate such fields for ¼th or 1/5th of the produce grown; or they may pay (to the king) as much as they can without entailing any hardship upon themselves (anavasitam bhagam), with the exception of their own private lands that are difficult to cultivate.

Those who cultivate irrigating by manual labour (hastapravartimam) shall pay 1/5th of the produce as water-rate (udakabhagam); by carrying water on shoulders (skandhapravartimam) ¼th of the produce; by water-lifts (srotoyantrapravartimam), 3rd of the produce; and by raising water from rivers, lakes, tanks, and wells (nadisarastata-kakupodghatam), 3rd or ¼th of the produce.

The superintendent shall grow wet crops (kedara), winter-crops (haimana), or summer crops (graishmika) according to the supply of workmen and water.

Rice-crops and the like are the best (jyashtha, *i.e.*, to grow); vegetables (shanda) are of intermediate nature; and sugarcane crops (ikshu) are the worst (pratyavarah, *i.e.*, very difficult to grow), for they are subject to various evils and require much care and expenditure to reap.

Lands that are beaten by foam (phenaghatah, *i.e.*, banks of rivers, etc.) are suitable for growing valliphala (pumpkin, gourd and the like); lands that are frequently overflown by water (parivahanta) for long pepper, grapes (mridvika), and sugarcane;

the vicinity of wells for vegetables and roots; low grounds (hariniparyantah) for green crops; and marginal furrows between any two rows of crops are suitable for the plantation of fragrant plants, medicinal herbs, cascus roots (usinara), hira, beraka, and pindaluka (lac) and the like. Such medicinal herbs as grow in marshy grounds are to be grown not only in grounds suitable for them, but also in pots (sthalyam).

The seeds of grains are to be exposed to mist and heat (tusharapayanamushnam cha) for seven nights; the seeds of kosi are treated similarly for three nights; the seeds of sugarcane and the like (kandabijanam) are plastered at the cut end with the mixture of honey, clarified butter, the fat of hogs, and cow-dung; the seeds of bulbous roots (kanda) with honey and clarified butter; cotton seeds (asthibija) with cow-dung; and water pits at the root of trees are to be burnt and manured with the bones and dung of cows on proper occasions.

The sprouts of seeds, when grown, are to be manured with a fresh haul of minute fishes and irrigated with the milk of snuhi (Euphorbia Antiquorum).

Where there is the smoke caused by burning the essence of cotton seeds and the slough of a snake, there snakes will not stay.

Always while sowing seeds, a handful of seeds bathed in water with a piece of gold shall be sown first and the following mantra recited:

"Prajapatye Kasyapaya devaya namah.
Sada Sita medhyatam devi bijeshu cha
dhaneshu cha. Chandavata he."

"Salutation to God Prajapati Kasyapa. Agriculture may always flourish and the Goddess (may reside) in seeds and wealth. Channdavata he."

Provisions shall be supplied to watchmen, slaves and labourers in proportion to the amount of work done by them.

They shall be paid a pana-and-a-quarter per mensem. Artisans shall be provided with wages and provision in proportion to the amount of work done by them.

Those that are learned in the Vedas and those that are engaged in making penance may take from the fields ripe flowers and fruits for the purpose of worshipping their gods, and rice and barley for the purpose of performing agrayana, a sacrificial performance at the commencement of harvest season, also those who live by gleaning grains in fields may gather grains where grains had been accumulated and removed from.

Grains and other crops shall be collected as often as they are harvested. No wise man shall leave anything in the fields, nor even chaff. Crops, when reaped, shall be heaped up in high piles or in the form of turrets. The piles of crops shall not be kept close, nor shall their tops be small or low. The threshing floors of different fields shall be situated close to each other. Workmen in the fields shall always have water but no fire.

The Superintendent of Liquor

By employing such men as are acquainted with the manufacture of liquor and ferments (kinva), the Superintendent of Liquor shall carry on liquor-traffic not only in forts and country parts, but also in camps.

In accordance with the requirements of demand and supply (krayavikrayavasena) he may either centralize or decentralize the sale of liquor.

A fine of 600 panas shall be imposed on all offenders other than those who are manufacturers, purchasers, or sellers in liquor-traffic.

Liquor shall not be taken out of villages, nor shall liquor shops be close to each other.

Lest workmen spoil the work in hand, and Aryas violate their decency and virtuous character, and lest firebrands commit indiscreet acts, liquor shall be sold to persons of well known character in such small quantities as one-fourth or half-a-kudumba, one kudumba, half-a-prastha, or one prastha. Those who are well known and of pure character may take liquor out of shop. Or all may be compelled to drink liquor within the shops and not allowed to stir out at once in view of detecting articles such as sealed deposits, unsealed deposits, commodities given for repair, stolen articles, and the like which the customer's may have acquired by foul means.

When they are found to possess gold and other articles not their own, the superintendent shall contrive to cause them to be arrested outside the shop. Likewise those who are too extravagant or spend beyond their income shall be arrested.

No fresh liquor other than bad liquor shall be sold below its price. Bad liquor may be sold elsewhere or given to slaves or workmen in lieu of wages; or it may form the drink of beasts for draught or the subsistence of hogs.

Liquor shops shall contain many rooms provided with beds and seats kept apart. The drinking room shall contain scents, garlands of flowers, water, and other comfortable things suitable to the varying seasons.

Spies stationed in the shops shall ascertain whether the expenditure incurred by customers in the shop is ordinary or extraordinary and also whether there are any strangers. They shall also ascertain the value of the dress, ornaments, and gold of the customers lying there under intoxication.

When customers under intoxication lose any of their things, the merchants of the shop shall not only make good the loss, but also pay an equivalent fine.

Merchants seated in half-closed rooms shall observe the appearance of local and foreign customers who, in real or false guise of Aryas lie down in intoxication along with their beautiful mistresses.

Of various kinds of liquor such as medaka, prasanna, asava, arista, maireya, and madhu:—

Medaka is manufactured with one drona of water, half, an adaka of rice, and three prastha of kinva (ferment).

Twelve adhakas of flour (pishta), five prasthas of kinva (ferment), with the addition of spices (jatisambhara) together with the bark and fruits of putraka (a species of tree) constitute prasanna.

One-hundred palas of kapittha (Feronia Elephantum) 500 palas of phanita (sugar), and one prastha of honey (madhu) form asava.

With an increase of one-quarter of the above ingredients, a superior kind of asava is manufactured; and when the same ingredients are lessened to the extent of one-quarter each, it becomes of an inferior quality.

The preparation of various kinds of arishta for various diseases are to be learnt from physicians.

A sour gruel or decoction of the bark of meshasringi (a kind of poison) mixed with jaggery (guda) and with the powder of long pepper and black pepper or with the powder of triphala (1 Terminalia Chebula, 2 Terminalia Bellerica, and 3 Phyllanthus Emblica) forms Maireya.

To all kinds of liquor mixed with jaggery, the powder of triphala is always added.

The juice of grapes is termed madhu. Its own native place (svadesa) is the commentary on such of its various forms as kapisayana and harahuraka. One drona of either boiled or unboiled paste of masha (Phraseolus Radiatus), three parts more of rice, and one karsha of morata (Alangium Hexapetalum) and the like form kinva (ferment).

In the manufacture of medaka and prasanna, five karshas of the powder of (each of patha (Clypea Hermandifolio), lodhra (Symplocos Racemosa), tejovati (Piper Chaba), elavaluka (Solanum Melongena) honey, the juice of grapes (madhurasa), priyangu (panic seeds), daruharidra (a species of turmeric) black pepper and long pepper are added as sambhara, requisite spices.

The decoction of madhuka (Bassia Latifolia) mixed with granulated sugar (katasarkara), when added to prasanna, gives it a pleasing colour.

The requisite quantity of spices to be added to asava is one karsha of the powder of each of chocha (bark of cinnamon), chitraka (Plumbago Zeylanica), vilanga, and gajapippali (Scindapsus Officinalis), and two karshas of the powder of each of kramuka (betel nut), madhuka (Bassia Latifolia), musta (Cyprus Rotundus), and lodhra (Symlocos Racemosa).

The addition of one-tenth of the above ingredients (*i.e.*, chocha, kramuka, etc.), is (termed) bijabandha.

The same ingredients as are added to prasanna are also added to white liquor (svetasura).

The liquor that is manufactured from mango fruits (sahakarasura) may contain a greater proportion of mango essence (rasottara), or of spices (bijottara). It is called mahasura when it contains sambhara (spices as described above).

When a handful (antarnakho mushtih, *i.e.*, so much as can be held in the hand, the fingers being so bent that the nails cannot be seen) of the powder of granulated sugar dissolved in the decoction of morata (Alangium Hexapetalum), palasa (Butea Frondosa), dattura (Dattura Fastuosa), karanja (Robinia Mitis), meshasringa (a kind of poison) and the bark of milky trees (kshiravriksha) mixed with one-half of the paste formed by combining the powders of lodhra (Symplocos Racemosa), chitraka (Plumbago Zeylanica), vilanga, patha (clypea Hermandifolia), musta (cyprus Rotundus), kalaya (leguminous seeds), daruharidra (Amonum Xanthorrhizon), indivara (blue lotus), satapushpa (Anethum Sowa), apamarga (Achyranthes Aspera) saptaparna (Echites Scholaris), and nimba (Nimba Melia) is added to (even) a kumbha of liquor payable by the king, it renders it very pleasant. Five palas of phanita (sugar) are added to the above in order to increase its flavour.

On special occasions (krityeshu), people (kutumbinah, *i.e.*, families) shall be allowed to manufacture white liquor (svetasura), arishta for use in diseases, and other kinds of liquor.

On the occasions of festivals, fairs (samaja), and pilgrimage, right of manufacture of liquor for four days (chaturahassaurikah) shall be allowed.

The Superintendent shall collect the daily fines (daivasikamatyayam, *i.e.*, license fees) from those who on these occasions are permitted to manufacture liquor.

Women and children shall collect 'sura,' and 'kinva,' 'ferment.'

Those who deal with liquor other than that of the king shall pay five percent as toll.

With regard to sura, medaka, arishta, wine, phalamla (acid drinks prepared from fruits), and amlasidhu (spirit distilled from molasses): Having ascertained the day's sale of the above kinds of liquor, the difference of royal and public measures (manavyaji), and the excessive amount of sale proceeds realised thereby, the Superintendent shall fix the amount of compensation (vaidharana) due to the king (from local or foreign merchants for entailing loss on the king's liquor traffic) and shall always adopt the best course.

The Duty of Revenue-collectors; Spies in the Guise of Householders, Merchants and Ascetics

Having divided the kingdom (janapada) into four districts, and having also subdivided the villages (grama) as of first, middle and lowest rank, he shall bring them under one or another of the following heads:—-Villages that are exempted from taxation (pariharaka); those that supply soldiers (ayudhiya); those that pay their taxes in the form of grains, cattle, gold (hiranya), or raw material (kupya); and those that supply free labour (vishti), and dairy produce in lieu of taxes (karapratikara).

It is the duty of Gopa, village accountant, to attend to the accounts of five or ten villages as ordered by the Collector-General.

By setting up boundaries to villages, by numbering plots of grounds as cultivated, uncultivated, plains, wet lands, gardens, vegetable gardens, fences (vata), forests, altars, temples of gods, irrigation works, cremation grounds, feeding houses (sattra), places where water is freely supplied to travellers (prapa), places of pilgrimage, pasture grounds and roads, and thereby fixing the boundaries of various villages, of fields, of forests, and of roads, he shall register gifts, sales, charities, and remission of taxes regarding fields.

Also having numbered the houses as taxpaying or non-taxpaying, he shall not only register the total number of the inhabitants of all the four castes in each village, but also keep an account of the exact number of cultivators, cow-herds, merchants, artizans, labourers, slaves, and biped and quadruped animals, fixing at the same time the amount of gold, free labour, toll, and fines that can be collected from it (each house).

He shall also keep an account of the number of young and old men that reside in each house, their history (charitra), occupation (ajiva), income (aya), and expenditure (vyaya). Likewise Sthanika, district officer, shall attend to the accounts of one quarter of the kingdom.

In those places which are under the jurisdiction of Gopa and Sthanika, commissioners (prodeshtarah) specially deputed by the Collector-general shall not only inspect the work done and the means employed by the village and district officers, but also collect the special religious tax known as bali (balipragraham kuryuh).

Spies under the disguise of householders (grihapatika, cultivators) who shall be deputed by the collector-general for espionage shall ascertain the validity of the accounts (of the village and district officers) regarding the fields, houses and families of each village—-the area and output of produce regarding fields, right of ownership and remission of taxes with regard to houses, and the caste and profession regarding families.

They shall also ascertain the total number of men and beasts (janghagra) as well as the amount of income and expenditure of each family.

They shall also find out the causes of emigration and immigration of persons of migratory habit, the arrival and departure of men and women of condemnable (anarthya) character, as well as the movements of (foreign) spies.

Likewise spies under the guise of merchants shall ascertain the quantity and price of the royal merchandise such as minerals, or products of gardens, forests, and fields or manufactured articles.

As regards foreign merchandise of superior or inferior quality arriving thither by land or by water, they shall ascertain the amount of toll, road-cess, conveyance-cess, military cess, ferry-fare, and one-sixth portion (paid or payable by the merchants), the charges incurred by them for their own subsistence, and for the accommodation of their merchandise in warehouse (panyagara).

Similarly spies under the guise of ascetics shall, as ordered by the Collector-general, gather information as to the proceedings, honest or dishonest, of cultivators, cow-herds, merchants, and heads of Government departments. In places where altars are situated or where four roads meet, in ancient ruins, in the vicinity of tanks, rivers, bathing places, in places of pilgrimage and hermitage, and in desert tracts, mountains, and thick grown forests, spies under the guise of old and notorious thieves with their student bands shall ascertain the causes of arrival and departure, and halt of thieves, enemies, and persons of undue bravery.

The Collector-general shall thus energetically attend to the affairs of the kingdom. Also his subordinates constituting his various establishments of espionage shall along with their colleagues and followers attend to their duties likewise.

2

Indian Feudalism

The term Indian feudalism is an attempt to classify Indian history according to a European model. Historians have become very reluctant to classify other societies into European models and today it is rare for Indian history to be described as feudal by academics; it still done in popular usage, however, but only for pejorative reasons to express disfavour, typically by critics. These include zamindar, jagir, desmukh, chowdhury. Most of these "systems" were abolished after the Independence of India and the rest of the sub-continent, but most still exist, officially or in its remnants.

Characteristics of European Feudalism

The evolution of highly diverse forms, customs, and institutions makes it almost impossible to accurately depict feudalism as a whole, but certain components of the system may be regarded as characteristic: strict division into social classes, *i.e.*, nobility, clergy, peasantry, and, in the later Middle Ages, burgesses; private jurisdiction based on local custom; and the landholding system dependent upon the fief or fee. Feudalism was based on contracts made among nobles, and although it was intricately connected with the manorial system, it must be considered as distinct from it. Although some men held their land in alod, without obligation to any person, they were exceptions to the rule in the Middle Ages.

In an ideal feudal society (a legal fiction, most nearly realized in the Crusaders' Latin Kingdom of Jerusalem), the ownership of all land was vested in the king. Beneath him was a hierarchy of nobles, the most important nobles holding land directly from the king, and the lesser from them, down to the seigneur who held a single manor. The political economy of the system was local and agricultural, and at its base was the manorial system. Under the manorial system the peasants, labourers, or serfs, held the land they worked from the seigneur, who granted them use of the land and his protection in return for personal services (especially on the demesne, the land he retained for his own use) and for dues (especially payment in kind).

The Fief

The feudal method of holding land was by fief; the grantor of the fief was the suzerain, or overlord, and the recipient was the vassal. The fief was formally acquired following the ceremony of homage, in which the vassal, kneeling before the overlord, put his hands in those of the lord and declared himself his man, and the overlord bound himself by kissing the vassal and raising him to his feet. The vassal then swore an oath of fealty, vowing to be faithful to the overlord and to perform the acts and services due him. This formal procedure served to cement the personal relationship between lord and vassal; after the ceremony the lord invested the vassal with the fief, usually by giving him some symbol of the transferred land. Honours or rights, as well as land, could be granted as fiefs. Gradually the system of subinfeudation evolved, by which the vassal might in his turn become an overlord, granting part of his fief to one who then became vassal to him. Thus very complex relationships, based on fiefs, developed among the nobles, and the personal ties between overlords and vassals were weakened. Originally the fief had to be renewed on the death of either party. With the advent of hereditary succession and primogeniture, renewal of the fief by the heir of the deceased became customary, and little by little the fief became hereditary.

Military Service

The feudal system rested on the unsettled conditions of the times and thus on the need of the lord for armed warriors and the need of the vassal for protection. The nobility was essentially a military class, with the knight as the typical warrior. Since equipping mounted fighters was expensive, the lord could not create his armed force without the obligation of the vassal to supply a stipulated number of armed men, a number that varied from the service of the vassal himself to the service of hundreds in private armies. The gradations of nobility were, therefore, based on both military service and landholding. At the bottom of the social scale was the squire, originally the servant of the knight. Above the knight were classes that varied in different countries-counts, dukes, earls, barons, and other nobles. The vassal owed, in addition to military service, other dues and services that varied with local custom and tended to become fixed. The obligation of the overlord in the feudal contract was always the protection of the vassal.

History of Feudalism in Europe

Origins

The feudal system first appears in definite form in the Frankish lands in the 9th and 10th century. A long dispute between scholars as to whether its institutional basis was Roman or Germanic remains somewhat inconclusive; it can safely be said that feudalism emerged from the condition of society arising from the disintegration of Roman institutions and the further disruption of Germanic inroads and settlements. Of course, the rise of feudalism in areas formerly dominated by Roman institutions meant the breakdown of central government; but in regions untouched by Roman customs the feudal system was a further step toward organization and centralization.

The system used and altered institutions then in existence. Important in an economic sense was the Roman villa, with the peculiar form of rental, the precarium, a temporary grant of land that the grantor could revoke at any time. Increasingly, the poor landholder transferred his land to a protector and received it back as a precarium, thus giving rise to the manorial system. It was also possible for the manorial system to develop from the Germanic village, as in England.

The development of fiefs was also influenced by the Roman institution of patricinium and the German institution of mundium, by which the powerful surrounded themselves with men who rendered them service, especially military service, in exchange for protection. More and more, this service-and-protection contract came to involve the granting of a beneficium, the use of land, which tended to become hereditary. Local royal officers and great landholders increased their power and forced the king to grant them rights of private justice and immunity from royal interference. By these processes feudalism became fixed in Frankish lands by the end of the 10th century.

The church also had great influence in shaping feudalism; although the organization of the church was not feudal in character, its hierarchy somewhat paralleled the feudal hierarchy. The church owned much land, held by monasteries, by church dignitaries, and by the churches themselves. Most of this land, given by nobles as a bequest or gift, carried feudal obligations; thus clerical land, like lay land, assumed a feudal aspect, and the clergy became participants in the temporal feudal system. Many bishops and abbots were much like lay seigneturs. This feudal connection between church and state gave rise to the controversy over lay investiture.

Spread

Feudalism spread from France to Spain, Italy, and later Germany and Eastern Europe. In England the Frankish form was imposed by William I (William the Conqueror) after 1066, although most of the elements of feudalism were already present. It was extended eastward into Slavic lands to the marches (frontier provinces), which were continually battered by new invasions, and it was adopted partially in Scandinavian countries. The important features of feudalism were similar throughout, but there existed definite national differences. Feudalism continued in all parts of Europe until the end of the 14th century.

Decline

The concentration of power in the hands of a few was always a great disruptive force in the feudal system. The rise of powerful monarchs in France, Spain, and England broke down the local organization. Another disruptive force was the increase of communication, which broke down the isolated manor, assisted the rise of towns, and facilitated the emergence of the burgess class. This process was greatly accelerated in the 14th century and did much to destroy the feudal classifications of society.

The system broke down gradually. It was not completely destroyed in France until the French Revolution (1789), and it persisted in Germany until 1848 and in Russia until 1917. Many relics of feudalism still persist, and its influence remains on the institutions of Western Europe.

Other Feudal Systems

Other ages and other lands have seen the development of feudal institutions. In Japan the feudal system was well ordered before the 10th century, and it persisted with modifications until the 19th century (see bushido; daimyo). In other areas, as in China, where feudal practices were in existence by 1100 B.C., society became feudalistic but not precisely feudal. Feudalism in India and in the Saracen and Ottoman civilizations was in many ways analogous to Western feudalism, but it proved less durable than its European counterpart. The existence of feudalism in several civilizations has given rise to theories of feudalism as a necessary and inevitable stage of political development. Some scholars, however, consider the European feudal system a unique phenomenon.

Introduction

India is a country remarkable for its diversity; biological and human. The biological diversity owes itself to the country's position at the trijunction of the African, the northern Eurasian and the Oriental realm; its great variety of environmental regimes, and its relative stability of biological production.

It is this biological wealth that has attracted to the sub-continent many streams of people at different times, from different directions; bringing together a great diversity of human genes and human cultures. Whereas in other lands the dominant human cultures have tended to absorb or eliminate others, in India the tendency has been to isolate and subjugate the subordinated cultures, thereby augmenting cultural diversity. This tendency to nurture diversity has been favoured by the diversity of the country's ecological regimes [Gadgil and Guha, 1992].

People migrate because of pulls from their destination and pushes in their homeland, often propelled along by some technological advantage. Thus in 16th century Europeans came to India in search of spices, pushed out by the little ice age that had gripped Europe, equipped with superior seagoing vessels and guns. That migration is well documented and understood; but it is the many earlier ones that have brought to India the bulk of human genes and cultural traits. It is our purpose in this paper to elucidate what we can of these many earlier migrations.

Role of Innovations

People have of course migrated out of India as well, but these out-migrations have been on a much smaller scale, and mostly over the last three centuries. This is related to the fact that India has never been the site of any significant technological innovations. A series of important innovations have, over the years taken place outside of India, innovations which have given an edge to people in control of these innovations, propelling major migrations [Habib, 1992].

In chronological order the most relevant of these include:

(i) Evolution of symbolic language, probably by the first modern Homo Sapiens, in Africa, perhaps around 100 kybp (kybp = thousand years before present);

(ii) Husbanding of wheat, barley, cattle, pig in the mideast around 10 kybp;

(iii) Husbanding of rice, buffalo in China and Southeast Asia around 8 kybp;

(iv) Domestication of horse in Central Asia around 6 kybp;

(v) Use of iron in Anatolia around 5 kybp;

(vi) Use of stirrup for horse riding in Central Asia around 2 kybp;

(vii) Use of gunpowder in China around 2 kybp;

(viii) Use of canons and guns in war in Arabia in 15th century

Our theme then is that these manifold innovations to the west, east and north of the Indian sub-continent have propelled many waves of people onto our land, giving rise to what is genetically as well as culturally the most diverse society in the world. There are diverse lines of evidence for these migrations-genetic, linguistic, archaeological, anthropological. We will endeavour to draw on all these disciplines to reconstruct the story of peopling of India.

Genetic Affinities

Genetically and culturally India is perhaps the most diverse country on the face of the earth. The most authoritative summary of genetics of human populations is provided by Cavalli-Sforza in his magnum opus, History and Geography of Human Genes [Cavalli-Sforza, et. al 1994].

He provides global maps of frequencies of 82 genes for 42 population aggregates of indigenous people covering the entire world. The 82 loci show the highest levels of heterozygosity, 0.35-0.37 for northwestern India, west Asia and continental Europe.

Parts of south and eastern India share slightly lower levels of 0.33-0.35 with Western China, Central Asia, Scandinavia and Northern Africa. The lowest levels of 0.21-0.23 occur in the New Guinea and Western Australia.

Such genetic data is however rather limited, based on traditional markers such as blood groups. Modern genetic techniques have greatly added to the wealth of genetic information that may be obtained from a single individual by looking at the nucleotide base sequences themselves. Amongst the most variable of such sequences occur in two hypervariable regions of mitochondria, which are purely maternally inherited in humans. We have collaborated with Cavalli-Sforza and his colleagues at Stanford Medical School to examine base pair sequences of 791 base pair lengths from the "D" loop region of mitochondrial DNA for 101 Indians [Mountain et al. 1995].

Of these 48 belonged to an upper caste group Haviks, and 43 to a scheduled caste group Mukris from the coastal Uttara Kannada District of Karnataka, 7 to a tribal population called Kadars from Kerala, and 3 to other Indians involved in field collection of samples of scrapings of cheek cells and scalp hair roots. 86 of these 791 sites demonstrated some variation amongst Indians, it was also possible to compare 745 from amongst these 791 sites with published data on 187 individuals from Africa, Europe, China and other parts of Asia along with one Australian and one Afro-American individual [Vigilant et al., 1991].

The tree has two distinct trunks rooted in M1 and M2. The first trunk includes 65 sequences; all! Kung, most pygmies, 10 other Africans and two Chinese; the second trunk includes 229 sequences including 11 pygmies, 55 other Africans and all the non-Africans with the exception of the two Chinese. It is evident then that the primary genetic differentiation of the human species is between Africans and non-Africans, with Indians intermingling with Europeans and Chinese.

The magnitude of base pair differences in these sequences can permit us to estimate the time elapsed since common ancestry.

Evidently the group of 65 dominated by Africans with a mode around 17, are far more diversified genetically than the 229 primarily non-African sequences with a mode around 10. The time estimated to have elapsed since common ancestry of course depends on the mutation rate, which is probably somewhere between 10-5 to 10-6 for this hypervariable region of mitochondrial DNA. That gives us a range of 22 to 220 kybp for the first and 13.6 and 136 kybp for the second trunk.

This is in conformity with the current view that modern Homo sapiens populations underwent a first expansion within Africa around 100 kybp, and a second expansion outside Africa around 65 kybp. The Homo sapiens peopling India are then a part of this second expansion around 65 kybp-an expansion that may have occurred in southern China [Ballinger et al., 1992] or in or close to the Indian sub-continent itself [Mountain et al 1995].

This data can also be used to construct a tree summarizing the relationship amongst the major human groups.

As expected this tree separates out Africans from non-Africans. Amongst the non-Africans the Europeans, Chinese and Indians are almost equally close to each other, being a little more separated from other Asians and New Guineans. The Indian population of today might then be surmised to have been put together by many ebbs and flows of people over the huge Eurasian continent.

Gene Analysis Reveals People Radiating out of the Middle East and the Orient

To assess the patterns of these ebbs and flows, Cavalli-Sforza et al (1994) have examined the frequencies of 69 genes from 42 populations covering all of Asia. Any given population is then represented as a point in the 69 dimensional space. This information can be summarized with the help of a multi-variate analysis technique called principal components. The first principal component for Asia explains 35.1% of the total variation in the gene frequency; the second principal component 17.7% of the variation.

Subsequent components explain relatively little. These two maps are most instructive. The first PC map suggests that genetic affinities amongst Asian populations decline with distance along east-west axis. This is compatible with movements of people radically fanning out of mid-east; although it could also result from a westward movement along a very broad front in eastern Asia. In a similar fashion the second principal component is compatible with fanning out of people from southeast Asia and China, although it could also result from a major movement originating in the northernmost reaches of Asia.

In both these cases, the first explanation, namely fanning out of people from middle-east and from China and Southeast Asia is far more likely. These are known to have been two independent centres of origin of cultivated plants, the middle east being the earliest in the world around 10 kybp and China and southeast Asia a little later around 8 kybp. Cultivation permits substantial increases in population density. This numerical superiority as well as availability of stored grain and meat on hoof as a buffer permits agricultural people to expand into regions till then under hunting-gathering economy, replacing and absorbing the local populations and leaving definite genetic footprints. Excellent archaeological evidence from Europe provides conclusive evidence of such a process of a northward fanning out of farming people. It is then very likely that Asian populations today represent two major radiations of people out of two centres of origin of cultivation, one in the middle-east. The other in China and Southeast Asia. The

Indian population too must have been profoundly influenced by these two migrations, one through its northwestern frontiers near Khyber Pass in present day Pakistan, and the other through the northeast near the China-Myanmar-India border in Manipur. The first one appears to be more significant, since it explains twice as much of the total variation.

Language Families Reveal People's Ancestries and Movements

Humans not only transmit genes from one generation to the next, they also transmit cultural traits. Some of these are extremely conservative, being transmitted quite faithfully from parents to offspring. Foremost amongst these is language; children almost invariably acquire their mother tongue from their parents and other relatives. Language and other conservative traits such as practices relating to disposal of the dead are therefore excellent devices to trace historical changes. If this be so linguistic and genetic divergence ought to go hand in hand. To test this proposition, Cavalli-Sforza et al (1994) plot genetic distance amongst members of a human groups against the number of different languages spoken by members of the group.

The excellent correlation confirms our faith in languages as good markers for unravelling the ancestries and movements of people.

The languages of the world have been classified in a number of major families. There are of course a few which are stand-alone, which cannot be assigned to any family. Nahali, a tribal language of Central India and Burushaski, spoken by a small group of people on the border of Pakistan and Afghanistan are two such.

But all other languages of India, can be assigned to one of four major language families-Austric, Dravidian, Indo-European and Sino-Tibetan. An excellent information base on the speakers of these languages is provided by the People of India project of the Anthropological Survey of India. This project involved assigning the entire Indian population to 4635 ethnic communities and putting together detailed information on each of them through interviews of over 25000 individual informants spread over all districts of India, along with compiling information from a variety of published sources [Joshi, et al., 1993]. This project records as the mother tongue the following number of languages of different families spoken by Indian ethnic communities:

Table 1: Global Distribution

Austric	Southeast Asia, Eastern and Central India
Dravidian	South and Central India, Pakistan, Iran
Indo-European	Europe, West Asia, North, West and East India
Sino-Tibetan	China, Southeast Asia, India bordering Himalayas

It is reasonable to assume that speakers of these four language families represent at least four major lineages [Parpola, 1974]. The first question to ask is whether these language families developed within the country, or came in with migrations of people from outside the sub-continent. The geographical range of distribution of Austric, Indo-European and Sino-Tibetan speakers is extensive; India harbours only a minority of the languages within these families. The geographical range of distribution of Dravidian languages is however restricted largely to India; there are only two outlying populations-Brahui in Baluchistan and Elamic in Iran. Dravidian languages might then have developed within India, others are less likely to have done so, for we have no evidence of any major technological innovations that could have served to carry speakers of those languages outside India.

Language and Economy

We may look for evidence on how long the lineages speaking different language families have been in India in two different ways.

Firstly we may examine the current levels of economic activities of the communities speaking those languages, and to compare them with levels of economic activities of speakers of other language families.

The tribal communities of India continue to extensively hunt and gather as well as practice low input shifting cultivation. These communities are likely to have migrated to India relatively early, perhaps prior to the beginning of agriculture and animal husbandry. Some tribal groups or other speak languages belonging to each of the four families. Korkus, Mundas, Santals, Khasis speak Austric languages; Gonds, Oraons Dravidian languages, Nagas and Kukis Sino-Tibetan languages and Bhils and Varlis speak Indo-European languages.

But it is amongst Austric speakers that all communities are exclusively tribals. Outside India also most Austric speaking communities practice very primitive technologies.

This suggests that Austric speaking people may be the oldest inhabitants of India. They may be amongst the first group of Homo sapiens to have reached India, perhaps some 50-65 kybp. Since over 98% of Austric speakers today lie in southeast Asia, they may have entered India from the northeast.

Sino-Tibetan speakers of India also include many tribal groups, though they also include communities like Maites of Manipur valley practising advanced agriculture. Their concentration is along the Himalayas; only one community of West Bengal has reached mainland India. Many of them report having moved into India from Myanmar or China within last few generations. They are therefore peripheral to the broader peopling of India.

The bulk of Indian mainland populations are Dravidian and Indo-European speakers. Both include communities at all economic levels from tribals to the most advanced cultivator, pastoral, trader or priestly groups. Many of the technologically less advanced amongst these communities such as Dravidians speaking Kanis of Kerala or Indo-European speaking Bhils of Rajasthan may have acquired these languages in more recent times through the influence of the economically more advanced mainstream societies. It is however notable that while there are several Dravidian speaking forest dwelling tribal communities such as Gonds or Oraons in a matrix of more advanced Indo-European speaking communities, there are no enclaves of forest dwelling tribal Indo-European speakers surrounded by more advanced Dravidian speaking communities. The tribal Indo-European speakers of south India are all nomadic communities such as Banjaras or Pardhis with known history of migration from Rajasthan to south India in recent centuries. This is strongly suggestive of Dravidians being older inhabitants of the Indian sub-continent, having been pushed southwards, surrounded by or converted to Indo-European languages by later arriving Indo-European speakers.

One may then suggest the following sequence of migrations of these major language speaking groups into India: Austric-Dravidian-Indo-European. If this be correct, another interesting prediction follows.

Austric languages having arrived in India earliest may show the most diversified vocabulary, Indo-European languages the least. To test this we have compiled words for universally used nouns such as mother, water, tree in several Austric, Dravidian, Indo-European and Sino-Tibetan languages. While a more objective analysis of the extent of such variation is under way, it appears true that Austric languages show the greatest and Indo-European the least divergence.

Archaeological Evidence

While tool using Homo erectus populations have been in India for over 500 kybp, fossil human remains appear only after 45-50 kybp, associated with middle palaeolithic, or stone age tools.

It has been suggested that these sites fall in two groups, the northern sites showing affinities with the Mousterian tool industries of Europe, while the southern sites show cultural antecedents in lower palaeolithic. This may reflect two separate streams of migration of newly expanding Homo sapiens populations; one coming into India from the northwest, the second from the northeast. One may surmise that the stream coming in from the northeast may have included early speakers of Austric languages.

The next important event on the Indian archaeological scene is the beginning of cultivation of plants and use of pottery.

Cultivation of plants evidently reached India simultaneously, around 6 kybp from two different directions, from the two centres of origin in the mid-east and China and Southeast Asia. The steady advance beyond this stage seems however to have been primarily driven by the crop-animal complex derived from the mid-east, reaching the tip of southern India some 4000 years later around 2 kybp. The diffusion of pottery traditions, which arise in response to the need to store and cook grain shows similar evidence of the two influences from northwest and northeast, with the western influence predominating over much of the country. Thus the Black and Red Ware reflects western, while the Cordedware Chinese influence.

It is likely that the farmers entering India from the northwest passage were either Dravidian or Indo-European speakers; those entering the sub-continent from the northeastern passage may have been Sino-Tibetan or perhaps Austric speakers. If, as the linguistic evidence suggests Dravidian speakers entered India well before Indo-European speakers then middle-eastern farmers entering India from the northwest may have been Dravidian speakers. The remnants of related languages, Elamite and Brahui in Iran and Pakistan is consistent with such a migration of Dravidian speakers from mid-east to India.

Horse and Iron as Pointers of Heritage

If this is true, then the Indo-European speakers must have come to India with some other major advantage. Two other technological innovations, known to have originated outside of India are excellent candidates. They are the domestication of horse, around 6 kybp on the shores of Black Sea in present Ukraine, and the use of iron, around 5 kybp in Anatolia in present day Turkey. Riding of horses or hitching them to carts greatly increases the mobility and the military or trading capabilities of a group. While cattle, sheep, goat, pig were all domesticated in mid-east around 10 kybp, the horse was domesticated 4000 years later in a separate centre in the Asian steppes.

The most favoured theory of the spread of India-European languages today is that it was the language of these horse people who came to dominate Europe, west Asia and much of India over the next 4000 years. As a ruling class, they are believed to have imposed their language over Europe, without making any major genetic contributions to the populations. They may have wielded parallel influence in India. The horse appears in archaeological records between 2000 to 500 years after the first appearance of cultivation of crops and husbanding of cattle, sheep, goat and pigs in different parts of India. Particular styles of burial appear to accompany the horse people. These burial styles show links with styles noted in Central Asian homeland of Indo-European speakers strengthening our belief in the possibility that the Indo-European speakers indeed made their way to India propelled by the advantage that the control over horses conferred.

The people associated with Vedic traditions and Sanskrit language definitely used horses, and may have been one group, though perhaps not the only group of Indo-European speakers to enter the sub-continent. These people also seem to have been associated with cremation as a method of disposal of the dead. Cremation is today the dominant mode amongst most Indo-European speaking communities of India, burial remains common amongst Dravidian speaking communities, especially those affected little by the process of Sanskritisation.

This also suggests that Indo-European speakers came to India after Dravidian speakers, probably associated with the use of horse and the practice of cremation. It is also possible that it was the use of iron that conferred an important advantage to certain groups of people migrating to India; groups that may have included speakers of Indo-European languages. The archaeological evidence suggests that use of iron is not necessarily associated with that of the horse, and appears either later than or ahead of the former in different parts of the country.

It is then likely that iron was brought to India by people other than horse people, people other than Vedic people. Indeed there may have been many waves of Indo-European speakers into India, waves that may have brought into the country different languages of that family. Thus some linguists believe that the present day Indo-European languages came to India in at least two distinct streams, the first stream bringing in languages related to Bengali, Oriya, Marathi, Sindhi and Kashmiri and the second stream languages related to Punjabi, Hindi and Rajasthani.

It is not at all clear whether the Harappan people spoke Dravidian or Indo-European languages. This civilization is contemporaneous with the first appearance of horse, most likely associated with Indo-European speakers in the archaeological record.

It could therefore have been a Indo-European speaking civilization. But there is a greater possibility that it may have emerged out of the earlier Dravidian speaking communities of agriculturists. What seems more plausible is the equation of Dasas of Vedic people with the earliest, probably Austric speaking hunter-gatherers and Dasyus with the Dravidian speaking cultivating communities. It is notable that the Vedic people were engaged in a far more violent conflict with Dasyus; such conflict may relate to struggle over fertile land [Possehl, 1979].

A Plausible Scenario

There are then many still unanswered questions pertaining to how our sub-continent was peopled. But the most plausible scenario. The earliest migrants into India, perhaps 50 kybp may have been the Austric speaking Homo sapiens, with the advantage conferred by the mastery over a symbolic language. Their genetic footprints may be discerned in the trends evident in the 2nd P.C of the synthetic genetic map of Asia.

The next major waves of migrations around 6 kybp may have been those of wheat cultivators from the middle east and the rice cultivators from China and south east Asia. The former are likely to have been Dravidian speakers and contributed to the trend evident in the 1st P.C. of the synthetic genetic map of Asia.

The latter may have been Sino-Tibetan speakers who would have contributed further to the trend revealed by 2nd P.C. The latest major migration around 4 kybp may have included several waves of Indo-European speakers equipped with horses and iron technology.

These might have been the most massive migrations peopling India. Others have followed, largely from the west, through the Khyber Pass on the northwestern frontiers of the sub-continent. These seem to have been propelled by superior weaponry, increasingly better control over horses and finally seagoing ships.

Such significant innovations may include some of the following. An important early development in weaponry was the composite angular bow which appeared in west Asia around 5 kybp. Bending through the length of the limb, releasing this bow string produced no kick leading to a smooth and accurate shot.

The extremely long draw length of over 1 m led to a greatly enhanced cast. A crucial piece of equipment associated with control over horse is stirrup, which helps in balancing the rider and permits him to stand up to threw the lance. The earliest form of the stirrup was a string with two loops on either side for the rider's foot. The first known instance of iron stirrups comes from China in sixth century A.D. reaching Iran by 7th century, and arriving in India with Turkish warriors in 11th century.

Another significant invention was the iron horse shoe first known from Siberia in 9th Century A.D., reaching India with Turkish warriors in 13th Century A.D. The gunpowder was invented in China around 100 A.D. and slowly reached Iran, Arabia and finally Europe with Mongols around 1400 A.D. It reached India with the arrival of the first Mughal emperor Babur who used it in the first battle of Panipat in 1526 A.D.

The early canons in India were made by welding together many iron rods. The Europeans introduced cast iron canons in the next century; these could fire more accurate and powerful volleys. The Europeans also developed superior ocean-going vessels from which canons could be fired by 16th century [Deloche, 1983; Habib, 1992].

These many developments taking place in China, Central Asia and finally Europe brought in many people, enjoying a military advantage.

The number of people thus coming in were probably not very large, but they contributed immensely to the cultural diversity of the country by bringing in new languages, new forms of religion, and of course new technologies. Amongst these technologies was spinning wheel, apparently invented in China and brought to Europe by Mongols around 12th Century A.D. It seems to have reached India in 13th-14th Century and created a tremendous commercial potential for textile production in India. Similarly Indian agriculture too must have been greatly influenced by the introduction of the Persian wheel, first referred to by Babur in 1526-30 in his memoir Babur Nama.

With these many streams of Homo sapiens coming into the country over 50,000 years or more, India has developed what Cavalli-Sforza calls an incredibly complex genetic landscape. Our mitochondrial DNA data on 101 Indians permits us to estimate the time to common ancestry of our people on the basis of the pairwise differences in the mitochondrial DNA sequences. These estimates of course, depend on the assumed value of mutation rates; but 65,000 years is close to a reasonable estimate for the modal value of 9.

So the Indian population has been put together by people drawn from many different streams ultimately derived from the major expansion of non-African Homo sapiens around this time.

A Segmented Society

What the Indian population is remarkable for is the segmentation of this large population into thousands of endogamous groups. The People of India data recognizes 4635 such ethnic communities. Many of these are however clusters of endogamous groups with similar traditional occupations and social status.

The actual number of endogamous groups is decidedly much larger, of the order of 50 to 60 thousand. This persistence of tribe like endogamous groups, characteristic of hunter-gatherer-shifting cultivation stage all over the world, in a complex agrarian, and now industrial society of India is a unique phenomenon. It seems to be a result of a peculiarly Indian tradition of subjugation and isolation, rather than the worldwide practice of elimination or assimilation of subordinated communities by the dominant groups.

Our mitochondrial DNA studies provide some notable insights into the structure of this social mosaic. For this purpose we chose two communities, Haviks and Mukris from the same district of Uttara Kannada. Haviks are a Brahmin group well known for their skills at growing multi-storeyed spice gardens of cardamom, pepper and betelnut. They also perform priestly functions, and are today prominent in many white collar occupations. Their current population is around 100,000 individuals concentrated in an area of about 20,000 km^2.

The Mukri, on the contrary are members of a scheduled caste, earlier treated as untouchable. Their current population numbers around 9000 individuals concentrated in an area of 2000 km^2. They continue to indulge in substantial amounts of hunting, gathering and fishing to this date and serve as unskilled labour on Havik and other farms. The neighbour joining phylogenetic tree for 48 Haviks, 43 Mukris, 7 Kadars and 3 other Indians. Note that Haviks and Mukris, although they lie at opposite ends of the social hierarchy do not constitute two distinct trunks.

Their sequences are intermingled suggesting past genetic exchanges, although these may have occurred well before the formation of the Indian caste society some 2000 years ago; indeed they may even derive from the time of common ancestry some 65 kybp, perhaps as a part of population expansion of non-Africans outside of India. But intermingled as they are, the Havik sequences form a distinctive star-like pattern with many short branches joining the centre, unlike the Mukri sequences which are bunched in a few clusters on long branches.

The star like Havik pattern is suggestive of a history of population expansion, the clustered Mukri pattern suggests long history of a stationary population, or a population that has experienced several bottlenecks. This is further brought out in the distribution of pairwise mitochondrial DNA base pair sequence differences for the Havik and Mukri populations.

The unimodal pattern for Haviks is compatible with a history of population growth, the multimodal Mukri pattern with a history of population stationarity or bottlenecks.

Such differences in genetic structure suggestive of different population histories have been suggested from other human populations earlier, but never before for two population groups living together in such a restricted geographical locality as a single district of Uttara Kannada. This reflects the unique history of Indian population, with dominant groups like Haviks enjoying high levels of resource access and expanding in numbers and range, while subjugated populations like Mukris existed side by side with much more limited resource access and stagnant populations.

Such scenarios have probably characterized the Indian social mosaic for long, perhaps since the beginnings of cultivation and animal husbandry 6000 years ago. As groups with technologies conferring superiority in resource appropriation have migrated into and spread throughout India, they have subjugated other groups, restricted their resource access and permitted their continued existence, while the dominant groups have themselves grown in numbers and expanded in geographical range, perhaps dividing further into more endogamous groups.

This process of maintenance of large number of communities in isolation from each other has been accompanied by extreme specialization of occupation. It is perhaps this specialization of occupation that has prevented Indians from cross-fertilization of ideas and innovations, so that the Indian society has always been at the receiving end of technological innovations.

Land Tenure in Ancient India

Ancient record show that land has been under cultivation in India for more than 5,000 years. In the beginning, tribes exercised control (especially delimitation and defence) over the areas they had taken possession of. This right of the conqueror was the initial from of land right. The tribes allotted to the individual families land for their utilization, usually by means of shifting cultivation.

The jungle which covered unlimited land, although economically useless, led to another form of land right, namely, the right of the first clearer. Whoever cleared a plot in the jungle also had the right to use this land. However, this individual right of utilization was only valid as long as the land was actually cultivated. As soon as it was abandoned, the power of disposition over it reverted to the tribe. The strenuous work of clearing, the necessity of mutual help, small scale defence measures, and the expansion of the families led, in the course of time, to the formation of villages which assumed the regulation of land rights. Two different forms developed in time.

The village which had individual land rights consisted of a group of families which had rights to the land on the basis of having cleared it. The claims of the families were limited to the cleared land. The uncultivab land in the vicinity of the village was jointly utilized, but no claims were made to it. It belonged to the ruler who, in later epochs, also granted permission to cultivate the land.

In the case of villages which held land rights jointly, the village community claimed the right to all land within the village boundaries and allotted it to individual families for utilization. The administration was not carried out by a village headman, but by the panchayat, a village council in which the individual families had their say.

Thus, at an early period already, there were individual and joint land rights. But landed property, as known in the West, did not exist at all. The rights were a privilege granting inheritable utilization rights and included social obligations, especially taking consideration of the village community's interests.

Because of the need for defence, authority concentrated in the course of time, and thus, a state was formed with one ruler at its head. Costs of governing were covered, at first, with gifts. Soon, however, it became obligatory to deliver a share of the grain yield- in other words-, a tax was introduced. The king was thus only given a right to a share of the yield, but to rights to the land and its utilization. However, he was entitled to all the uncultivated land that lay between the villages.

It was necessary to establish an official hierarchy to collect the taxes. The tax collectors were remunerated by being given a share of the collected taxes and a plot of crown land. This "watan" land was free of tax, inheritable, and transferrable, and represented a new form of land rights, namely, land rights on account of the government allotting land to government officials.

In the course of time, the tasks of the central government increased. In this huge country where transport conditions were difficult, possibilities of simplifying administration played an important role. Therefore, the ruler allotted the tax revenue from specific areas to people who had to maintain troops in the provinces, make roads passable, and keep the passes open. At first, the transfer of the right to these taxes was valid only for the time during which these tasks were carried out. Even priests and favourites were provided for in that way, at first for life, later on, all these cessions became inheritable. This right to the land on the basis of the transfer of the right to taxes included taxes only, but not ownership of the land as in the case of 'watan' lands.

In pre-Islamic times already, there had been a diversification in the land rights. In addition to the land claims of the village community and the farmers based on the right of the conqueror and the first clearer, the ruler's claims to a share of the yield and the uncultivated land between the villages were generally recognized. In addition, the right to collect taxes for certain regions was transferred to specific people and land rights to officials. These were only allotted crown land. The traditional rights of the cultivators remained unaltered. The Moguls who conquered India in the 12th century left the land to the cultivators at first in exchange for the usual taxes. Often, former small rulers were employed as tax collectors and were given 10% of the collected amount as remuneration for their trouble. They were even allowed to keep the land they had held before and were exempted from paying taxes. They were strictly controlled to prevent them from collecting more taxes than was lawful.

Emperor Akbar (1556-1605) implemented radical reforms. He replaced the payment of taxes in kind by a monetary tax which was no longer fixed as a share of the actual but rather of the average yield. Thus, it was not calculated according to the yield, but according to the area sown, and the cropping risk was shifted to the cultivators. In addition, the taxes were increased to amount to half of the average yield. Although this resulted in evil times for the rural population, the Moguls did not make any claims to the land itself after their conquest. Tax administration was high level; a land register was introduced; and taxes were levied according to criteria such as quality of the soil, and so on.

After Aurangzeb's death in 1707, the power of the central government decreased rapidly, and the control over the tax revenues was lost. In order to obtain revenues at all, tax collectors' posts were leased to the highest bidders in exchange for fixed sums. On the basis of their knowledge of the local conditions, the tax collectors were free to extort as much as possible from the rural population and keep for themselves the difference between the collected taxes and the amount to be remitted. These "assignees" were the first intermediary step in the direct tax relations between the government and cultivators.

The transfer of tax collection rights, known already in pre-Mogul times, for specific regions as remuneration for services rendered became so common that, under Aurangzeb's reign, 90% of all tax revenues fell to such privileged parties, and only 10% to the ruler. These grants of land with the right to collect taxes from it were also conferred on favourites. The conferment of such "jagir" transferred all the rights the government held, *i.e.*, taxes, claims to uncultivated land, police power, etc., but no claims to the cultivators' land. Whenever tax collectors became landlords in the course of time, this was due to their reclaiming waste land or their confiscating the land of people who owed taxes.

Towards the end of the Mogul era, a type of "right" to land developed which was in the hands of sometimes parasitical rent collectors who did not perform any work. But this refers to the government's tax rights, not to a direct claim to landed property, or land utilization, on peasants' land. Their old saying 'Taxes are the king's wealth, the land belongs to me" was still valid.

Changes in Land Tenure under British Rule

India's invasion by the British brought about, in the course of time, a complete transformation in the country's land tenure system. The East India Company experienced difficulty in its trading because the sale of British goods in India was insignificant. On the other hand, the exportation of gold and silver from England to pay for Indian goods was soon prohibited. The company found a solution by securing money from India to pay for Indian goods.

It collected taxes for the Indian rulers which, in the beginning, brought revenues of only 10% of the levied taxes, but, since the control over the amount of levied taxes became lax at the end of the Mogul period, its revenues increased. In addition, they were assigned areas as "jagir:°' The decisive breakthrough came when, in 1765, the office of 'dewan' for Bengal, Orissa, and Bihar, namely the financial sovereignty for these areas, was assigned to the Company with the concession for levying taxes in exchange for a global sum of Rs.2.6 million per annum.

After some time of experimentation, in 1793, Cornwallis' Permanent Settlement brought a final regulation of the procedure for levying taxes, which led to decisive changes in land tenure. The British did as if all the land belonged to the state and was thus at their disposal. They registered the local tax collectors, who were called zamindars, as owners of the land in their district. These zamindars had to collect and deliver the taxes; the amount was fixed at the beginning and remained the same permanently. To give them an incentive, they were free to decide how much to demand from the cultivators. On the other hand, the fixed lump tax sum was an incentive to put more land under cultivation and, thus, have more tax-payers in one region. In order to do so, one could not bleed the individual farmers too much.

The right to the land conferred on the zamindars was alienable, rentable, and heritable. This meant the introduction of a complete novelty, in India. The privilege of utilizing land had become a saleable good. Those who had been cultivators until then obtained the status of 'occupancy tenants.' These occupancy rights were heritable and transferrable and were not tampered with as long as the holders paid their taxes. In contrast to these, the tenants who cultivated land owned by the tax collectors were" tenants at will', *i.e.*, they could be evicted.

In the beginning, there were hardly any problems. The scarcity of cultivators prevented the zamindars from demanding too high taxes. They were interested in attracting people to cultivate the land and, thus, to increase the number of tax payers in order to increase the difference between the revenues and the fixed amount that had to be remitted.

The detrimental consequences of recognizing the tax collectors as landlords and of introducing the legal institution of saleable private landed property first became evident as, later, considerable changes occurred in India in the demographic and economic situation. The industrial revolution in England, namely, brought about a change in the British policy in India. The objective was no longer to import from India, but to sell English products in India. Since the textile industry played an important role at the beginning of industrialization in England, very large amounts of cheap products manufactured by mechanical looms were exported to India and this soon led to a collapse in the textile home industry in India. A large number of weavers became unemployed.

In order to secure a basis of existence, they migrated to the rural areas and tried to lease land they could farm. The scope of this migration-Dacca's inhabitants alone decreased from 150,000 to 20,000 between 1824 and 1837-caused pressure on the rural areas and brought about a complete change in the relationships between zamindars and tenants. The monopoly of controlling the means to secure livelihood shifted power unilaterally into the hands of the zamindars who were able to extort more and more taxes as the demand for land increased. This led to indebtedness and often to the loss of occupancy rights and relegation to tenants at will.

The great discrepancy between the fixed amount of taxes to be remitted and the increasing revenues made the zamindars wealthy. Soon they no longer went to the trouble of collecting the taxes themselves but rather sub-leased this office to others while they themselves lived on the remainder between the amount claimed as taxes and that paid to the "sub-assignees." The difference between the revenues and the amounts to be remitted was so great that even the "sub-assignees" tried to sub-lease. After some time, it became quite common to have 10 to 20 intermediaries, more or less without a specific function, between the government and the farmers, and they all had a share in the cultivation yield.

In addition, abwabs, supplements and fees for the most curious reasons were introduced; for example, for using an umbrella, for permission to sit down in the zamindar's office, for being allowed to stand up again, etc. Moreover, the "began" unpaid work which the tenants were forced to perform on the zamindar's land, took on larger and larger proportions. On the average, it amounted to 20 25% of the lease.

Under the effect of these developments which should be regarded as late consequences of the changes in the land tenure brought about by the "Permanent Settlement," more and more cultivators became indebted, lost their occupancy rights, and dropped in status to tenants at will or agricultural labourers. On the other hand, the wealth of the zamindars kept increasing on account of the income they earned from the difference between the amount of taxes and the rentals, the increase in cultivated areas, money lending, and expropriation of debtors. In the course of time, the zamindari region was characterized by the marked difference between wealth, power, and prospects in life. Even the government experienced drawbacks on account of this system. Changes in the monetary value, prices, and the amount of cultivated areas turned the fixed tax, after 150 years, into nothing but a token sum, and considerable tax tosses ensued.

The zamindari system was not introduced in the whole of India. Because of the experience made with the system, better knowledge of the conditions in India, and liberal influences on the colonial policy, the provinces which became British possessions later were assigned other taxation systems. The ryotwari system was introduced in Madras, Bombay, and Assam. Under that system, the government claimed the property rights to all of the land, but allotted it to the cultivators on the condition that they pay the taxes. They could use, sell, mortgage, bequeath, and lease the land as long as they paid their taxes. Otherwise, they were evicted. This direct tax relation between the government and the cultivators was meant to prevent sub-tax collectors, thus increasing purchasing power, and, in that way, improving the marketing prospects for English products. Here, the taxes were only fixed in a temporary settlement for a period of thirty years and then revised. This way, the government increased its revenue.

In North India and in the Punjab where villages with joint land rights were common, an attempt was made to utilize this structure in the Mahalwari system. Taxation was imposed with the village community as theoretical landlord, since it had the land rights. The village community had to distribute these taxes among the cultivators who owed taxes individually and jointly. Everyone was thus liable for the others' arrears. A village inhabitant, the lambardar, collected the amounts and remitted them in bulk. Here, too, tax assessment was revised at intervals.

Despite this different system, the conditions for cultivators constantly deteriorated in these regions as well. The high taxes fixed by the government half to two thirds of the net yield was the usual amount made investments impossible. Because of fragmentation resulting from inheritance, the farms became smaller and smaller. The fact that land could be used as collateral made it possible to borrow money to pay taxes in the case of crop failures. But, in that way, more and more farms passed into the husbands of moneylenders, often better off cultivatorsin the village. In the course of time, these ceased to cultivate their land themselves and sub-leased it instead. Finally, the ryotwari region was no longer a self-cultivator region. More than one third of the land was leased and in many districts more than two thirds. The great demand for land owing to the population growth made it possible to let others work for oneself. In the Mahalwari region as well, sub-leasing and indebtedness became, more and more common. Indeed, it was not possible to transfer the land to people who were not from the locality, but the result was that landed property became concentrated in the hands of a few wealthy people, whereas the others lost their rights. A constantly increasing number of people were or became landless. While in the middle of the last century there were still no landless, in 1931 and 1945, respectively 33 and 70 million landless labourers were registered. Others succeeded in renting some land, but on less favourable terms. Share tenancy, in particular, increased greatly.

The British land policy which lasted 150 years as well as the consequences of economic changes and the drastic population growth led to a complete change in the land tenure system in India. Whereas, formerly, the cultivators possessed the right of use and the government the right to impose taxes, now the rights in land were split into many pieces. In this process, not only did a large number of cultivators lose their valid land rights and fell in status to unprotected tenants and labourers. At the same time, the tax collectors became landlords and large landowners. A stratum of intermediaries who did not have a specific function developed, and the land passed into the hands of moneylenders. This caused an enormous differentiation in financial conditions, whereby, the mass of farmers lived in abject poverty.

To explain the further development following India and Pakistan's independence, it is very important to note that, admittedly, the economic situation of the different groups of the rural population had developed very differently, and a large part of the population became poor, but, in its main traits, the social system remained intact, There existed namely a complicated relationship pattern between landlords, cultivators, and landless people which was based on mutual rights and obligations and which provided everyone with a place-even if a poor one am within the rural society. The system aimed at satisfying the needs of everyone in the economic and social sector, and was based on the fact that all members depended upon one another.

Thus, the landlords owned land, it is true, but were dependent upon the landless tenants, agricultural labourers, and village craftsmen to cultivate it. Inversely, the landless could not utilize their labour in an agrarian society if the landlords did rot give them the possibility of working on the fields. This made it necessary for the landlords to maintain the landless' economic situation at least at a level which was not detrimental to their capacity to work, nor caused them to migrate. This not only forced the existence of a minimum wage, although very low, but also induced financial aid in emergencies, crop failures, etc. In addition, the landlords preferred to face want than not meet the obligations resulting from their labour relationships.

Such mutual relationships existed even in the social sector. The landlord assured the protection and representation of their workers externally, whereas the landless adopted a loyal attitude towards their employers and were, so to say, automatically on his side. This secured him power and influence and put him in a position to represent their interests well externally. In the wars of time these behavioural patterns became so ingrained that the obligations of the strong towards the weak became social norms, and paternalistic behaviour was a prerequisite for being recognized as a leading personality. This norm, which is typical for rural societies, sets obvious limits to exploitation. It is true that the level of these limits are very low, but they guaranteed a subsistence. It is also important to observe that the rights had been unilaterally shifted to the benefit of the landlords, but the landless did not consider themselves to be exploited. Here, religion may have played an important role, but the existence of mutual relationships even if they were unequal which granted security against threat to existence were also of extreme importance.

3

Historic Aspects of Craft and Trade in India

Although the courtly culture of the Mughal rulers of the Indian sub-continent is the most well known, a cosmopolitan outlook was not new to India; several sources point to a thriving system of international trade that linked the ports of Southern India with those of Ancient Rome. The chronicles of the Greek Periplus reveal that Indian exports included a variety of spices, aromatics, quality textiles (muslins and cottons), ivory, high quality iron and gems.

Considered items of luxury in those days, these were in high demand. While a good portion of Indo-Roman trade was reciprocal, (Rome supplying exotic items such as cut-gems, coral, wine, perfumes, papyrus, copper, tin and lead ingots), the trade balance was considerably weighted in India's favour. The balance of payments had to be met in precious metals, either gold or silver coinage, or other valuables like red coral (*i.e.* the hard currency of the ancient world). India was particularly renowned for its ivory work and its fine muslins (known in Roman literature as 'woven air').

However, these items must have been quite expensive since the Roman writer Pliny (AD 23-79) complained of the cost of these and other luxury commodities that were imported from India. "Not a year passed in which India did not take fifty million sesterces away from Rome", wrote Pliny. This trade surplus gave rise to prosperous urban centres that were linked to an extensive network of internal trade. Literary records from that period paint a picture of abundance and splendour. The Silappathikaarum (The Ankle Bracelet), a Tamil romance (roughly dated to the late second century AD), provides a glimpse of the maritime wealth of the cosmopolitan cities of South India. Set in the prosperous port city of Puhar (Kaveripattanam), the story refers to ship owners described as having riches 'the envy of foreign kings'. Puhar is portrayed as a city populated by enterpreneurial merchants and traders, where trade was well regulated: "The city of Puhar possessed a spacious forum for storing bales of merchandise, with markings showing the quantity, weight, and name of the owner." The Silappathikaarum suggests that the markets offered a great variety of precious commodities prized in the ancient world.

Special streets were earmarked for merchants that traded in items such as coral, sandalwood, jewellery, faultless pearls, pure gold, and precious gems. Skilled craftspeople brought their finished goods such as fine silks, woven fabrics, and luxurious ivory carvings. Archealogical finds of spectacular burial jewellery in southern India appear to corroborate such accounts. Northern India also had its flourishing urban centres. This can be inferred from descriptions of an archealogical site in ancient Taxila.

Vladimir Zwalf (in Jewellery, 7000 years-Hugh Tait, Editor) notes: "The site has yielded magnificent and well-preserved gold jewellery, notably necklaces, ear-pendants and finger-rings, characterised by a mastery of granulation and inlay." While most ornaments from that period have not survived, sculpture from several sites shows heavy adornment. Patliputra (now Patna) during the Mauryan period was described by travellers as one of the grandest cities of that period.

Textiles

The antiquity of Indian textile exports can be established from the records of the Greek geographer Strabo (63 BC-AD 20) and from the first century Greek source Periplus, which mentions the Gujarati port of Barygaza, (Broach) as exporting a variety of textiles. Archaeological evidence from Mohenjodaro, establishes that the complex technology of mordant dyeing had been known in the sub-continent from at least the second millennium BC.

The use of printing blocks in India may go as far back as 3000 BC, and some historians are of the view that India may have been the original home of textile printing. "The export of printed fabrics to China can be dated to the fourth century BC, where they were much used and admired, and later, imitated." (Stuart Robinson: 'A History of Printed Textiles').

The thirteenth-century Chinese traveller Chau Ju-kua refers to Gujarat as a source of cotton fabrics of every colour and mentions that every year these were shipped to the Arab countries for sale. " The discovery at Broach of a hoard of gold and silver coins, mostly fourteenth-century and belonging to the Mamluk kingdom of Egypt and Syria, suggests the maintenance of the advantageous trading system recorded since Roman times whereby Indian textiles and other renewable resources were traded for precious metals".- (John Guy, 'Arts of India, 1550-1900').

Also in the thirteenth century, Marco Polo recorded the exports of Indian textiles to China and South East Asia from the Masulipattinam (Andhra) and Coromandel (Tamil) coasts in the "largest ships" then known.

It is conjectured that the initial development of this trade accompanied the spread of Indian cultural influence in South-East Asia. John Guy in the "Arts of India, 1550-1900", points out that "textile patterns on sculptures of Indian deities in central Java and elsewhere in the region very probably reflect the prestige cloths in circulation in the late first millennium". Chou Ta-kuan, the Chinese observer of life at the Khmer capital of Angkor at the end of the thirteenth century, wrote that "preference was given to the Indian weaving for its skill and delicacy."

Robyn Maxwell (in Textiles of Southeast Asia) observes that elaborately decorated Indian textiles were the most highly valued and notes: " Many spectacular Indian trade cloths, most now two or three centuries old, have been treasured as heirlooms throughout Southest Asia into the twentieth century, making only rare appearances at important ceremonies or at times of crisis".

Prestige trade textiles such as Patola (double ikat silk in natural dyes) from Patan and Ahmedabad, and decorative cottons in brilliant colour-fast dyes from Gujarat and the Coromandel coast were sought after by the Malaysian royalty and wealthy traders of the Phillipines.

The port city of Surat (in Gujarat) emerged as the major distribution point for patola destined for South-East Asia, and was frequented by the ships of the Dutch East India Company. "The right to wear patola was widely claimed as a prerogative of the Indonesian nobility, a practice encouraged by the Dutch East India Company who distributed patola to local rulers as part of the incentives offered to win local trading concessions and co-operation." (-John Guy, 'Arts of India') Textiles also comprised a significant portion of the Portuguese trade with India.

These included embroidered bedspreads and wall hangings possibly produced at Satgaon, the old mercantile capital of Bengal, (near modern Calcutta).

Quilts of embroidered wild silk (tassar, munga or eri) on a cotton or jute ground, combining European and Indian motifs were comissioned by the Portuguese who had been attracted to Bengal, (as traders had been since the early centuries AD), by the quality of the region's textiles.

J.H. van Linschoten, who was based in Goa as secretary to the archbishop in the 1580s, observed that Cambay also produced silk embroidered quilts. Textiles from Golconda and further south also found favour in Europe and South East Asia.

In the early 1600s, Dutch and English trading settlements were established in Golconda territory. Produced in the Golconda hinterland, kalamkaris, *i.e.* finely painted cotton fabrics were bought or commissioned from the port city of Masulipattinam.

Buying at source enabled the Dutch and English merchants to procure these textiles at rates thirty per cent lower. 'Palampores'- painted fabrics based on the "tree of life" motif that had become popular in the Mughal and Deccan courts were also highly regarded.

The attractiveness of fast dyed, multi-colored Indian prints on cotton (*i.e.* chintz) in Europe led to the formation of the London East India Company in 1600, followed by Dutch and French counterparts.

By the late 1600s, there was such overwhelming demand for Indian chintz (whether from Chittagong in Bengal, or Patna or Surat, that ultimately French and English wool and silk merchants prevailed on their governments to ban the importation of these imported cottons from India.

The French ban came in 1686, while the English followed in 1701. (Not all textile producing centres were associated with ports. Several textile producing centres that catered to the internal market, and to the overland international trade were located in Northern and Central India, in the kingdoms of the Rajputs and the Mughals, each with their own unique specialization.

While Kashmir was well known for its woollen weaves and embroidery, cities like Benaras, Ujjain, Indore and Paithan (near Aurangabad) were known for their fine silks and brocades. Rajasthan specialized in all manner of patterned prints and dyed cloths. Fine collections of Indian Textiles can be seen in the Calico Museum in Ahmedabad and in the Crafts Museum in Delhi.

Carpets

According to texts dating from the Buddhist era, woollen carpets were known in India as early as 500 B.C. References to woven mats and floor coverings are not infrequent in ancient and medieval Indian literature.

By the 16th century, carpet-weaving centres were established in all the major courts of the sub-continent.

However, it is the output of the Mughal period that is now attracting international attention. Dismissed by earlier scholars as mechanical derivatives of Persian carpets, Indian carpets of the Mughal period are slowly gaining recognition as the most technically accomplished classical carpets of all times.

Daniel Walker, curator at the Metropolitan Museum of Art (New York) has described pile-woven carpets of the Mughal era as "among the most beautiful works of art ever created".

He suggests that the large-scale production from the imperial workshops of Akbar "set the tone for subsequent carpet weaving in India and resulted in carpets whose jewel-like beauty is still breathtaking". *(Ref. Flowers Underfoot, Indian Carpets of the Mughal Era)*

Decorative Crafts

Under the patronage of the various royal clans that ruled India, particularly the Mughals, the Rajputs and the Deccani nawabs, the decorative arts and crafts reached unprecedented heights. (These traditions were continued, and even augmented by later regional nawabs in Bengal, Mysore, Central India, Punjab, Awadh and Kashmir).

European traders did not fail to notice the relatively high quality of Indian craftsmanship and proceeded to set up their own "karkhanas" i.e factories, that rivalled the Mughal and Deccani establishments.

Hardwood furniture was a major product of Portuguese patronage, usually richly decorated with inlaid woods and ivory. Catering to the European markets, the items preserved the general forms of European furniture, but were embellished with expensive inlays and carvings that took their inspiration from Indian styles, particularly the Mughal.

Several production centres, principally in Sind, Gujarat and the Deccan serviced this trade based in Goa. Mother-of-pearl was one of the materials often used in the decoration of such items, particularly small storage chests.

These were produced principally in Ahmedabad and Cambay, and later in Surat. Gujarati furniture with mother-of-pearl inlay is recorded in the Baburnama (early 16th century).

The technique of setting mother-of-pearl in a black lac ground, had been employed on wooden tomb-covers of the early seventeenth century in Ahmedabad and Cambay, where a good proportion of such work catered to the Turkish market, as evinced by examples preserved in the Topkapi Saraye Museum of Istanbul.

The craft of papier mache, extensively promoted by the Mughals and later the Rajputs, also found favour with 17th century European traders who commissioned Kashmiri artists to produce for the European market.

Jewellery

Since the Indian sub-continent invariably carried a trade surplus, precious and semi-precious stones, or gold and silver from the international trade complemented internally mined supplies, leading several visitors to India to note the enormous wealth of some of India's most well known kingdoms. They would describe overflowing treasuries, replete with a variety of precious metals and gems.

Bazaars exclusively devoted to trade in precious metals and stones were not uncommon. As already mentioned, Tamil texts dating to the 2nd Century AD refer to them, as do the chronicles of the 14th century traveller Ibn Batuta of Tunisia, and Europeans who visited the Vijaynagar, or Golconda kingdoms.

Vladimir Zwalf (in Jewellery, 7000 years-Hugh Tait, Editor) observes: "The ostentatious display of jewels at the Mughal court mentioned by all visitors to it is borne out by contemporary miniature paintings and a large quantity of extant pieces. Jewellery was worn by both men and women, and was also used in the ornamentation of arms and armour, furniture and vessels.

Gems dominate Mughal jewellery. India was a major source and trading centre for precious stones." Shah Jahan was particularly knowledgeable about gems, and personally supervised some of the works executed in the "karkhanas".

Several fine examples of jewellery from the courts of the Mughals and Rajputs, and other regional nawabs can be seen in the collection in the National Museum, including selections from Benaras, Bengal and Southern India.

Metallurgy

Two quotes well summarize the development of metallurgical skills prior to modern industrialisation. Sir Thomas Holland, (chairman of the Indian Industrial Commission from 1916-18) reported in 1908: "The high quality of the native made iron, the early anticipation of the process now employed in Europe for the manufacture of high-class steels, and the artistic products in copper and bronze gave India a prominent position in the metallurgical world."

D.H. Buchanan wrote in 'Development of Capitalist Enterprise in India, 1934': "In India, steel was used for weapons, for decorative purposes and for tools, and remarkably high grade articles were produced. The old weapons are second to none, and it is said that the famous damascus blades were forged from steel imported from Hyderabad in India. The iron column, called the Kutub pillar at Delhi, weighs over six tons and carries an epitaph composed about 415 A.D. No one yet understands how so large a forging could have been produced at that time."

The craft of Bidri-ware which originated in the Deccan, in Bidar and spread northwards to centres like Lucknow, required not insignificant metallurgical skills.

The delicate inlay work required discipline and expertise, and additionally, required the knowledge of extraction of zinc (a primary constituent of the Bidri alloy). Unlike copper or iron, zinc was not easily extractable from its ore. Consequently, in Europe, the metal could not be used on an industrial scale until an Englishman patented his zinc distillation process in 1738. However, in India, zinc was first produced in the 1st C. BC (The Rasvatnakar mentions the distillation of Zinc in Zawar, Rajasthan, and excavations by the M.S. University.

4

Caste System in Ancient India

All developed social systems are stratified. No society is a mass of individuals. European society was organized along class, guilds, and religion (Jews and gentiles, Protestants and Catholics, etc.) India had castes, or more properly, jatis.

As a political category, caste is a British invention. The British introduced the category of caste for purposes of counting population in the census that began in 1871. The British began to rank order castes by status and economics. Many petitions were filed by new resurgent groups to seek higher ranking. Caste began to be organized as political movement. In a similar fashion, the counting of people by tribal identity in Africa led to tribalism. Sikhism was defined as a separate religion by the British, and it became so. These points are elaborated in an excellent book by Nicholas Dirks, Castes of Mind: Colonialism and the Making of Modern India, 2001.

Castes in India are different than classes in the West. Castes are not economically structured. Each caste has its own rich and its own poor. There are rich Brahmins and poor Brahmins. As a general rule, Brahmins were among the poorest section of society. This observation runs counter to the prevalent view that Indian society is Brahmin dominated and Brahmin exploited. Different castes in India are like different ethnic groups within the United States. There are rich Italians and poor Italians, rich Irish and poor Irish. Also like caste groups in India, till recently the ethnic groups in America married in their own community, i.e. Jews would marry other Jews, the Polish would marry other Polish, and so on.

The caste system in ancient times was not static. Castes rose and fell. Castes became static and rigid during extended foreign rule. Under Muslim rule, some caste groups that fought against domination were pushed to the outer edges of the social system. I have been told that among the sweeper castes in India, one finds many Rajput gotras.

Why is caste denied in the West and replaced by 'class'? Why are dowry murders denied when husbands in the West shoot their wives more frequently than dowry murders in India? Why is idolatry denied when Westerners worship celebrities and money and brand names as their idols? Is the American flag not an idol that is worshipped by the Pledge of Allegiance? The third world non Christian phenomenon is always given a separate term so as to be able to demonize it whereas the western equivalent is spared by saying the term does not apply.

This is linguistic sleigh of hand.

"The European colonizers wanted to impose their ideal of equality so profoundly contrary to that of liberty, that the Western peoples sought to impose their ideas, culture, religion, language, and ways of living and thinking on the people of their empires who preferred to live and think differently. Whole races and civilizations have been destroyed by the European conqueror so that he can preserve the illusion of living in a world of justice, equality, and democracy."

"The moneyed elite in the United States have long coveted their neighbours' land, resources, and cheap labour forces. Eager to invade, annex, and exploit, the plutocracy began to disseminate the warped notion of Manifest Destiny in the Nineteenth Century. Purporting to have the unwavering support of the Almighty, the "superior" Anglo-Saxons rationalized slavery, the Native American Genocide, the conquest of half of Mexico, the annexation of Hawaii, and their eradication of over 300,000 "savages" in conquering the Philippines."

Racial and Social inequities continue to plague modern Western industrial societies who claim to be the beacon of Human Rights.

Historically, nations in Europe and America have had a similar structure: the class system. A Westerner who has had occasion to witness the rise of the new castes in industrial societies, or status-oriented thinking and bureaucratic hierarchies would not praise the modern or industrial culture. Exploitation exists in all societies-in India, it is caste, while in the West, it is based on class. Casteism in India is a terrible injustice. No thoughtful person will deny that. So is crime, homelessness, social inequality and racism in Western nations. Ancient Hindus have never discriminated against people based on their colour or race. Hindus worship God Krishna and Goddess Kali. Both, Krishna and Kali, means black and are depicted as such as well.

> *"In Europe and America, which are said to be the most democratic and highly individualistic, individual life is least regarded. In the land of liberty, fundamentalism, Ku Klax Klan, and Nordic assaults on all other races and cultures prevail."*

Degeneration of the Varna System

The Varna system was started as analogous to professional guilds, but as a result of exploitation by some priests, and socioeconomic elements of society, this system became hereditary and degenerated over the centuries. The ancient culture of India was based upon a system of social diversification according to spiritual development.

Four orders of society were recognized based upon the four main goals of human beings and established society accordingly. These four groups were the Brahmins, the priests or spiritual class; the Kshatriya, the nobility or ruling class; the Vaishya, the merchants and farmers; and the Shudras or servants. These four orders of society were called "varna", which has two meanings; first it means "colour" and second it means a "veil". As colour it does not refer to the colour of the skin of people, but to the qualities or energies of human nature. As a veil it shows the four different ways in which the Divine Self is hidden in human beings.

In ancient India, these divisions were not based on birth but based on qualifications. According to the Bhagavad Gita this Aryan family system broke down in India over three thousand years ago at the time of Krishna. Hence after three thousand years this system of determining natural aptitude has degenerated into the caste system which resembles it now only in form.

As the Varna system became increasingly rigid and based on inheritance, it was enveloped by another system known as the caste system. Thus, this varna system determined the social structure of ancient Hindu society. The caste system could not have been part of Hindu religious philosophy, since it violates fundamental Hindu doctrine, according to which there is no absolute distinction between individuals, since the atman dwells in the hearts of all beings. There is no religious sanction whatsoever to the concept of the caste system in Hinduism.

Swami Sivananda (The Divine Life Society, Rishikesh), in his commentary on Gita, Ch.18, verses 41, and 45 says: "Mankind is organized into the four castes and each man's life is divided into four stages, according to the nature of the Gunas (traits) and the degree of growth or evolution.

This is the division of labour for which each caste is fitted according to its own nature. The duty prescribed is your sole support, each devoted to his own duty in accordance with his own nature or caste, and the highest service you can render to the Supreme is to carry it out wholeheartedly, without expectation of fruits, with the attitude of dedication to the Lord. The caste system is, indeed, a splendid thing. It is quite flawless. But the defect came in from somewhere else. The classes gradually neglected their duties. The test of ability and character slowly vanished. Birth became the chief consideration in determining castes. All castes fell from their ideals and forgot all about their duties."

Varna-Not Racial Colour

Varna was conferred on the basis of the intrinsic nature of an individual, which is a combination of the three gunas. The term, 'Varna', has nothing to do with racial colour. It is related to the three 'gunas' or traits-white (sattva or sagacity), red (rajas or aggressiveness), and dark (tamas or ignorance) which all men and also all living beings possess, albeit in different proportions-varying from species to species, from man to man and even from sibling to sibling.

Alain Danielou has said: "That abusive caste practices were introduced when the administrative power ceased to be in Hindu hands, thus making the repression of abuses legally impossible. Such abuses as there are have been greatly exaggerated in order to justify Western domination and are normally quite local. In most of India, the caste system functions today as it always has; as a harmonious whole in which each is satisfied with his social lot, in which the freedom of each tribe, and religious group to live according to its customs, traditions, and convictions is respected as it is in no other country and no other form of society.

Manu Smrti: Not a Religious Book:

"The Seniority of Brahmans is from Sacred Knowledge, that of Kshatriyas from valour, that of Vaishyas from wealth in grain, but that of Sudras is from age alone." (Manu Smriti II, 155)

"Manu has declared that those Brahmans who are thieves, outcasts, eunuchs, or atheists are unworthy to partake of oblations offered to gods and ancestors." (Manu Smriti III, 150)

" A Brahmin who departs from the Rule of Noble Conduct, does not gain the fruit described in the Veda, but he who duly follows the Rule of Noble Conduct, will obtain the full reward." (Manu Smriti I,109)

" He who possesses faith may receive pure learning even from a man of lower caste, the highest law even from the lowest, and an excellent wife even from a base family." (Manu Smriti II, 238)

Manu Smriti which outlines the scheme of the four varnas (socioeconomic classes) and four ashramas (stages of life of the individual) refuses a provide for the fifth varna. The four classes are adequate to cover all the sections of the society. Manu Smriti is a sociological treatise and not a religious or theological work. It has never been held on par with the Vedas and has never been claimed to be a Holy Book whose authority is unquestionable. Manu Smriti does not deal with the Absolute, a field specialized in by the Upanishads. Manu Smriti is as this-worldly as the Arthashastra is. Manu was also only a Codifier (Documenter of the then-existing codes) of the Caste System and was not to be interpreted as the creator of the Caste System.

"Only the British administrators and jurists who dominated the scene since 1757 found it expedient for their purposes to present it as a religious code binding all the Hindus. The original text of Manu Smriti has been tampered with is acknowledged by Sir William Jones who introduced it as the law book of the Hindus, as he agrees that ' it is accommodated to the improvements of a commercial age'. The extant text of Manu Smriti is a doctored version, doctored to benefit the commercial class of Britain which had sponsored the East India Company, the company for which he was serving as a judge at Calcutta."

Varnashrama Dharma, said to be the mainstay of the Hindu Social Order has no sanction in the Vedas.

In ancient India, these divisions were not based on birth but based on qualifications. According to the Bhagavad Gita this Aryan family system broke down in India over three thousand years ago at the time of Krishna. Hence after three thousand years this system of determining natural aptitude has degenerated into the caste system which resembles it now only in form.

Manu made it clear that superiority is not by birth but by Conduct. This Principle was further emphasized later by Maharishi Veda Vyasa in Mahabharata. Manu himself says that if there is anything in his Smriti which is not acceptable to the conscience of any person, that person should reject it and act according to his/her own conscience.

> *"For choosing your course of conduct at any time and place, keep in view the instructions given first in Sruti (Vedas), then in Smritis, Itihaas (History of great personalities) and finally you act according to your conscience." (Manu Smriti, 11, 6).*
>
> *"Just as a wooden toy elephant cannot be real elephant, and a stuffed deer cannot be a real deer, so, without studying scriptures and the Vedas and the development of intellect, a Brahmin by birth cannot be considered a Brahmin. " (Manu Smriti 11-157).*

Louis Francois Jacolliot (1837-1890), who worked in French India as a government official and was at one time President of the Court in Chandranagar, translated numerous Vedic hymns, the Manusmriti, and the Tamil work, Kural. His masterpiece, La Bible dans l'Inde, stirred a storm of controversy.

Manu-Hindu Law: The Hindu law were codified by Manu more than 3,000 years before the Christian era, copied by entire antiquity and notably by Rome, which alone has left us a written law-the code of Justanian, which has been adopted as the base of all modern legislations.

Jurisprudence: "Observe, enpassant, this striking coincidence with French law, that the Hindu wife, in default of her husband's authority may release from her incapacity, by authority of justice. " "The contract made by a man who is drunk, foolish, imbecile or grievously disordered in his mental condition...." Manu further adds, "What is held under comprehension-held by force is declared null."

Would not this be thought a mere commentary on the Code of Napoleon? Of 4-5,000 years after "How far is all this from those barbarous customs of first ages, when every question was solved by violence and force, and what admiration should we feel for a people who, at the epoch at which Biblical fall would date the world's creation, had already reached the extraordinary degree of civilization indicated by laws so simple and so practical."

Caste System and Code of Manu

The Hindus have been an intensely practical people. The magnificence of daring glimpses into the cosmos as their meditations or scientific investigations revealed to them, convinced them beyond doubt that the complexity of earthly existence could be reduced to some order and the march of human progress subjected to some form of control. They embraced in their researches such subjects as astronomy, physics, chemistry, biology, medicine, ethics, logic, psychology, aesthetics, politics, economics, sociology, and metaphysics. Indeed, in sociology alone, they have left us over twenty treatises; and the Code of Manu, the subject of the present study, is only one of them.

Manu, Manas, manava, all have the same philological root, man, to think. Manu's Code, therefore, is a treatise of social relations for human beings. It lays emphasis on reason, the thinking faculty (manas), in the ordering of man's social relations. It stands for a planned society. Manu's social theory is an art of life; it is a technique, not mere congeries of consistent concepts.

An individual's life is divided into four parts—1. studentship, 2. householding 3. partial retirement or hermitage, 4. and complete retirement. Correspondingly, there are four groups: 1. the manual worker, 2. the merchant, 3. the warrior, and 4. the teacher. A unity of function ties each stage of individual life to the corresponding group. This unity, which lays emphasis on harmonious relations, is the dharma, or the ethics of Manu. There are thus presented four social institutions: 1. the educational, 2. the family-economic, 3. the political, 4. and the religious.

Stable Human Societies

Alain Danielou says: "The Hindus assert that their social formula meets the requirements of man's individual and collective nature. The fact that the Hindu civilization has been able to survive over thousand of years, despite disorders caused by invasions, schisms, and internal wars, and has been capable of constant renewal, as demonstrated by one brilliant period after another, merits all our attention in the study of a social system whose longevity is unique in history."

Aryan Invasion Theory and Caste System

Guy Sorman visiting scholar at Hoover Institution at Stanford and the leader of new liberalism in France, writes: "The Invasion theory has today become the standard explanation for the caste system, though it came up only in the 19th century. Besides, all we have to attest the Aryan invasion is a specious interpretation of the Mahabharata, which is like searching the origins of European aristocracy in the works of Homer! In any case, it is doubtful whether a single invasion, which was more likely a slow infiltration of the North, could have succeeded in structuring so perfectly Indian society along ethnic lines for over three thousand years. Finally, in South India the caste system among the dark, skinned Dravidians is as rigid as it is in the North, though the Aryans in all probability never reached there.

The racial origin of caste hypothesis tells us little about India but it does tell us a great deal about the 19th century Westerners who invented the Aryan invasion theory. It was at the same time that Sieyes and Augustin Thierry claimed that the French nobility was of Germanic stock, whereas the lower classes were of Gallic origin; so the 1789 Revolution was a race war rather than a class war! It was also in the 19th century that appeared the myth of the Indo-Europeans being at the source of all Western civilization and for this we have to thank British authors who were taken up with evolutionist theory. Indian historians trained in Europe have fallen victim to this myth but that does not make it any more authentic. Later on, at the beginning of the 20th century, it became fashionable to support the Marxist theory which replaced race with class, though its premises were just as shaky."

Genetic Evidence of Indian Caste

The origins and affinities of the 1 billion people living on the subcontinent of India have long been contested.

This is owing, in part, to the many different waves of immigrants that have influenced the genetic structure of India. In the most recent of these waves, Indo-European-speaking people from West Eurasia entered India from the Northwest and diffused throughout the subcontinent. They purportedly admixed with or displaced indigenous Dravidic-speaking populations. Subsequently they may have established the Hindu caste system and placed themselves primarily in castes of higher rank.

To explore the impact of West Eurasians on contemporary Indian caste populations, we compared mtDNA (400 bp of hypervariable region 1 and 14 restriction site polymorphisms) and Y-chromosome (20 biallelic polymorphisms and 5 short tandem repeats) variation in 265 males from eight castes of different rank to 750 Africans, Asians, Europeans, and other Indians. For maternally inherited mtDNA, each caste is most similar to Asians. However, 20%-30% of Indian mtDNA haplotypes belong to West Eurasian haplogroups, and the frequency of these haplotypes is proportional to caste rank, the highest frequency of West Eurasian haplotypes being found in the upper castes.

In contrast, for paternally inherited Y-chromosome variation each caste is more similar to Europeans than to Asians. Moreover, the affinity to Europeans is proportionate to caste rank, the upper castes being most similar to Europeans, particularly East Europeans.

These findings are consistent with greater West Eurasian male admixture with castes of higher rank. Nevertheless, the mitochondrial genome and the Y-chromosome each represents only a single haploid locus and is more susceptible to large stochastic variation, bottlenecks, and selective sweeps.

Thus, to increase the power of our analysis, we assayed 40 independent, biparentally inherited autosomal loci (1 LINE-1 and 39 Alu elements) in all of the caste and continental populations (600 individuals). Analysis of these data demonstrated that the upper castes have a higher affinity to Europeans than to Asians, and the upper castes are significantly more similar to Europeans than are the lower castes. Collectively, all five datasets show a trend toward upper castes being more similar to Europeans, whereas lower castes are more similar to Asians. We conclude that Indian castes are most likely to be of proto-Asian origin with West Eurasian admixture resulting in rank-related and sex-specific differences in the genetic affinities of castes to Asians and Europeans.

Shared Indo-European languages (i.e., Hindi and most European languages) suggested to linguists of the nineteenth and twentieth centuries that contemporary Hindu Indians are descendants of primarily West Eurasians who migrated from Europe, the Near East, Anatolia, and the Caucasus 3000–8000 years ago (Poliakov 1974; Renfrew 1989a,b). These nomadic migrants may have consolidated their power by admixing with native Dravidic-speaking (e.g., Telugu) proto-Asian populations who controlled regional access to land, labour, and resources (Cavalli-Sforza et al. 1994), and subsequently established the Hindu caste hierarchy to legitimize and maintain this power (Poliakov 1974; Cavalli-Sforza et al. 1994). It is plausible that these West Eurasian immigrants also appointed themselves to predominantly castes of higher rank. However, archaeological evidence of the diffusion of material culture from Western Eurasia into India has been limited (Shaffer 1982). Therefore, information on the genetic relationships of Indians to Europeans and Asians could contribute substantially to understanding the origins of Indian populations.

Previous genetic studies of Indian castes have failed to achieve a consensus on Indian origins and affinities. Various results have supported closer affinity of Indian castes either with Europeans or with Asians, and several factors underlie this inconsistency. First, erratic or limited sampling of populations has limited inferences about the relationships between caste and continental populations (i.e., Africans, Asians, Europeans).

These relationships are further confounded by the wide geographic dispersal of caste populations. Genetic affinities among caste populations are, in part, inversely correlated with the geographic distance between them (Malhotra and Vasulu 1993), and it is likely that affinities between caste and continental populations are also geographically dependent (e.g., different between North and South Indian caste populations).

Second, it has been suggested that castes of different rank may have originated from or admixed with different continental groups (Majumder and Mukherjee 1993). Third, the size of caste populations varies widely, and the effects of genetic drift on some small, geographically isolated castes may have been substantial. Fourth, most of the polymorphisms assayed over the last 30 years are indirect measurements of genetic variation (e.g., ABO typing), have been sampled from only a few loci, and may not be selectively neutral. Finally, only rarely have systematic comparisons been made with continental populations using a large, uniform set of DNA polymorphisms (Majumder 1999).

To investigate the origin of contemporary castes, we compared the genetic affinities of caste populations of differing rank (i.e., upper, middle, and lower) to worldwide populations. We analysed mtDNA (hypervariable region 1 [HVR1] sequence and 14 restrictionsite polymorphisms [RSPs]), Y-chromosome (5 shorttandem repeats [STRs] and 20 biallelic polymorphisms), and autosomal (1 LINE-1 and 39 Alu inserts) variation in 265 males from eight different Teluguspeaking caste populations from the state of Andhra Pradesh in South India (Bamshad et al. 1998). Comparisons were made to 400 individuals from tribal and Hindi-speaking caste and populations distributed across the Indian subcontinent (Mountain et al. 1995; Kivisild et al. 1999) and to 350 Africans, Asians, and Europeans (Jorde et al. 1995, 2000; Seielstad et al. 1999).

Results: Analysis of mtDNA Suggests a Proto-Asian Origin of Indians MtDNA HVR1 genetic distances between caste populations and Africans, Asians, and Europeans are significantly different from zero ($p < 0.001$) and reveal that, regardless of rank, each caste group is most closely related to Asians and is most dissimilar from Africans. The genetic distances from major continental populations (e.g., Europeans) differ among the three caste groups, and the comparison reveals an intriguing pattern. As one moves from lower to upper castes, the distance from Asians becomes progressively larger. The distance between Europeans and lower castes is larger than the distance between Europeans and upper castes, but the distance between Europeans and middle castes is smaller than the upper caste-European distance. These trends are the same whether the Kshatriya and Vysya are included in the upper castes, the middle castes, or excluded from the analysis. This may be owing, in part, to the small sample size ($n = 10$) of each of these castes. Among the upper castes the genetic distance between Brahmins and Europeans (0.10) is smaller than that between either the Kshatriya and Europeans (0.12) or the Vysya and Europeans (0.16). Assuming that contemporary Europeans reflect West Eurasian affinities, these data indicate that the amount of West Eurasian admixture with Indian populations may have been proportionate to caste rank.

Conventional estimates of the standard errors of genetic distances assume that polymorphic sites are independent of each other, that is, unlinked. Because mtDNA polymorphisms are in complete linkage disequilibrium (as are polymorphisms on the nonrecom-bining portions of the Y-chromosome), this assumption is violated. Alternatively, the mtDNA genome can be treated as a single locus with multiple haplotypes.

However, even if this assumption is made, mtDNA distances do not differ significantly from one another even at the level of the three major continental populations (Nei and Livshits 1989), the standard errors being greater than the genetic distances. Considering that the distances between castes and continental populations are less than those between different continental populations, the estimated mtDNA genetic distances between upper castes and Europeans versus lower castes and Europeans would not be significantly different from each other. Therefore, to resolve further the relationships of Europeans and Asians to contemporary Indian populations, we defined the identities of specific mtDNA restriction-site haplotypes. The presence of the mtDNA restriction sites

Ddei 10,394 and Alui 10,397 defines a haplogroup (a group of haplotypes that share some sequence variants), M, that was originally identified in populations that migrated from mainland Asia to Southeast Asia and Australia (Ballinger et al. 1992; Chen et al. 1995; Passarino et al. 1996) and is found at much lower frequency in European and African populations. Most of the common haplotypes found in Telugu-and Hindi-speaking caste populations belong to haplogroup M and do not differentiate into language-specific clusters in a phylogenetic reconstruction. Furthermore, these Indian haplogroup-M-haplotypes are distinct from those found in other Asian populations and indicate the existence of Indian-specific subsets of haplogroup M (e.g., M3). As expected if the lower castes are more similar to Asians than to Europeans, and the upper castes are more similar to Europeans than to Asians, the frequencies of M and M3 haplotypes are inversely proportional to caste rank.

Of the non-Asian mtDNA haplotypes found in Indian populations, most are of West Eurasian origin. However, most of these Indian West-Eurasian haplotypes belong to an Indian-specific subset of haplogroup U, that is, U2i (Kivisild et al. 1999), the oldest and second most common mtDNA haplogroup found in Europe (Torroni et al. 1994). In agreement with the HVR1 results, the frequency of West Eurasian mtDNA haplotypes is significantly higher in upper castes than in lower castes ($p < 0.05$), the frequency of U2i haplotypes increasing as one moves from lower to higher castes. In addition, the frequency of mtDNA haplogroups with a more recent coalescence estimate (i.e., H, I, J, K, T) was fivefold higher in upper castes (6.8%) than in lower castes (1.4%). These haplotypes are derivatives of haplogroups found throughout Europe (Richards et al. 1998), the Middle East (Di Rienzo and Wilson 1991), and to a lesser extent Central Asia (Comas et al. 1998). Collectively, the mtDNA haplotype evidence indicate that contemporary Indian mtDNA evolved largely from proto-Asian ancestors with Western Eurasian admixture accounting for 20%-30% of mtDNA haplotypes.

Y-Chromosome Variation

Confirms: Indo-European Admixture Genetic distances estimated from Y-chromosome STR polymorphisms differ significantly from zero ($p < 0.001$) and reveal a distinctly different pattern of population relationships. In contrast to the mtDNA distances, the Y-chromosome STR data do not demonstrate a closer affinity to Asians for each caste group. Upper castes are more similar to Europeans than to Asians, middle castes are equidistant from the two groups, and lower castes are most similar to Asians. The genetic distance between caste populations and Africans is progressively larger moving from lower to middle to upper caste groups.

Genetic distances estimated from Y-chromosome biallelic polymorphisms differ significantly from zero ($p < 0.05$), and the patterns differ from the mtDNA results even more strikingly than the Y-chromosome STRs. For Y-chromosome biallelic polymorphism data, each caste group is more similar to Europeans, and as one moves from lower to middle to higher castes the genetic distance to Europeans diminishes progressively. This pattern is further accentuated by separating the European population into Northern, Southern, and Eastern Europeans; each caste group is most closely related to Eastern Europeans. Moreover, the genetic distance between upper castes and Eastern Europeans is approximately half the distance between Eastern Europeans and middle or lower castes. These results suggest that Indian Y-chromosomes, particularly upper caste Y-chromosomes, are more similar to European than to Asian Y-chromosomes. This underscores the close affinities between Hindu Indian and Indo-European Y-chromosomes based on a previously reported analysis of three Y-chromosome polymorphisms (Quintana-Murci et al. 1999b).

Overall, these results indicate that the affinities of Indians to continental populations varies according to caste rank and depends on whether mtDNA or Ychromosome data are analysed. However, conclusions drawn from these data are limited because mtDNA and the Y-chromosome is each effectively a single haploid locus and is more sensitive to genetic drift, bottlenecks, and selective sweeps compared to autosomal loci.

These limitations of our analysis can be overcome, in part, by analyzing a larger set of independent autosomal loci. Consequently, we assayed 1 LINE-1 and 39 unlinked Alu polymorphisms.

Affinities to Europeans and Asians Stratified

Genetic distances estimated from autosomal Alu elements correspond to caste rank, the genetic distance between the upper and lower castes being more than 2.5 times larger than the distance between upper and middle or middle and lower castes (upper to middle, 0.0069; upper to lower, 0.018; middle to lower, 0.0071). These trends are the same whether the Kshatriya and Vysya are included in the upper castes, the middle castes, or excluded from the analysis (data not shown). Furthermore, a neighbour-joining network of genetic distances between separate castes clearly differentiates castes of different rank into separate clusters. This is similar to the relationship between genetic distances and caste rank estimated from mtDNA (Bamshad et al. 1998). It is important to note, however, that the autosomal genetic distances are estimated from 40 independent loci. This afforded us the opportunity to test the statistical significance of the correspondence between genetic distance and caste status. The Mantel correlation between interindividual genetic distances and distances based on social rank was low but highly significant for individuals ranked into upper, middle, and lower groups ($r = 0.08$; $p < 0.001$) and into eight separate castes ($r = 0.07$; $p < 0.001$). Given the resolving power of this autosomal dataset, we next tested whether we could reconcile the results of the analysis of mtDNA and Ychromosome markers in castes and continental populations.

Genotypic differentiation was significantly different from zero ($p < 0.0001$) between each pair of caste populations and between each caste and continental population. Similar to the results of both the mtDNA and Y-chromosome analyses, the distance between upper castes and European populations is smaller than the distance between lower castes and Europeans. However, in contrast to the mtDNA results but similar to the Ychromosome results, the affinity between upper castes and Europeans is higher than that of upper castes and Asians. If the Kshatriya and Vysya are excluded from the analysis or included in the middle castes, the genetic distance between the upper caste (Brahmins) and Europeans remains smaller than the distance between the lower castes and Europeans and the distance between upper castes and Asians. Analysis of each caste separately reveals that the genetic distance between the Brahmins and Europeans (0.013) is less than the distance between Europeans and Kshatriya (0.030) or Vysya (0.020). Nevertheless, each separate upper caste is more similar to Europeans than to Asians.

Because historical evidence suggests greater affinity between upper castes and Europeans than between lower castes and Europeans (Balakrishnan 1978, 1982; Cavalli-Sforza et al. 1994), it is appropriate to use a one-tailed test of the difference between the corresponding genetic distances.

The 90% confidence limits of Nei's standard distances estimated between upper castes and Europeans (0.006-0.016) versus lower castes and Europeans (0.017-0.037) do not overlap, indicating statistical significance at the 0.05 level. Significance at 0.05 is not achieved if the Kshatriya and Vysya are excluded. These results offer statistical support for differences in the genetic affinity of Europeans to caste populations of differing rank, with greater European affinity to upper castes than to lower castes.

Discussion: Previous genetic studies have found evidence to support either a European or an Asian origin of Indian caste populations, with occasional indications of admixture with African or proto-Australoid populations (Chen et al. 1995; Mountain et al. 1995; Bamshad et al. 1996, 1997; Majumder et al. 1999; Quintana-Murci et al. 1999a).

Our results demonstrate that for biparentally inherited autosomal markers, genetic distances between upper, middle, and lower castes are significantly correlated with rank; upper castes are more similar to Europeans than to Asians; and upper castes are significantly more similar to Europeans than are lower castes. This result appears to be owing to the amalgamation of two different patterns of sex-specific genetic variation. The majority of Indian mtDNA restriction-site haplotypes belong to Indian-specific subsets (e.g., M3) of a predominantly Asian haplogroup M, although a substantial minority of mtDNA restriction site haplotypes belong to West Eurasian haplogroups. A higher proportion of proto-Asian mtDNA restriction-site haplotypes is found in lower castes compared to middle or upper castes, whereas the frequency of

West Eurasian haplotypes is positively correlated with caste rank, that is, is highest in the upper castes.

For Y-chromosome STR variation the upper castes exhibit greatest similarity with Europeans, whereas the lower caste groups are most similar to Asians. For Y-biallelic polymorphism variation, each caste group is more similar to Europeans than to Asians, and the affinity to Europeans is proportional to caste rank, that is, is highest in the upper castes.

Importantly, five different types of data (mtDNA HVR1 sequence, mtDNA RSPs, Y-chromosome STRs, Ychromosome biallelic polymorphisms, and autosomal Alu polymorphisms) support the same general pattern: relatively smaller genetic distances from European populations as one moves from lower to middle to upper caste populations. Genetic distances from Asian populations become larger as one moves from lower to middle to upper caste populations. It is especially noteworthy that the analysis of Y biallelic polymorphisms, which involved an independent set of comparative Asian, European, and African populations, again indicated the same pattern. Additional support is offered by the fact that the autosomal polymorphisms yielded a statistically significant difference between the uppercaste-European and lower-caste-European genetic distances.

With additional loci, other differences (e.g., the distances between different caste groups and Asians) may also reach statistical significance. The most likely explanation for these findings, and the one most consistent with archaeological data, is that contemporary Hindu Indians are of proto-Asian origin with West Eurasian admixture. However, admixture with West Eurasian males was greater than admixture with West Eurasian females, resulting in a higher affinity to European Y-chromosomes. This supports an earlier suggestion of Passarino et al. (1996), which was based on a comparison of mtDNA and blood group results. Furthermore, the degree of West Eurasian admixture was proportional to caste rank. This explanation is consistent with either the hypothesis that proportionately more West Eurasians became members of the upper castes at the inception of the caste hierarchy or that social stratification preceded the West Eurasian incursion and that West Eurasians tended to insert themselves into higher-ranking positions.

One consequence is that shared Indo-European languages may not reflect a common origin of Europeans and most Indians, but rather underscores the transfer of language mediated by contact between West Eurasians and native proto-Indians.

West Eurasian admixture in Indian populations may have been the result of more than one wave of immigration into India. Kivisild et al. (1999) determined the coalescence (50,000 years before present) of the Indian-specific subset of the West Eurasian haplotypes (i.e., U2i) and suggested that West Eurasian admixture may have been much older than the purported Dravidian and Indo-European incursions.

Our analysis of Indian mtDNA restriction-site haplotypes that do not belong to the U2i subset of West Eurasian haplotypes (i.e., H, I, J, K, T) is consistent with more recent West Eurasian admixture. It is also possible that haplotypes with an older coalescence were introduced by Dravidians, whereas haplotypes with a more recent coalescence belonged to Indo-Europeans. This hypothesis can be tested by a more detailed comparison to West Eurasian mtDNA haplotypes from Iran, Anatolia, and the Caucasus. Alternatively, the coalescence dates of these haplotypes may predate the entry of West Eurasians populations into India. Regardless of their origin, West Eurasian admixture resulted in rank-related differences in the genetic affinities of castes to Europeans and Asians. Furthermore, the frequency of West Eurasian haplotypes in the founding middle and upper castes may be underestimated because of the upward social mobility of women from lower castes (Bamshad et al. 1998). These women were presumably more likely to introduce proto-Asian mtDNA haplotypes into the middle and upper castes.

Our analysis of 40 autosomal markers indicates clearly that the upper castes have a higher affinity to Europeans than to Asians. The high affinity of caste Y-chromosomes with those of Europeans suggests that the majority of immigrating West Eurasians may have been males. As might be expected if West Eurasian males appropriated the highest positions in the caste system, the upper caste group exhibits a lower genetic distance to Europeans than the middle or lower castes. This is underscored by the observation that the Kshatriya (an upper caste), whose members served as warriors, are closer to Europeans than any other caste (data not shown). Furthermore, the 32-bp deletion polymorphism in CC chemokine receptor 5, whose frequency peaks in populations of Eastern Europe, is found only in two Brahmin males (M. Bamshad and S.K. Ahuja, unpubl.). The stratification of Y-chromosome distances with Europeans could also be caused by malespecific gene flow among caste populations of different rank. However, we and others have demonstrated that there is little sharing of Y-chromosome haplotypes among castes of different rank (Bamshad et al. 1998; Bhattacharyya et al. 1999).

The affinity of caste populations to Europeans is more apparent for Y-chromosome biallelic polymorphisms than Y-chromosome STRs. This could be attributed to the use of different European populations in comparisons using STRs and biallelic polymorphisms.

Alternatively, it may reflect, in part, the effects of high mutation rates for the Y-chromosome STRs, which would tend to obscure relationships between caste and continental populations. A lack of consistent clustering at the continental level has been observed in several studies of Y-chromosome STRs (Deka et al. 1996; Torroni et al. 1996; de Knijff et al. 1997). The autosomal Alu and biallelic Y-chromosome polymorphisms, in contrast, have a slower rate of drift than Ychromosome STRs because of a higher effective population size, and their mutation rate is very low. Thus, the Y-chromosome biallelic polymorphisms and autosomal Alu markers may serve as more stable markers of worldwide population affinities.

Our analysis may help to explain why estimates of the affinities of caste groups to worldwide populations have varied so widely among different studies. Analyses of recent caste history based on only mtDNA or Y-chromosome polymorphisms clearly would suggest that castes are more closely related to Asians or to Europeans, respectively. Furthermore, we attempted to minimize the confounding effect of geographic differences between populations by sampling from a highly restricted region of South India. Because of the ubiquity of the caste system in India's history, it is reasonable to predict similar patterns in caste populations living in other areas. Indeed, any genetic result becomes more compelling when it is replicated in other populations. Therefore, comparable studies in caste populations from other regions of

India must be completed to test the generality of these results. The dispersal and subsequent growth of Indian populations since the Neolithic Age is one of the most important events to shape the history of South Asia.

However, the origin and dispersal route of the aboriginal inhabitants of the Indian subcontinent is unclear.

Our findings suggest a proto-Asian origin of the Indian-specific haplogroup-M-haplotypes. Haplogroup-M-haplotypes are also found at appreciable frequencies in some East African populations-18% of Ethiopians (Quintana-Murci et al. 1999a) and 16% of Kenyans (M. Bamshad and L.B. Jonde, unpubl.). A comparison of haplogroup-M-haplotypes from East Africa and India has suggested that this southern route may have been one of the original dispersal pathways of anatomically modern humans out of Africa (Quintana-Murci et al. 1999a). Together, these data support our previous suggestion (Kivisild et al. 1999) that India may have been inhabited by at least two successive late Pleistocene migrations, consistent with the hypothesis of Lahr and Foley (1994). It also adds to the growing evidence that the subcontinent of India has been a major corridor for the migration of people between Africa, Western Asia, and Southeast Asia (Cavalli-Sforza et al. 1994).

It should be emphasized that the DNA variation studied here is thought to be selectively neutral and thus represents only the effects of population history.

These results permit no inferences about phenotypic differences between populations. In addition, alleles and haplotypes are shared by different caste populations, reflecting a shared history. Indeed, these findings underscore the longstanding appreciation that the distribution of genetic polymorphisms in India is highly complex. Further investigation of the spread of anatomically modern humans throughout South Asia will need to consider that such complex patterns may be the norm rather than the exception.

Methods

Sample Collection: All studies of South Indian populations were performed with the approval of the Institutional Review Board of the University of Utah, Andhra University, and the government of India. Adult males living in the district of Visakhapatnam, Andhra Pradesh, were questioned about their caste affiliations and surnames and the birthplaces of their parents. Those who were unrelated to any other subject by at least three generations were considered eligible to participate.

We classified caste populations based upon the traditional ranking of these castes by varna, occupation, and socioeconomic status. According to various Sanskrit texts, Hindu populations were partitioned originally into four categories or varna: Brahmin, Kshatriya, Vysya, and Sudra (Tambia 1973; Elder 1996). Those in each varna performed occupations assigned to their category. Brahmins were priests; Kshatriya were warriors; Vysya were traders; and Sudra were to serve the three other varna (Tambia 1973; Elder 1996). Each varna was assigned a status; Brahmin, Kshatriya, and Vysya were considered of higher status than the Sudra because the Brahmin, Kshatriya, and Vaishya are considered the twice-born Bamshad et al. castes and are differentiated from all other castes in the caste hierarchy. This is the rationale behind classifying them as the upper group of castes (Tambia 1973).

The Kapu and the Yadava are called once-born castes that have traditionally been classified in the Sudra, the lowest of the original four varna. However, the status of the Sudra was actually higher than that of a fifth varna, the Panchama. This fifth varna was added at a later date to include the so-called untouchables, who were excluded from the other four varna (Elder 1996). The untouchable varna includes the Mala and Madiga. The position of the Relli in the caste hierarchy is somewhat ambiguous, but they have usually been classified in the lower caste group. Therefore, prior to the collection of any data, males from eight different Telugu-speaking castes (n = 265) were ranked into upper (Niyogi and Vydiki Brahmin, Kshatriya, Vyshya [n = 80]), middle (Telega and Turpu Kapu, Yadava [n = 111]), and lower (Relli, Madiga, Mala [n = 74]) groups (Bamshad et al. 1998). This ranking has been used by previous investigators (Krishnan and Reddy 1994).

After obtaining informed consent, 8 mL of whole blood or 5 plucked scalp hairs were collected from each participant. Extractions were performed at Andhra University using established methods (Bell et al. 1981).

DNA Polymorphisms

The mtDNA data consisted of 68, 116, and 73 HVR1 sequences and 79, 159, and 72 restriction-site haplotypes from largely the same individuals in upper, middle, and lower castes, respectively. These data were compared to data from 143 Africans (15 Sotho-Tswana, 7 Tsonga, 14 Nguni, 24 San, 5 Biaka Pygmies, 33 Mbuti Pygmies, 9 Alur, 18 Hema, and 18 Nande), 78 Asians (12 Cambodians, 17 Chinese, 19 Japanese, 6 Malay, 9 Vietnamese, 2 Koreans, and 13 Asians of mixed ancestry), and 99 Europeans (20 unrelated males of the French CEPH kindreds, 69 unrelated Utah males of Northern European descent, and 10 Poles) (Jorde et al. 1995, 1997).

In addition to our samples, the phylogenetic analyses also included data from 98 published HVR1 sequences from two castes (48 Havlik and 43 Mukri), and a tribal population (7 Kadar) living in south-western India (Mountain et al. 1995) and restriction-site haplotypes from one caste (62 Lobana) from Northern India, three tribal populations from Northern (12 Tharu and 18 Bhoksa) and Southern (86 Lambadi) India, and 122 individuals from various caste populations in Uttar Pradesh (Kivisild et al. 1999). Phylogenetic relationships of HVR1 sequences assigned to haplogroupMwere estimated for Indians (this study), Turks (this study), Central Asian populations (Comas et al. 1998), Mongolians (Kolman et al. 1996), Chinese (Horai et al. 1996), and Japanese (Horai et al. 1996; Seo et al. 1998).

The mtDNA HVR1 Sequence was Determined by Fluorescent: Sanger sequencing using a Dye terminator cycle sequencing kit (Applied Biosystems) according to the manufacturer's specifications (Bamshad et al. 1998). Sequencing reactions were resolved on an ABI 377 automated DNA sequencer, and sequence data were analysed using ABI DNA analysis software and SEQUENCHER software (Genecodes). To identify mtDNA haplotypes and haplogroups (a group of haplotypes that share some sequence variants), major continent-specific genotypes (Torroni et al. 1994, 1996; Wallace 1995) for the following polymorphic mtDNA restriction sites were determined: Hpai 3592, Ddei 10394, Alui 10397, Alui 13262, Bamhi 13366, Alui 5176, Haeiii 4830, Alui 7025, Hinfi 12308, Acci 14465, Avaii 8249, Alui 10032, Bstoi 13704, and Haeii 9052.

Y-Chromosome and Autosomal Polymorphisms

Y-chromosome-specific STRs (DYS 19, DYS 288, DYS 388, DYS 389A, DYS 390) were amplified using published conditions (Hammer et al. 1998). PCR products were separated on an ABI 377 automated sequencer and scored using ABI Genotyper software. Y-chromosome STR data were collected from 622 males including 280 South Indians, 200 Africans (Seielstad et al. 1999; this study), 40 Asians, and 102 Europeans. Autosomal data were collected from 608 individuals including 265 South Indians, 155 Africans, 70 Asians, and 118 Europeans. The Y-chromosome-specific biallelic polymorphisms tested included: DYS188792, DYS194469, DYS 211105, DYS 221136, DYS 257108, DYS 87, M3, M4, M9, M12, M15, SRY 4064, SRY 10831.1, SRY 10831.2, p12f2, PN1, PN2, PN3, RPS 4Y711, and Tat (Hammer and Horai 1995; Hammer et al. 1997, 1998, 2000; Underhill et al. 1997; Zerjal et al. 1997; Karafet et al. 1999). All individuals tested negative for the Y Alu insert (DYS287). A complete description of the Ychromosome STR loci can be found in Kayser et al. (1997). For the Y-chromosome biallelic dataset, comparisons were made to a different set of worldwide populations including: East Asians from Japan, Korea, China, and Vietnam (n = 460); Western Europeans from Britain and Germany (n = 77); Southern Europeans from Italy and Greece (n = 148); and Eastern Europeans from Russia and Romania (n = 102) (M.F. Hammer, unpubl.). The complete dataset of Indians consisted of 55 Brahmin, 111 Yadava and Kapu, and 74 Relli, Mala, and Madiga.

Statistical Analysis

Genetic distances for Y-chromosome STRs were estimated using the method of Shriver et al. (1995), which assumes a stepwise mutation model. Genetic distances for mitochondrial and autosomal markers were calculated as pairwise FST distances, using the ARLEQUIN package (Schneider et al. 1997).

For autosomal polymorphisms, Nei's standard distances and their standard errors were estimated using DISPAN; and 90% confidence intervals were estimated by multiplying the standard error by 1.65. The significance of the FST distances between populations was estimated by generating a null distribution of pairwise FST distances by permuting haplotypes between populations. The p-value of the test is the proportion of permutations leading to an FST value larger than or equal to the observed one. Genotypic differentiation was estimated using GENEPOP (Raymond and Rousset 1995) vers. 3.2. The null hypothesis tested is that there is a random distribution of K different haplotypes among r populations. Estimates of significance for the correlation between interindividual caste rank differences and interindividual autosomal genetic distances were made by forming two n - n matrices, where n is the number of individuals. For the first matrix, interindividual genetic distances were based on the proportion of Alu insertions/deletions shared by each pair of individuals. To form the second matrix, each individual was assigned a score according to his rank in the caste hierarchy for caste groups (i.e., upper caste = 1, middle caste = 2, lower caste = 3) and also for separate castes (i.e., Brahmin = 1, Kshatriya = 2, Vyshya = 3, Kapu = 4, Yadava = 5, Relli = 6, Mala = 7, and Madiga = 8). An interindividual matrix of score distances was formed by comparing the absolute value of the difference between the scores of each pair of individuals. The matrix of genetic distances was compared to 10,000 permuted matrices of score distances using a Mantel matrix comparison test (Mantel 1967). To illustrate phylogenetic relationships we constructed reduced median (Bandelt et al. 1995) and neighbour-joining networks (Felsenstein 1989). Coalescence times were calculated as in Forster et al. (1996), using the estimator, which is the average transitional distance from the founder haplotype.

Acknowledgments: We thank all participants, the faculty and staff of Andhra University for their discussion and technical assistance, as well as Henry Harpending for comments and criticisms. We acknowledge the contributions of an anonymous reviewer who suggested that the Kshatriya and Vyshya be analysed separately from the other upper castes. Genetic distances between STRs were estimated by the program DISTNEW, kindly provided by L. Jin. This work was supported by NSF SBR-9514733, SBR-9700729, SBR-9818215, NIH grants GM-59290 and PHS MO1-00064, the Estonian Science Fund (1669 and 2887), and the Newcastle University small grants committee. The publication costs of this article were defrayed in part by payment of page charges. This article must therefore be hereby marked "advertisement" in accordance with 18 USC section 1734 solely to indicate this fact.

5

Position of Women in Ancient India

Hindu Family Dharma

Hindu value system placed very high degree of importance to morality where a woman does not accept the seed form anyone other than her husband. We are talking of normal circumstances of life. We speak of rules not exceptions!

Family Structure and Allocation of Powers and Responsibilities: Each family would have a head known as Karta whose decision would be final in case of family disputes and disagreements. This authority would be vested in the Karta with the responsibility to be just and fair to all in the family, and not to base crucial decisions on personal preferences. In all his visible judgments and decisions, he would be expected to demonstrate justice and fairness.

Children of the family would grow up 'learning to value' these qualities of justice and fairness. This process of living through just and fair dealings, would inculcate those qualities in them, through the course of their growing up process.

This was a living reality of Hindu social life.

This was a living reality of Hindu social life or else, different visitors from different nations over different centuries would not have mentioned so consistently of this quality among Hindus. Now, it is quite true that during the two thousand years which precede the time of Mahmud of Ghazni, Bhaarat Varsh has had but few foreign visitors, and few foreign critics; still it is extremely strange that whenever, either in Greek, or in Chinese, or in Persian, or in Arab writings, we meet any attempts at describing the distinguishing features in the national character of the Bhartiyas (*Hindus), regard for truth and justice should always be mentioned first. Max Muller, p 50

Hindu Joint Family Structure of Earlier Times and its Strengths: Returning to the Hindu family structure of earlier days, Karta would normally be the able-bodied able-minded eldest male member of the family. Position of authority and responsibility would be distributed in a hierarchical manner in the sense that elder the member greater the authority coupled with greater responsibility. Younger members would be groomed on the same pattern to learn to assume the authority as well as discharge corresponding responsibility, as they would grow up in the hierarchy.

The respect for the elders would be an unwritten law, and it would be expected of all to observe it without any reservation. With that elders would have the equal amount of responsibility to stay worthy of such respect by their thoughts and actions. This would be the balancing factor for maintaining necessary equilibrium in the family.

Adult male members of the family would have the responsibility of earning for the family to meet its needs, and to provide shelter and protection to the female members and children of the family. Female members would have the responsibility of taking care of the in-house needs of male members of family, and raising the kids in line with the culture and traditions of the family. Elder female members of the family would have the responsibility of grooming up the younger female members of the family in the desired direction.

Each new generation would learn the family values from their mothers and grandmothers, and in this manner the female members of the family would play the crucial role through the formative years of growing children. Spirituality would be an essential part of the family values, and women folk would be the custodian and deliverer of these values to each next generation through their growing up process.

Single spouse system and fidelity would be the norm. Exceptions would be found in the context of political marriages where a king would offer his daughter to another king and thus, the two ruling families would unite and not be threat to each other. Such marriages would primarily be conducted for maintaining power-balance and political equilibrium. These would be exceptions not rule, and we have references to many kings having only one wife.

How Hindu family structure changed so drastically that now we hardly see any evidence of our earlier system.

The whole system, however, changed after brutal onslaught of Islam and its direct interference in Hindu way of family life through forced conversions and forced marriages of Hindu girls and Hindu women into Muslim powerful families. This is when family values started deteriorating substantially though it did preserve a lot of it, as we can see from the testimonies of Sir Thomas Munro as presented below, even after thousand years of inhumane oppression that Max Muller called an inferno and wondered "how any nation could have survived such an inferno without being turned into devils themselves."

If a good system of agriculture, unrivalled manufacturing skill, a capacity to produce whatever can contribute to either convenience or luxury, schools established in every village for teaching, reading, writing, and arithmetic, the general practice of hospitality and charity amongst each other, and above all, a treatment of the female sex full of confidence, respect, and delicacy, are among the signs which denote a civilized people-then the Hindus are not inferior to the nations of Europe, and if civilization is to become an article of trade between England and Bhaarat Varsh, I am convinced that England will gain by the import cargo. Sir Thomas Munro, quoted in Mill's History, vol. i. p. 371, re-quoted by Max Muller, p 57 p 231

The True Culprits have remained unidentified all along. There was so much of beauty left even until early 19th century that the eminent Governor of the then Madras Presidency wrote:

If civilization is to become an article of trade between England and Bhaarat Varsh, I am convinced that England will gain by the import cargo.

This would mean that real downfall has occurred during past 170 years. All factors remaining constant the only variable has been Christian English education system forcibly imposed on the Hindus by systematic elimination of ancient Hindu education system [documentary evidence in Hidden face of Christianity].

Hindu Family Values were totally transformed by the Christian English Education system, which was predominantly guided by the values propagated by Jesus Christ in the Christian Bible.

Oxford Dictionary p 1249, p 792, p 1143 New Testament is the second part of the Christian Bible; Gospel is the record of Christ's life and teachings in the first four books of the New Testament; St. Matthew was an Apostle, and the author of the first Gospel; p 1099 St. Luke was an evangelist, and the author of the third Gospel; p 1928, p 77 St. Thomas was an Apostle; Each of the twelve chief disciples of Jesus Christ is an Apostle.

Christian Bible New Testament Matthew 10:34 Think not that I am come to send peace on earth: I came not to send peace, but a sword. 10:35 For I am come to set a man at variance against his father, and the daughter against the mother, and the daughter in law against her mother in law. 10:36 And a man's foe shall be they of his own household. 10:37 He that loveth father or mother more than me is not worthy of me. 12: 30 He that is not with me is against me.

Christian Bible New Testament Luke 12:51 Suppose ye that I am come to give peace on earth? I tell you, Nay; but rather division: 12:52 For from henceforth there shall be five in one house divided, three against two, and two against three. 12:53 The father shall be divided against the son, and the son against the father; the mother against the daughter, and the daughter against the mother; the mother in law against her daughter in law, and the daughter in law against her mother in law. 14:26 If any man come to me, and hate not his father, and mother, and wife, and children, and brethren, and sisters, yea, and his own life also, he cannot be my disciple.

Gospel of Thomas 16 Jesus said: Perhaps men think that I came to cast peace on the world; and they do not know that I came to cast division upon earth, fire, sword, war. For five will be in a house; there will be three against two and two against three, the father against the son and the son against the father. And they will stand because they are single ones. 56 Jesus said: He who will not hate his father and his mother cannot be my disciple. And he who will not hate his brothers and sisters, and carry his cross as I have, will not become worthy of me.

To understand Jesus's agenda, as documented in the pages of Christian Bible, you may want to study Christianity in a different Light. Christian missionary educators taught the Hindus for past six generations and media experts created the image in the minds of the Hindus that ancient Hindu Joint Family structure was essentially an evil social structure. This paved the way for promoting Split Family structure which has now been refined to such levels that gradually Single Parent system is becoming the norm in the Christian World that we mistakenly identify as Western world, and aping them faithfully we too are rapidly following their footsteps.

Marriages under Hindu Joint Family System

Marriage was one of the most significant aspects of Family Dharm. Marriage was not considered simply as union of two bodies. Marriage was a significant social event. It was union of two families and family traditions.

Marriages were decided with great care. Several aspects were considered. Not only boy and girl were important, but their parents were also important; so were family lineage, parental characters, parental nature, their values, their traditions, their health, their history and so many things.

Today boy and girl argue, why we need to look at parents, and what character and values they represent; we do not have to marry parents, we have to marry each other. Fine as it sounds, and nice as it feels, we tend to forget 'science' that we are so proud of, which has started understanding a little bit of the relevance of genes in human behavioural pattern. The hereditary attributes play their role in the long run and we find these lovebirds start splitting after a while. Few years ago, I looked at divorce rates in North America exceeding 50%, while these statistics did not tell us the full story, for they covered only those who were legally married, and such couples often find separation and divorce process pretty demanding, considering future of children involved and therefore, not all broken marriages result in legal divorce.

A very large segment of married couple in North America (I speak of Canada, and assume it would be same in USA) are those called common-law where the boy and girl live together like husband and wife, have children, file tax returns as common-law spouses, for most purposes they are like married couple except they are not legally married.

Most of them are youngsters who have not yet planned children, and these marriages break fairly easy as compared to legal marriages, for all they need is to split, and start living separate. These are high ratio cases. Thus, if we were to take these into account, then total divorces (where divorce would mean essentially all failed marriages), would probably exceed 75%.

What a great system it is that does not stand the test of time, that does not stand the test of success in the desired venture that fails and fails, and finally gets reduced to multiple experiments with life! This, we call modern social structure, and we gloat at its supposedly advanced nature. There is lot to learn from the systems of olden days that we look down upon thinking we have progressed! Have we? Except that we satisfy our ego by consoling ourselves with such inflated self-estimates! The Secret of Stable Hindu marriages of yesteryears—a meticulous system of mathematics applied to human lives.

We may have occasionally heard about extraordinary accomplishments of Hindu mathematics. The Christian World, however, prefers to attribute them to the Greeks and (pre-Islamic) Arabs who basically imported the knowledge from the Hindus and then popularized with the people of Europe.

The foundation of Family Dharm was on the premises of the institution of marriage. Arranged marriages demonstrated great stability and reflected high success rate.

This was ensured by a meticulous system of mathematics applied to human lives. Based on time and place of birth of a human being, it could calculate with fair amount of accuracy the life span of the individual. This helped match-making in a manner that one of the spouses does not have to live very long without the other.

The system could calculate the ego development of the marrying partners. This helped match-making with due caution to conflicting egos between the boy and the girl in consideration.

The system could calculate with fair amount of accuracy the degree of magnetic control or amenability either spouse will have on the other. This helped match-making with a view to harmony between the two.

The system could calculate with considerable accuracy the sexual compatibility between the boy and girl in question. This helped match-making with regard to this very essential factor in a satisfying marriage.

The system considered sexual compatibility in physical as well as emotional context. It may be difficult for modern people to visualize that a mathematical system could be capable of ascertaining such details without reference to medical and psychological systems.

Well, that difficulty in perception is natural because modern education system has not tried to evolve mathematical modules applied to human lives. It has not tried so because the modern Christian education system is based on an inflated ego that it has nothing to learn from ancient Hindu systems. More significantly, the modern education system is based on knowledge base of the Christian World, which would not want to entertain the thought that Hindu world could have had better developed modules for social, economical, judicial and other processes.

Returning to the mathematical system we have been referring to, it had developed the capability of determining the psychological dispositions of the intended couple. This helped in (a) ascertaining mental qualities and (b) estimating likely affection for each other, this being very significant element in matchmaking. Then the system calculated the temperament and character of the couple concerned where compatibility of temperament was looked at for a satisfactory marriage union.

Finally, system looked at nervous energy indicating the physiological and to certain extent hereditary factors. This helped matchmaking with a view to the children that would be borne of such couple, for a marriage was not meant only for the present generation but also for the future generation of the society to come.

All these factors could be translated into mathematical module because the Creation and maintenance of this Universe itself works on a mathematical module of high precision. The method was widely followed and its results have shown over thousands of years of its application.

In modern times its use has dwindled, for an image has been successfully created that whatever modern Christian education system does not teach us is essentially superstitious. The result of our modernity has already started showing on our present day family structure.

The technique was not an end in itself.

Here, you need to understand another fundamental relating to this Creation. That is: nothing is stand alone in isolation to the exclusion of everything else. Do not think that any one aspect of esoteric knowledge would suffice for you to understand the entire gamut of complexities involved in the process of Creation.

Simply put you need to understand that the module I spoke of ~ applied mathematics to human lives ~ is not stand alone. Its well understood application does ensure substantially a stable married life but in itself, it is not the only means to that end.

Election of the right partner at the initial stage by application of that mathematical module can ensure a stable beginning and a stable journey but then that needs to be complemented with some other equally significant modules relevant to human lives. You cannot ignore other modules and expect the entire fruit by sticking to only one. There are several aspects of esoteric knowledge that have not only remained limited within the boundaries of

Science but graduated beyond to the State of Art where they have become relevant to human lives in manners that you may not begin to think because your Christian English educators have systematically buried them over the past two centuries. I am not going to discuss them here but I will return with them someday.

In today's circumstances this clarification is all the more necessary because it is the age of quick fix where every one tends to look for an allopathic medicine for every headache ~ a pill that would instantly relieve you of the headache not bothering to fix the root problem. Besides, the close association with and total dependence on Christian English education system for six generations has made us not only forget those essentials but also treat them as meaningless superstitions because an ignorant education system can give you no better knowledge ~ a culture that cares not to understand Mother Nature but only attempts to conquer it like all arrogant fools do can give you no better understanding of matters that truly affect your lives. All they do is whole lot of trial and errors and give them impressive names like psychiatry and various derivatives of those kinds which are nothing but a huge money making racket in the name of scientific education.

How we lost all that.

Christian British systematically destroyed ancient Hindu education system. They withdrew all governmental support to any form of education that remotely related to Hindu system. Through Christian English education system they filled the minds of Hindu children that all of Hindu system of knowledge was nothing but superstition. Through six generations of Christian English education you have learned to think of them as superstition. Superstition is something that you believe in blindly. Aren't you doing the same thing? Didn't you believe blindly what those ignorant Christian British educators told you. Neither did they examine the validity of Hindu branches of knowledge, nor did you examine them. And, you blindly believed them all to be superstition. This belief of yours ~ isn't it a superstition by itself?

They killed our knowledge base, they let it get lost. If few kept it alive through generations without adequate support system and if they lost most of it, you call them quacks. Who is responsible for the degeneration of Hindu knowledge base? Are these whom you call quacks? Or, are those who methodically wiped it out over the period of time?

Sati was Started for Preserving Caste

With the much discussed subject, now in India, about a so called "sati" of Charanshah, in village Satpura in Uttar Pradesh, some information about this evil in Hindu social system, may be not only informative but also educative to the masses who wish to build a new India on new values.

Condition of Widows in Ancient India

In India, the condition of women in general, was made more dreadful than that of a slave, but the lot of widows was always very hard and they were forced to lead a horrible life of torture, disfigurement, tonsure and deprivation, with an enforced strict ban on remarriage. They were compelled to undergo sex with other men for procreation under the system of Niyoga. As if this was not enough, a peculiar system existed in India, whereby widows were burnt alive on the funeral pyre of their dead husbands. The practice existed among the higher castes mainly, though it was given a honourable and prestigious outlook among the masses by various means adopted by the Brahmins.

Why this system started in India? It was for maintaining the caste, which was very important for the welfare of those, who are benefited by it. And as the caste system grew more rigid, the sati become more strict. Notable example is Bengal, where it was enforced more strictly because of "Kulin system", where any of the hundreds of disgruntled young wives could easily poison the old man.

Position of Women

Ms. Shakuntala Rao Shastri, in her "Women in Sacred Laws" very aptly describes the pitiable condition of women before the Britishers came to India:

"True it is that anyone who has witnessed the pathetic condition of women in India at the dawn of British rule cannot but be

shocked at it: the enforced child marriage, the exposure of female children, putting to death female children by throwing them at the junction of the Ganges and the sea, the violence used to make women follow the Sati rite and thus end their miserable existence, the shameful treatment accorded to a widow, the (in)famous kulinism which made marriage a profession rather than a sacrament, made woman not only an object of pity but many a woman sighed in the secret recess for her heart and wished that she had never been born a woman in this unfortunate country." [Shastri Shakuntala Rao, "Women in Sacred Laws" p. 171]

The situation described by the learned Vedic Scholar is at the time of dawn of British occupation, but since how long it was in existence? The reply is that this was the situation since the fall of Buddhism around tenth century AD. That the women enjoyed high position in Buddhist period can be judged by a mere glance at the Buddhist law being practiced in India before tenth century AD and which is practiced in all the Buddhist countries even now.

Today after passing of Ambedkar's Hindu Code, piece meal, the Hindu Laws of Marriage, Adoption, Succession, and other related Laws have been changed to a great extent. But prior to 1956, the Old Hindu Brahmanic Law was in force, under which the condition of women was pitiable. To get some idea of how these laws were made more and more cruel is seen if one considers that original law of India was Buddhist Law. BUDDHIST LAW WAS THE NATIONAL LAW OF INDIA, BECAUSE FROM THE HISTORICAL PERIOD, THE RELIGION OF INDIA WAS BUDDHISM. IT WAS THE MAIN STREAM. The Brahmins succeeded in causing the fall of Buddhism, at the cost of women and Shudras. They had to bear the brunt of all evils, to maintain the supremacy of the Brahmins.

Epigraphic Evidences of Sati

Ms. Shakuntala Rao Shastri describes the "Memorial stelae". They are small stone uprights sculptured with figures and inscriptions, and are called Devli, and are found in abundance in Rajputana. They are erected in commemoration of women immolating themselves on funeral pyres of their husbands. The earliest one found in Jodhpur state at Gatiyala is dated 890 AD. The earliest of these stelae is found in Eran in Sagar District in M.P. and is dated 510 A. D. Thus the practice of Sati was coming to vogue in sixth century AD. [Shastri Shakuntala Rao, Ibid. p. 130]

The Annals of Kashmir by Kallahna of 12th century, mentions some instances where, in addition to wife / wives others like concubines, slaves, mother nurse, friends and followers also practiced Anumaran. Earliest mentioned was in 902 King Samkaravarman, in 1081 King Ananta, in 1161 King Malla, and the last one mentioned was in 12th century of King Sussala. [Shastri Shakuntala Rao, Ibid. p.130]

Not only it was practiced in North, West and Central India, the examples of Inscriptions from Epigraphica Carnataka show that the custom existed in South India also. Anumarana was practiced after deaths of various kings like-in 1130 AD Kadamba King Tailapa, Ganga King Nitimarga, and Satyavakya Kongunivarman Lord of Nandagiri, both of whom lived in 915 AD, in 1220 AD King Ballala, and in 1180 King Bammarasa. [Ibid. p. 132 ff.]

When a Tomar King in Gujrath died, his 90,000 queens were requested not to commit sati. They consulted their Kula-brahmana, who advised them to commit sati as Veda verse 18/877 mentions "Agne" and not "Agre", just for the sake of golden coins, thus condemning these 90,000 women to flames. 3000 queens committed sati with king of Vijaynagar. On conquest of Jaselmere by Muslims, 24 thousand queens committed sati. Old cremation place has got inscriptions mentioning names of those committing sati. 112 queens of king Amarsing of Bundi, 88 queens of Keshosing, Jagirdar of Dharampur, 78 queens of Surendrasing of Palitana. Some social reformists tried to prevent sati of 95 queens of Bharatpur, but they had to commit sati.

Why Sati was Started: Thus we find that excepting the solitary instance mentioned by Diodoras, which occured in a foreign land, and the persons involved were perhaps from foreign tribes settled in India during those times, the practice started from the time of decline and ultimate fall of Buddhism after seventh century. Still we find Banabhatta (7th century) in the court of Harshavardhana and later Medhatithi (9th century) condemning the practice. The more important question is why this system started, developed and why it attained such a high respect. Sati custom in India has to be considered in combination with other customs of Child girl marriage with an elderly man and prohibition of widows to remarry. All these customs were imposed by the Brahmins in order to prevent transgression of caste rules. This was explained by Dr. Ambedkar as early as in 1919, while dealing with genesis and mechanism of Castes. The following are the salient points from it.

Endogamy is the only characteristic peculiar to caste. No civilized society in today's world shows more survivals of primitive times than Indian society. One such primitive practice is of exogamy long given up by the world but is still favoured in India. Though there are no clans in India, clan system is savoured, as there is prohibition on not only "sapinda" marriages but also on "sagotra" marriages among the Hindus. The various gotras and other totemic organizations have always been exogamus. When endogamy was superimposed over sagotra exogamy, a caste was formed.

To preserve and maintain this caste, inter caste marriages were banned. In case of death of a spouse, the other spouse was likely to marry outside the caste. To prevent this happening various means were adopted. These are:

1. Sati or burning of a widow on the funeral pyre of her deceased husband.
2. Enforced widowhood by which she is forced not to marry and
3. Girl marriage with an aged man.

All the medieval Brahmanic texts eulogize these customs in very glamourous language but give no reasons for them. Dr. Ambedkar, who calls all this eulogy as a sugar coating of the barbarous pill, gives the reasons:

> *"... Sati, enforced widowhood and girl marriage are customs that were primarily intended to solve the problem of the surplus man and surplus woman in a caste and to maintain its endogamy. Strict endogamy could not be preserved without these customs, while caste without endogamy is a fake." [Ibid., p.14]*

The Brahmins enclosed themselves into a caste, thus forcing others to be the other caste. This was divided and further subdivided into multiple non-Brahmin castes and the institution of castes spread through the length and breadth of India. This spread was due to the tendency of imitation of Brahmins by the others.

As these customs were very harsh and barbarous, the imitation was imperfect and we find that nearer a caste is to Brahmins more strictly it insisted on observance of these customs. Example of Kulinism in Bengal, which also was a movement to preserve the Caste and ensure supremacy of Brahmins, is discussed elsewhere. That the reason, these customs had to be enforced strictly in Bengal following Kulinism, was to prevent any one among the hundreds of dissatisfied wives of a kulin man from easily poisoning him, could be easily appreciated.

6

Religious and Social Revolution-Buddhism

The History of Buddhism spans from the 6th century BC to the present, starting with the birth of the Buddha Siddhartha Gautama. This makes it one of the oldest religions practised today. Throughout this period, the religion evolved as it encountered various countries and cultures, adding to its original Indian foundation Hellenistic as well as Central Asian, East Asian and Southeast Asian cultural elements. In the process, its geographical extent became considerable so as to affect at one time or another most of the Asian continent. The history of Buddhism is also characterized by the development of numerous movements and schisms, foremost among them the Theravada, Mahayana and Vajrayana traditions, punctuated by contrasting periods of expansion and retreat.

Life of the Buddha

According to the Buddhist tradition, the historical Buddha Siddhartha Gautama was born to the Shakya clan, at the beginning of the Magadha period (546-324 BC), in the plains of Lumbini, Southern Nepal. He is also known as the Shakyamuni (literally "The sage of the Shakya clan").

After an early life of luxury under the protection of his father, Suddhodana, the ruler of Kapilavastu (later to be incorporated into the state of Magadha), Siddhartha entered into contact with the realities of the world and concluded that real life was about inescapable suffering and sorrow. Siddhartha renounced his meaningless life of luxury to become an ascetic. He ultimately decided that asceticism was also meaningless and instead chose a middle way, a path of moderation away from the extremes of self-indulgence and self-mortification.

Under a fig tree, now known as the Bodhi tree, he vowed never to leave the position until he found Truth. At the age of 35, he attained Enlightenment. He was then known as Gautama Buddha, or simply "The Buddha", which means "the enlightened one".

For the remaining 45 years of his life, he travelled the Gangetic Plain of central India (region of the Ganges/Ganga river and its tributaries), teaching his doctrine and discipline to an extremely diverse range of people. The Buddha's reluctance to name a successor or to formalise his doctrine led to the emergence of many movements during the next 400 years: first the schools of Nikaya Buddhism, of which only Theravada remains today and then the formation of Mahayana, a pan-Buddhist movement based on the acceptance of new scriptures.

Early Buddhism

Before the royal sponsorship of Ashoka the Great in the 3rd century BC, Buddhism seems to have remained a relatively minor phenomenon and the historicity of its formative events is poorly established. Two formative councils are supposed to have taken place, although our knowledge of them is based on much later accounts. The councils tend to explain the formalization of the Buddhist doctrine and the various subsequent schisms inside the Buddhist movement.

Asian Expansion

In the areas east of the Indian subcontinent (today's Burma), Indian culture strongly influenced the Mons. The Mons are said to have been converted to Buddhism around 200 BC under the proselytizing of the Indian king Ashoka, before the fission between Mahayana and Hinayana Buddhism. Early Mon Buddhist temples, such as Peikthano in central Burma, have been dated between the 1st and the 5th century AD. The Buddhist art of the Mons was especially influenced by the Indian art of the Gupta and post-

Gupta periods and their mannerist style spread widely in South-East Asia following the expansion of the Mon kingdom between the 5th and 8th centuries. The Theravada faith expanded in the northern parts of Southeast Asia under Mon influence, until it was progressively displaced by Mahayana Buddhism from around the 6th century AD.

Sri Lanka was allegedly proselytized by Ashoka's son Mahinda and six companions during the 2nd century BC. They converted the king Devanampiya Tissa and many of the nobility. This is when the Mahavihara monastery, a centre of Sinhalese orthodoxy, was built. The Pali Canon was put in writing in Sri Lanka during the reign of king Vittagamani (r. 29-17 BC) and the Theravada tradition flourished there, harbouring some great commentators such as Buddhaghosa (4th-5th century). Although Mahayana Buddhism gained some influence at that time, Theravada ultimately prevailed and Sri Lanka turned out to be the last stronghold of Theravada Buddhism, from where it would expand again to South-East Asia from the 11th century.

There is also a legend, not directly validated by the edicts, that Ashoka sent a missionary to the north, through the Himalayas, to Khotan in the Tarim Basin, then the land of the Tocharians, speakers of an Indo-European language.

In the areas west of the Indian subcontinent, neighbouring Greek kingdoms had been in place in Bactria (today's northern Afghanistan) since the time of the conquests of Alexander the Great around 326 BC: first the Seleucids from around 323 BC, then the Greco-Bactrian kingdom from around 250 BC.

The Greco-Bactrian king Demetrius I invaded India in 180 BC as far as Pataliputra, establishing an Indo-Greek kingdom that was to last in various part of northern India until the end of the 1st century BC. Buddhism flourished under the Indo-Greek kings and it has been suggested that their invasion of India was intended to show their support for the Mauryan empire and to protect the Buddhist faith from the alleged religious persecutions of the Sungas (185-73 BC), accounts which are disputed by historians.

One of the most famous Indo-Greek kings is Menander (reigned c. 160-135 BC). He apparently converted to Buddhism and is presented in the Mahayana tradition as one of the great benefactors of the faith, on a par with king Ashoka or the later Kushan king Kanishka. Menander's coins bear the mention "Saviour king" in Greek and sometimes designs of the eight-spoked wheel. Direct cultural exchange is also suggested by the dialogue of the Milinda Panha between Menander and the monk Nagasena around 160 BC. Upon his death, the honour of sharing his remains was claimed by the cities under his rule and they were enshrined in stupas, in a parallel with the historic Buddha (Plutarch, Praec. reip. ger. 28, 6). Several of Menander's Indo-Greek successors inscribed the mention "Follower of the Dharma" in the Kharoshthi script on their coins and depicted themselves or their divinities forming the vitarka mudra.

The interaction between Greek and Buddhist cultures may have had some influence on the evolution of Mahayana, as the faith developed its sophisticated philosophical approach and a man-god treatment of the Buddha somewhat reminiscent of Hellenic gods. It is also around that time that the first anthropomorphic representations of the Buddha are found, often in realistic Greco-Buddhist style: "One might regard the classical influence as including the general idea of representing a man-god in this purely human form, which was of course well familiar in the West and it is very likely that the example of westerner's treatment of their gods was indeed an important factor in the innovation" (Boardman, "The Diffusion of Classical Art in Antiquity").

Rise of Mahayana (1st c.BC-2nd c.AD)

The rise of Mahayana Buddhism from the 1st century BC was accompanied by complex political changes in northwestern India. The Indo-Greek kingdoms were gradually overwhelmed and their culture assimilated by the Indo-Scythians and then the Yuezhi, who founded the Kushan Empire from around 12 BC.

The Kushans were supportive of Buddhism and a fourth Buddhist council was convened by the Kushan emperor Kanishka, around 100 AD at Jalandhar or in Kashmir and is usually associated with the formal rise of Mahayana Buddhism and its secession from Theravada Buddhism. Theravada Buddhism does not recognize the authenticity of this council and it is sometimes called the "council of heretical monks".

It is said that Kanishka gathered 500 bhikkhus in Kashmir, headed by Vasumitra, to edit the Tripitaka and make references and remarks. Allegedly, during the council there were all together three hundred thousand verses and over nine million statements compiled and it took twelve years to complete. This council did not rely on the original Pali canon (the Tipitaka). Instead, a set of new scriptures was approved, as well as fundamental principles of Mahayana doctrine. The new scriptures, usually in the Gandhari vernacular and the Kharosthi script, were rewritten in the classical language of Sanskrit, to many scholars a turning point in the propagation of Buddhist thought.

The new form of Buddhism was characterized by an almost God-like treatment of the Buddha, by the idea that all beings have a Buddha-nature and should aspire to Buddhahood and by a syncretism due to the various cultural influences within northwestern India and the Kushan Empire.

Mahayana Expansion (1st c.AD-10th c.AD)

From that point on and in the space of a few centuries, Mahayana was to flourish and spread in the East from India to South-East Asia and towards the north to Central Asia, China, Korea and finally to Japan in 538 AD.

India

After the end of the Kushans, Buddhism flourished in India during the dynasty of the Guptas (4th-6th century). Mahayana centres of learning were established, especially at Nalanda in northeastern India, which was to become the largest and most influential Buddhist university for many centuries, with famous teachers such as Nagarjuna. The Gupta style of Buddhist art became very influential from South-East Asia to China as the faith was spreading there. Indian Buddhism had weakened in the 6th century following the White Hun invasions and Mihirkulas persecution.

Xuanzang reports in his travels across India during the 7th century of Buddhism being popular in Andhra, Dhanyakataka and Dravida which today roughly correspond to the modern day

Indian states of Andhra Pradesh and Tamil Nadu. While reporting many deserted stupas in the area around modern day Nepal and the persecution of Buddhists by Sanka in the Kingdom of Gouda. (In modern day West Bengal.) Xuanzang compliments the patronage of Harshavardana during the same period.

After Harshavardanas kingdom, the rise of many small kingdoms that lead to the rise of the Rajputs across the gangetic plains and marked the end of Buddhist ruling clans along with a sharp decline in royal patronage until a revival under the Pala Empire in the Bengal region. Here Mahayana Buddhism flourished and spread to Bhutan and Sikkim between the 8th and the 12th century before the Palas collapsed under the assault of the Hindu Sena dynasty.

The Palas created many temples and a distinctive school of Buddhist art. Xuanzang noted in his travels that in various regions Buddhism was giving way to Jainism and Hinduism. By the 10th century Buddhism had experienced a sharp decline beyond the Pala realms in Bengal under a resurgent Hinduism and the incorporation in Vaishnavite Hinduism of Buddha as the 9th incarnation of Vishnu.

A milestone in the decline of Indian Buddhism in the North occurred in 1193 when Turkic Islamic raiders under Muhammad Khilji burnt Nalanda. By the end of the 12th century, following the Islamic conquest of the Buddhist strongholds in Bihar and the loss of political support coupled with social and caste pressures, the practice of Buddhism retreated to the Himalayan foothills in the North and Sri Lanka in the south. Additionally, the influence of Buddhism also waned due to Hinduism's revival movements such as Advaita, the rise of the bhakti movement and the missionary work of Sufis.

Central and Northern Asia

Central Asia: Central Asia had been influenced by Buddhism probably almost since the time of the Buddha. According to a legend preserved in Pali, the language of the Theravada canon, two merchant brothers from Bacteria, named Tapassu and Bhallika, visited the Buddha and became his disciples. They then returned to Bacteria and built temples to the Buddha (Foltz).

Central Asia long played the role of a meeting place between China, India and Persia. During the 2nd century BC, the expansion of the Former Han to the west brought them into contact with the Hellenistic civilizations of Asia, especially the Greco-Bactrian Kingdoms. Thereafter, the expansion of Buddhism to the north led to the formation of Buddhist communities and even Buddhist kingdoms in the oases of Central Asia. Some Silk Road cities consisted almost entirely of Buddhist stupas and monasteries and it seems that one of their main objectives was to welcome and service travellers between east and west.

The Hinayana traditions first spread among the Turkic tribes before combining with the Mahayana forms during the 2nd and 3rd centuries BC to cover modern-day Pakistan, Kashmir, Afghanistan, eastern and coastal Iran, Uzbekistan, Turkmenistan and Tajikistan.

These were the ancient states of Gandhara, Bacteria, Parthia and Sogdia from where it spread to China. Among the first of these Turkic tribes to adopt Buddhism was the Turki-Shahi who adopted Buddhism as early as the 3rd century BC. It was not, however, the exclusive faith of this region. There were also Zoroastrians, Hindus, Nestorian Christians, Jews, Manichaeans and followers of shamanism, Tengrism and other indigenous, nonorganized systems of belief.

Various Nikaya schools persisted in Central Asia and China until around the 7th century AD. Mahayana started to become dominant during the period, but since the faith had not developed a Nikaya approach, Sarvastivadin and Dharmaguptakas remained the Vinayas of choice in Central Asian monasteries. Various Buddhism kingdoms rose and prospered in both the Central Asian region and downwards into the Indian sub-continent such as Kushan Empire prior to the White Hun invasion in the 5th century where under the King Mihirkula they were heavily persecuted.

Buddhism in Central Asia started to decline with the expansion of Islam and the destruction of many stupas in war from the 7th century. The Muslims accorded them the status of dhimmis as "people of the Book", such as Christianity or Judaism and Al-Biruni wrote of Buddha as prophet "burxan".

Buddhism saw a surge during the reign of Mongols following the invasion of Genghis Khan and the establishment of the II Khanate and the Chagatai Khanate who brought their Buddhist influence with them during the 13th century, however within a 100 years the Mongols would convert to Islam and spread Islam across all the regions across central Asia.

Parthia: Buddhism expanded westward into Arsacid Parthia, at least to the area of Merv, in ancient Margiana, today's territory of Turkmenistan.

Soviet archeological teams have excavated in Giaur Kala, near Merv, a Buddhist chapel, a gigantic Buddha statue, as well as a monastery. Parthians were directly involved in the propagation of Buddhism: An Shigao (c. 148 AD), a Parthian prince, went to China and is the first known translator of Buddhist scriptures into Chinese.

Tarim Basin: The eastern part of central Asia (Chinese Turkestan, Tarim Basin, Xinjiang) has revealed extremely rich Buddhist works of art (wall paintings and reliefs in numerous caves, portable paintings on canvas, sculpture, ritual objects), displaying multiple influences from Indian and Hellenistic cultures. Serindian art is highly reminiscent of the Gandharan style and scriptures in the Gandhari script Kharosthi have been found.

Central Asians seem to have played a key role in the transmission of Buddhism to the East. The first translators of Buddhists scriptures into Chinese were either Parthian (Ch: Anxi) like An Shigao (c. 148 AD) or An Hsuan, Kushan of Yuezhi ethnicity like Lokaksema (c. 178 AD), Zhi Qian and Zhi Yao, or Sogdians like Kang Sengkai. Thirty-seven early translators of Buddhist texts are known and the majority of them have been identified as Central Asians.

Central Asian and East Asian Buddhist monks appear to have maintained strong exchanges until around the 10th century, as shown by frescoes from the Tarim Basin.

These influences were rapidly absorbed however by the vigorous Chinese culture and a strongly Chinese particularism develops from that point.

China

Buddhism probably arrived in China around the 1st century AD from Central Asia (although there are some traditions about a monk visiting China during Ashoka's reign) and through to the 8th century it became an extremely active centre of Buddhism.

The year 67 AD saw Buddhism's official introduction to China with the coming of the two monks Moton and Chufarlan. In 68 AD, under imperial patronage, they established the White Horse Temple, which still exists today, close to the imperial capital at Luoyang. By the end of the second century, a prosperous community had been settled at Pengcheng (modern Xuzhou, Jiangsu).

The first known Mahayana scriptural texts are translations made into Chinese by the Kushan monk Lokaksema in Luoyang, between 178 and 189 AD. Some of the earliest known Buddhist artifacts found in China are small statues on "money trees", dated circa 200 AD, in typical Gandharan style (drawing): "That the imported images accompanying the newly arrived doctrine came from Gandhara is strongly suggested by such early Gandhara characteristics on this "money tree" Buddha as the high ushnisha, vertical arrangement of the hair, moustache, symmetrically looped robe and parallel incisions for the folds of the arms." ("Crossroads of Asia" p209)

Buddhism flourished during the beginning of the Tang Dynasty (618-907). The dynasty was initially characterized by a strong openness to foreign influences and renewed exchanges with Indian culture due to the numerous travels of Chinese Buddhist monks to India from the 4th to the 11th century. The Tang capital of Chang'an (today's Xi'an) became an important centre for Buddhist thought. From there Buddhism spread to Korea and Japanese embassies of Kentoshi helped gain footholds in Japan.

However foreign influences came to be negatively perceived towards the end of the Tang Dynasty. In the year 845, the Tang emperor Wu-Tsung outlawed all "foreign" religions (including Christian Nestorianism, Zoroastrianism and Buddhism) in order to support the indigenous Taoism. Throughout his territory, he confiscated Buddhist possessions, destroyed monasteries and temples and executed Buddhist monks, ending Buddhism's cultural and intellectual dominance.

Pure Land and Chan Buddhism, however, continued to prosper for some centuries, the latter giving rise to Japanese Zen. In China, Chan flourished particularly under the Song dynasty (1127-1279), when its monasteries were great centres of culture and learning.

Today, China boasts one of the richest collections of Buddhist arts and heritages in the world. UNESCO World Heritage Sites such as the Mogao Caves near Dunhuang in Gansu province, the Longmen Grottoes near Luoyang in Henan province, the Yungang Grottoes near Datong in Shanxi province and the Dazu Rock Carvings near Chongqing are among the most important and renowned Buddhist sculptural sites. The Leshan Giant Buddha, carved out of a hillside in the 8th century during Tang Dynasty and looking down on the confluence of three rivers, is still the largest stone Buddha statue in the world.

Korea

Buddhism was introduced around 372 AD, when Chinese ambassadors visited the Korean kingdom of Goguryeo, bringing scriptures and images. Buddhism prospered in Korea and in particular Seon (Zen) Buddhism from the 7th century onward. However, with the beginning of the Confucean Yi Dynasty of the Joseon period in 1392, Buddhism was strongly discriminated against until it was almost completely eradicated, except for a remaining Seon movement.

Japan

Japan discovered Buddhism in the 6th century when Korean monks travelled to the islands together with numerous scriptures and works of art. The Buddhist religion was adopted by the state in the following century. Being geographically at the end of the Silk Road, Japan was able to preserve many aspects of Buddhism at the very time it was disappearing in India and being suppressed in Central Asia and China.

From 710 AD numerous temples and monasteries were built in the capital city of Nara, such as the five-story pagoda and Golden Hall of the Horyuji, or the Kofuku-ji temple. Countless paintings and sculptures were made, often under governmental sponsorship. The creation of Japanese Buddhist art was especially rich between the 8th and 13th century during the periods of Nara, Heian and Kamakura.

From the 12th and 13th, a further development was Zen art, following the introduction of the faith by Dogen and Eisai upon their return from China. Zen art is mainly characterized by original paintings (such as sumi-e and the Enso) and poetry (especially haikus), striving to express the true essence of the world through impressionistic and unadorned "non-dualistic" representations. The search for enlightenment "in the moment" also led to the development of other important derivative arts such as the Chanoyu tea ceremony or the Ikebana art of flower arrangement. This evolution went as far as considering almost any human activity as an art with a strong spiritual and aesthetic content, first and foremost in those activities related to combat techniques (martial arts).

Buddhism remains very active in Japan to this day. Around 80,000 Buddhist temples are preserved and regularly restored.

South-East Asia

During the 1st century AD, the trade on the overland Silk Road tended to be restricted by the rise in the Middle-East of the Parthian empire, an unvanquished enemy of Rome, just as Romans were becoming extremely wealthy and their demand for Asian luxury was rising.

This demand revived the sea connections between the Mediterranean and China, with India as the intermediary of choice. From that time, through trade connection, commercial settlements and even political interventions, India started to strongly influence Southeast Asian countries. Trade routes linked India with southern Burma, central and southern Siam, lower Cambodia and southern Vietnam and numerous urbanized coastal settlements were established there.

For more than a thousand years, Indian influence was therefore the major factor that brought a certain level of cultural unity to the various countries of the region. The Pali and Sanskrit languages and the Indian script, together with Theravada and Mahayana Buddhism, Brahmanism and Hinduism, were transmitted from direct contact and through sacred texts and Indian literature such as the Ramayana and the Mahabharata.

From the 5th to the 13th century, South-East Asia had very powerful empires and became extremely active in Buddhist architectural and artistic creation. The main Buddhist influence now came directly by sea from the Indian subcontinent, so that these empires essentially followed the Mahayana faith. The Sri Vijaya Empire to the south and the Khmer Empire to the north competed for influence and their art expressed the rich Mahayana pantheon of the Bodhisattvas.

Vietnam

Srivijayan empire (5th-15th century): Srivijaya, a maritime empire centred at Palembang on the island of Sumatra in Indonesia, adopted Mahayana and Vajrayana Buddhism under a line of rulers named the Sailendras. Yijing described Palembang as a great centre of Buddhist learning where the emperor supported over a thousand monks at his court. Atisha studied there before travelling to Tibet as a missionary.

Sriviijaya spread Buddhist art during its expansion in Southeast Asia. Numerous statues of Bodhisattvas from this period are characterized by a very strong refinement and technical sophistication and are found throughout the region. Extremely rich architectural remains are visible at the temple of Borobudur (the largest Buddhist structure in the world, built from around 780 AD), in Java, which has 505 images of the seated Buddha. Srivijaya declined due to conflicts with the Chola rulers of India, before being destabilized by the Islamic expansion from the 13th century.

Khmer Empire (9th-13th century): Later, from the 9th to the 13th century, the Mahayana Buddhist and Hindu Khmer Empire dominated much of the South-East Asian peninsula. Under the Khmer, more than 900 temples were built in Cambodia and in neighbouring Thailand. Angkor was at the centre of this development, with a temple complex and urban organization able to support around one million urban dwellers. One of the greatest

Khmer kings, Jayavarman VII (1181-1219), built large Mahayana Buddhist structures at Bayon and Angkor Thom.

Following the destruction of Buddhism in mainland India during the 11th century, Mahayana Buddhism declined in Southeast Asia, to be replaced by the introduction of Theravada Buddhism from Sri Lanka.

Emergence of the Vajrayana (5th Century): Vajrayana Buddhism, also called Tantric Buddhism, first emerged in eastern India between the 5th and 7th centuries AD. It is sometimes considered a sub-school of Mahayana and sometimes a third major "vehicle" (Yana) of Buddhism in its own right. The Vajrayana is an extension of Mahayana Buddhism in that it does not offer new philosophical perspectives, but rather introduces additional techniques (upaya, or 'skilful means'), including the use of visualizations and other yogic practices. Many of the practices of Tantric Buddhism are also derived from Hinduism (the usage of mantras, yoga, or the burning of sacrificial offerings). This school of thought was founded by the Brahmin Padmasambhava.

Early Vajrayana practitioners were forest-dwelling mahasiddas who lived on the margins of society, but by the 9th century Vajrayana had won acceptance at major Mahayana monastic universities such as Nalanda and Vikramshila. Along with much of the rest of Indian Buddhism, the Vajrayana was eclipsed in the wake of the late 12th century Muslim invasions. It has persisted in Tibet, where it was wholly transplanted from the 7th to 12th centuries and became the dominant form of Buddhism to the present day and on a limited basis in Japan as well where it evolved into Shingon Buddhism.

Theravada Renaissance (11th Century AD): From the 11th century, the destruction of Buddhism in the Indian mainland by Islamic invasions led to the decline of the Mahayana faith in South-East Asia. Continental routes through the Indian subcontinent being compromised, direct sea routes between the Middle-East through Sri Lanka and to China developed, leading to the adoption of the Theravada Buddhism of the Pali canon, introduced to the region around the 11th century AD from Sri Lanka.

King Anawrahta (1044-1077); the historical founder of the Burmese empire, unified the country and adopted the Theravada Buddhist faith. This initiated the creation of thousands of Buddhist temples at Pagan, the capital, between the 11th and 13th century. Around 2,000 of them are still standing.

The power of the Burmese waned with the rise of the Thai and with the seizure of the capital Pagan by the Mongols in 1287, but Theravada Buddhism remained the main Burmese faith to this day. The Theravada faith was also adopted by the newly founded ethnic Thai kingdom of Sukhothai around 1260. Theravada Buddhism was further reinforced during the Ayutthaya period (14th-18th century), becoming an integral part of the Thai society.

In the continental areas, Theravada Buddhism continued to expand into Laos and Cambodia in the 13th century. However, from the 14th century, on the coastal fringes and in the islands of South-East Asia, the influence of Islam proved stronger, expanding into Malaysia, Indonesia and most of the islands as far as the southern Philippines.

However, since 1966 with Soeharto's rise of power in the aftermath of the bloody events after the so called "September 30th, 1965 murders", allegedly executed by the Communists Party, there has been a remarkable renaissance of Buddhism in Indonesia. This is partly due to the Soeharto's New Order's requirements for the people of Indonesia to adopt one of the five official religions: Islam, Protestantism, Catholicism, Hinduism or Buddhism. Today it is estimated there are some 10 millions Buddhists in Indonesia. A large part of them are people of Chinese ancestry.

Expansion of Buddhism to the West: After the Classical encounters between Buddhism and the West recorded in Greco-Buddhist art, information and legends about Buddhism seem to have reached the West sporadically. During the 8th century, Buddhist Jataka stories were translated into Syriac and Arabic as Kalilag and Damnag. An account of Buddha's life was translated in to Greek by John of Damascus and widely circulated to Christians as the story of Barlaam and Josaphat. By the 1300s this story of Josaphat had become so popular that he was made a Catholic saint.

The next direct encounter between Europeans and Buddhism happened in Medieval times when the Franciscan friar William of Rubruck was sent on an embassy to the Mongol court of Mongke by the French king Saint Louis in 1253. The contact happened in Cailac (today's Qayaliq in Kazakhstan) and William originally thought they were wayward Christians (Foltz, "Religions of the Silk Road").

Major interest for Buddhism emerged during colonial times, when Western powers were in a position to witness the faith and its artistic manifestations in detail. European philosophy was strongly influenced by the study of oriental religions during that period.

The opening of Japan in 1853 also created a considerable interest for the arts and culture of Japan and provided access to one of the most thriving Buddhist cultures in the world. Buddhism started to enjoy a strong interest from the general population in the West during the 20th century, following the perceived failure of social utopias, from Fascism to Marxism. After the Second World War, the focus of progress tended to shift to personal self-realization, on the material as well as spiritual plane.

In this context, Buddhism has been displaying a strong power of attraction, due to its tolerance, its lack of deist authority and determinism and its focus on understanding reality through self inquiry. According to the latest census it is now the fastest growing religion in Britain.

Theravada Buddhist Council in 1871 (5th Buddhist Council)

Another Buddhist Council, this time presided by Theravada monks took place in Mandalay Burma now known as Myanmar in 1871 in the reign of King Mindon. The chief objective of this meeting was to recite all the teachings of the Buddha and examine them in minute detail to see if any of them had been altered, distorted or dropped. It was presided over by three Elders, the Venerable Mahathera Jagarabhivamsa, the Venerable Narindabhidhaja and the Venerable Mahathera Sumangalasami in the company of some two thousand four hundred monks (2,400). Their joint Dhamma recitation lasted for five months. It was also the work of this council to cause the entire Tripitaka to be inscribed for posterity on seven hundred and twenty-nine marble slabs in the Myanmar script after its recitation had been completed and unanimously approved. This monumental task was done by some two thousand four hundred (2,400) erudite monks and many skilled craftsmen who upon completion of each slab had them housed in beautiful miniature 'pitaka' pagodas on a special site in the grounds of King Mindon's Kuthodaw Pagoda at the foot of Mandalay Hill where it and the so called 'largest book in the world', stands to this day.

Buddhist Philosophy

The Four Noble Truths are one of the most fundamental Buddhist teachings, they appear many times throughout the most ancient Buddhist texts, the Pali Canon. They are among the truths the Buddha realised during his enlightenment experience. Why the Buddha taught in this way is illuminated by the social context of the time in which he lived. The Buddha was a Sramaa, a wandering ascetic whose "aim was to discover the truth and attain happiness". The Buddha claimed to have achieved this aim while under a bodhi tree near the Ganges River; the Four Noble Truths are a formulation of his understanding of "suffering", the fundamental cause of all suffering, the escape from suffering and what effort a person can go to so that they themselves can "attain happiness."

These truths are not expressed as a theory or tentative idea, rather the Buddha says:

"These Four Noble Truths, monks, are actual, unerring, not otherwise. Therefore, they are called noble truths."

The Buddha said that he taught them...

"...because it is beneficial, it belongs to the fundamentals of the holy life, it leads to disenchantment, to dispassion, to cessation, to peace, to direct knowledge, to enlightenment, to Nirvana. That is why I have declared it."

This teaching was the basis of the Buddha's first discourse after his enlightenment. Mahayana Buddhism contains within itself an alternative version of the Four Noble Truths, in which the immortality of the Buddha occupies a central position.

Four Noble Truths

1. *Suffering (Dukkha)*: Now this, monks, is the noble truth of suffering: Birth is suffering, aging is suffering, sickness is suffering, death is suffering; union with what is displeasing is suffering; separation from what is pleasing is suffering; not to get what one wants is suffering; in brief, the five aggregates subject to clinging are suffering.
2. *Source of Suffering (Samudaya)*: Now this, monks, is the noble truth of the origin of suffering: It is this craving which leads to renewed existence, accompanied by delight and lust, seeking delight here and there; that is, craving for sensual pleasures, craving for existence, craving for extermination.
3. *The Cessation of Suffering (Nirodha)*: Now this, monks, is the noble truth of the cessation of suffering: It is the remainder less fading away and cessation of that same craving, the giving up and relinquishing of it, freedom from it and non-reliance on it.
4. *The Way Leading to the Cessation of Suffering (Magga)*: Now this, monks, is the noble truth of the way leading to the cessation of suffering: It is this Noble Eightfold Path; that is, right view, right intention, right speech, right action, right livelihood, right effort, right mindfulness, right concentration."

Variant Four Noble Truths in Mahayana Buddhism

Certain major Mahayana sutras, including the Mahaparinirvana Sutra and the Angulimaliya Sutra, present variant versions of the Four Noble Truths in line with their own metaphysics and soteriology. In the Mahaparinirvana Sutra, the Buddha declares that:

the Truth of Suffering relates to the failure to recognise the eternity of the Buddha;

the Truth of the Cause of Suffering concerns the perversion and distortion of the True Dharma;

The Truth of the Cessation of Suffering relates to the correct meditative cultivation of the tathagatagarbha (indwelling Buddha

Essence in all beings) and not erroneously viewing it as non-Self and empty; cessation of suffering also arises with the elimination of inner defilements, when one can then enter into the Buddhic Essence within oneself: "When the afflictions have been eradicated, then one will perceive entry into the tathagata-garbha"; the Truth of the Path to the Cessation of Suffering entails envisioning the Buddha, Dharma and Sangha as eternal, immovable and indestructible.

The Angulimaliya Sutra similarly emphasises the seeing and knowing of the Buddha's eternality, immutability and peace as the key factors in liberation from suffering; failure to see this eternal nature of ultimate reality is said to constitute the primary cause of beings' continued entrapment in the sufferings of samsara.

Noble Eightfold Path

The Noble Eightfold Path is, in the Buddhist tradition as taught by the Buddha Sakyamuni, considered to be the way that leads to the end of suffering. It forms the fourth part of the Four Noble Truths, which are the most fundamental Buddhist teachings.

The Noble Eightfold Path is essentially a practical guide of ethics, mental rehabilitation and mind deconditioning and is believed, by Buddhists, to result in an end to dukkha, or suffering, which is a goal that has informed and driven the entire Buddhist tradition since its inception 2500 years ago. As the name indicates, there are eight elements in the Noble Eightfold Path and these are further subdivided into three basic categories as follows:

- Wisdom (Sanskrit: prajna, Pali: panna)
  1. Right understanding
  2. Right intention
- Ethical conduct (Sanskrit: sila, Pali: sila)
  3. Right speech
  4. Right action
  5. Right livelihood
- Mental discipline (Sanskrit and Pali: samadhi)
  6. Right effort

7. Right mindfulness
8. Right concentration

In all of the elements of the Noble Eightfold Path, the word "right" is a translation of the word samyanc (Sanskrit) or samma (Pali), which denotes completion, togetherness and coherence and which can also carry the sense of "perfect" or "ideal".

Though the path is numbered one through eight, it is generally not considered to be a series of linear steps through which one must progress; rather, as the Buddhist monk and scholar Walpola Rahula points out, the eight elements of the Noble Eightfold Path "are to be developed more or less simultaneously, as far as possible according to the capacity of each individual. They are all linked together and each helps the cultivation of the others".

In Buddhist symbology, the Noble Eightfold Path is often represented by means of the Dharma wheel (Sanskrit: dharmacakra, Pali: dhammacakka), whose eight spokes represent the eight elements of the path.

Wisdom (Prajna-Panna)

The "wisdom" subdivision of the Noble Eightfold Path is constituted by those elements that refer primarily to the mental or cognitive aspect of a Buddhist practitioner's practice.

Right Understanding

Right understanding can also be translated as "right view" or "right perspective". This element of the Noble Eightfold Path refers explicitly to the Four Noble Truths of Buddhism, stating that these must be fully understood by the Buddhist practitioner. In the Mahasatipathana Sutta, one of the Buddha Sakyamuni's discourses, right understanding is explained directly in terms of the Four Noble Truths:

> *And what, O bhikkhus, is right understanding? To understand suffering, to understand the origination of suffering, to understand extinction of suffering, to understand the path leading to the extinction of suffering; this is called right understanding.*

Additionally, right understanding is sometimes considered to encompass an understanding of the Buddhist idea of the non-permanence, or even nonexistence, of the self, an idea known as anatman in Sanskrit and anatta in Pali.

There are two stages for every stage of the eightfold path, a preliminary stage and the higher stages gradually obtained through the journey towards enlightenment. The preliminary stage of Right Views or right understanding is the knowledge of the Four Noble Truths. The higher stage require more than the comprehension of the Four Noble Truths, it also includes the knowledge and understanding of the not-self doctorine, imperminence, dependent origination, the five aggregates, kamma and rebirth and so on.

Right Thought

Right thought can also be translated as "right intention", "right resolve", or "right aspiration". This element of the Noble Eightfold Path deals, fundamentally, with the Buddhist practitioner's reasons for practising Buddhism and with his or her outlook towards the world. It enjoins renunciation of worldly things and an accordant greater commitment to spiritual matters; good will; and a commitment to non-violence, or ahimsa, towards other living beings. In the Magga-vibhanga Sutta, it is simply explained as follows:

> *And what is right thought? Being resolved on renunciation, on freedom from ill will, on harmlessness: This is called right thought.*

Ethical Conduct (Sila-Sila)

The "ethical conduct" (Sila) subdivision of the Noble Eightfold Path is constituted by those elements that are driven by and ultimately conducive to the Buddhist idea of karuga, which is generally translated as compassion and somewhat akin to the Christian notion of agape, or "unconditional love". This aspect of the Noble Eightfold Path is the most outward-oriented aspect of the Noble Eightfold Path insofar as it deals directly with a Buddhist practitioner's relationship with other members of his or her society.

Right Speech

Right speech (samyag-vac, samma-vaca), as the name implies, deals with the way in which a Buddhist practitioner would best make use of his or her words. In the Magga-vibhanga Sutta, this aspect of the Noble Eightfold Path is explained as follows:

> *And what is right speech? Abstaining from lying, abstaining from divisive speech, abstaining from abusive speech, abstaining from idle chatter: This, monks, is called right speech.*

Walpola Rahula glosses this by stating that not engaging in such "forms of wrong and harmful speech" ultimately means that "one naturally has to speak the truth, has to use words that are friendly and benevolent, pleasant and gentle, meaningful and useful".

Right Action

Right action (samyak-karmanta, samma-kammanta) can also be translated as "right conduct" and, as the name implies, deals with the proper way in which a Buddhist practitioner would act in his or her daily life. In the Magga-vibhanga Sutta, this aspect of the Noble Eightfold Path is explained as follows:

> *And what, monks, is right action? Abstaining from taking life, abstaining from stealing, abstaining from unchastity: This, monks, is called right action.*

Together with the idea of ahimsa and right speech, right action constitutes the Five Precepts (Sanskrit: pancasila, Pali: pancasila), which form the fundamental ethical code undertaken by lay followers of Buddhism and which are as follows:

1. To refrain from destroying living beings.
2. To refrain from stealing.
3. To refrain from sexual misconduct (adultery, rape, etc.).
4. To refrain from false speech (lying).
5. To refrain from intoxicants which lead to heedlessness.

Right Livelihood

Right livelihood (samyag-ajiva, samma-ajiva) is based around the concept of ahimsa, or harmlessness and essentially states that Buddhist practitioners ought not to engage in trades or occupations which, either directly or indirectly, result in harm to other living beings. Such occupations include "trading in arms and lethal weapons, intoxicating drinks, poisons, killing animals, [and] cheating", among others. "Business in human beings"-such as slave trading and prostitution-is also forbidden, as are several other dishonest means of gaining wealth, such as "scheming, persuading, hinting, belittling, [and] pursuing gain with gain".

Mental Development (Samadhi)

The "mental development" subdivision of the Noble Eightfold Path is constituted by those elements that deal with how a Buddhist practitioner can best go about shaping his or her outlook towards the world.

Right Effort

Right effort (samyag-vyayama, samma-vayama) can also be translated as "right endeavour" and involves the Buddhist practitioner's continuous effort to, essentially, keep his or her mind free of thoughts that might impair his or her ability to realize or put into practice the other elements of the Noble Eightfold Path; for example, wishing ill towards another living being would contradict the injunction-contained in the "Right thought" element-to have good will towards others and the "Right effort" element refers to the process of attempting to root out such an ill wish and replace it with a good wish. The Buddhist monk Ajahn Chah, of the Thai forest tradition of Theravada Buddhism, described right effort as follows:

> *Proper effort is not the effort to make something particular happen. It is the effort to be aware and awake in each moment, the effort to overcome laziness and defilement, the effort to make each activity of our day meditation.*

By making right effort, a Buddhist practitioner is considered to be engaging in an effort that is wholesome in terms of karma; that is, in terms of that effort's ultimate consequences to the practitioner.

Right Mindfulness

Right mindfulness, also translated as "right memory", together with right concentration, is concerned broadly with the practice of Buddhist meditation. Roughly speaking, "mindfulness" refers to the practice of keeping the mind alert to phenomena as they are affecting the body and mind. In the Magga-vibhanga Sutta, this aspect of the Noble Eightfold Path is explained as follows:

And what, monks, is right mindfulness?

(i) There is the case where a monk remains focused on (his/her) body in and of itself... ardent, aware and mindful... having already put aside worldly desire and aversion.

(ii) (He/she) remains focused on feelings in and of themselves... ardent, aware and mindful... having already put aside worldly desire and aversion.

(iii) (He/she) remains focused on the mind in and of itself... ardent, aware and mindful... having already put aside worldly desire and aversion.

(iv) (He/she) remains focused on mental qualities in and of themselves... ardent, aware and mindful... having already put aside worldly desire and aversion.

This, monks, is called right mindfulness.

Bhikkhu Bodhi, a monk of the Theravadin tradition, further glosses the concept of mindfulness as follows:

The mind is deliberately kept at the level of bare attention, a detached observation of what is happening within us and around us in the present moment. In the practice of right mindfulness the mind is trained to remain in the present, open, quiet and alert, contemplating the present event. All judgments and interpretations have to be suspended, or if they occur, just registered and dropped.

Right Concentration

Right concentration (samyak-samadhi, samma-samadhi), together with right mindfulness, is concerned broadly with the practice of Buddhist meditation.

And what, monks, is right concentration?

(i) Quite withdrawn from sensuality, withdrawn from unwholesome states, a monk enters in the first jhana: rapture and pleasure born from detachment, accompanied by movement of the mind onto the object and retention of the mind on the object.

(ii) With the stilling of directed thought and evaluation, (he/she) enters and remains in the second jhana: rapture and pleasure born of concentration; fixed single-pointed awareness free from movement of the mind onto the object and retention of the mind on the object; assurance.

(iii) With the fading of rapture, (he/she) remains in equanimity, mindful and fully aware and physically sensitive of pleasure. (He/She) enters and remains in the third jhana which the Noble Ones declare to be "Equanimous and mindful, (he/she) has a pleasurable abiding."

(iv) With the abandoning of pleasure and pain...as with the earlier disappearance of elation and distress...(he/she) enters and remains in the fourth jhana: purity of equanimity and mindfulness, neither in pleasure nor in pain.

This, monks, is called right concentration.

The Ninth and Tenth Elements

In the Great Forty Sutra (Mahacattarisaka Sutta), which appears in the Pali Canon, the Buddha explains that cultivation of the Eightfold Path leads to the development of two further stages once enlightenment has been reached. These also fall under the category of panna and are Right Knowledge (sammanana) and Right Liberation (or Right Release; sammavimutti). Some consider Right Association as an implicit ninth aspect of the Path.

The Noble Eightfold Path and Cognitive Psychology

From the standpoint of modern cognitive psychology, the Noble Eightfold Path can be seen as rooted in what is called cognitive dissonance, which is the perception of incompatibility between two cognitions. In the essay "Buddhism Meets Western Science", Gay Watson explains this dissonance as it relates to Buddhist teaching:

Buddhism has always been concerned with feelings, emotions, sensations and cognition. The Buddha points both to cognitive and emotional causes of suffering. The emotional cause is desire and its negative opposite, aversion. The cognitive cause is ignorance of the way things truly occur, or of three marks of existence: that all things are unsatisfactory, impermanent and without essential self.

The Noble Eightfold Path is, from this psychological viewpoint, an attempt to resolve this dissonance by changing patterns of thought and behaviour. It is for this reason that the first element of the path is right understanding, which is how one's mind views the world. Under the wisdom (panna) subdivision of the Noble Eightfold Path, this worldview is intimately connected with the second element, right thought, which concerns the patterns of thought and intention that controls one's actions. These elements can be seen at work, for example, in the opening verses of the Dhammapada:

Preceded by perception are mental states,
For them is perception supreme,
From perception have they sprung.
If, with perception polluted, one speaks or acts,
Thence suffering follows
As a wheel the draught ox's foot.
Precded by perception are mental states,
For them is perception supreme,
From perception have they sprung.
If, with tranquil perception, one speaks or acts,
Thence ease follows
As a shadow that never departs.

Thus, by wilfully altering one's distorted worldview-as well as the behaviours stemming from that worldview-and bringing out "tranquil perception" in the place of "perception polluted", one is enabled to potentially escape from suffering and develop one's mind. Watson points this out from a psychological standpoint:

The Five Precepts

The five precepts constitute the basic Buddhist code of ethics, undertaken by lay followers of the Buddha Gautama in the Theravadin tradition.

The laity undertake to follow these training rules at the same time as they become Buddhists, taking refuge in the Triple Gem: In the Buddha (teacher), in the Dharma (teaching) and thirdly in the Sangha (community of monks and nuns). A lay practitioner who has undertaken the precepts is called an Upasaka.

The Buddha is said to have taught the five precepts out of compassion, not out of any desire to control his followers and so they are to be undertaken voluntarily rather than as commandments from a god. They are to be seen as guidelines to how one who is awakened lives, not as mere moral injunctions imposed from outside and to be obeyed literally at all times.

The Buddha said that undertaking the precepts is a gift to oneself and others. He also described the rewards of following the precepts and the bad consequences of breaking the precepts.

The following are the five precepts rendered in English and then Pali.

1. I undertake the precept to refrain from taking the life (killing) of living beings.

   Panatipata veramani sikkhapadam samadiyami
2. I undertake the precept to refrain from stealing.

   Adinnadana veramani sikkhapadam samadiyami
3. I undertake the precept to refrain from sexual misconduct (adultery, rape, etc.).

   Kamesu micchacara veramani sikkhapadam samadiyami
4. I undertake the precept to refrain from false speech (lying).

   Musavada veramani sikkhapadam samadiyami
5. I undertake the precept to refrain from intoxicants which lead to heedlessness.

   Sura meraya majja pamadatthana veramani sikkhapadam samadiyami

Chinese Version of Five Precepts

The Chinese version as found in the Supplement to the Canon hardly differs:

1. As the Buddha refrained from killing until the end of his life, so I too will refrain from killing until the end of my life.
2. As the Buddha refrained from stealing until the end of his life, so I too will refrain from stealing until the end of my life.
3. As the Buddha refrained from sexual misconduct until the end of his life, so I too will refrain from sexual misconduct until the end of my life.
4. As the Buddha refrained from false speech until the end of his life, so I too will refrain from false speech until the end of my life.
5. As the Buddha refrained from alcohol until the end of his life, so I too will refrain from alcohol until the end of my life.

Nirvana

Nirvana, is a Sanskrit word from India that literally means extinction (as in a candle flame) and/or extinguishing (*i.e.* of the passions).

It is a mode of being that is free from mind-contaminants (Kilesa) such as lust, anger or craving. It is thus a state of great inner peace and contentment-the end of suffering, or Dukkha. The Buddha in the Dhammapada says of Nirvana that it is "the highest happiness." This is not the transitory, sense-based happiness of everyday life, but rather an enduring, transcendental happiness integral to the calmness attained through enlightenment.

The Buddha describes the abiding in nirvana as 'deathlessness' (Pali: amata or amaravati) or 'the unconditioned' and as the highest spiritual attainment, the natural result that accrues to one who lives a life of virtuous conduct in accordance with Dharma. Such a life (called Brahmacarya in India) dissolves the causes for future becoming (Skt, Karma; Pali, Kamma) that otherwise keep beings forever wandering through realms of desire and form (samsara).

There are many synonyms for Nirvana, as shown by the following passage:

World Honoured One, the ground of fruition is bodhi, nirvana, true suchness, the Buddha-nature, the amala-consciousness, the empty treasury of the Thus Come One, the great, perfect mirror-wisdom. But although it is called by these seven names, it is pure and perfect, its substance is durable, like royal vajra, everlasting and indestructible. (Surangama Sutra IV 207)

Overview: Nirvana (Pali nibbana) in sutra is "bhavanirodha nibbanam" (The cessation of becoming means Nirvana). Nirvana in sutra is never conceived of as a place, but the antinomy of samsara which itself is synonymous with ignorance (avidya, Pali avijja). "This said:

'the liberated mind (citta) that no longer clings' means Nibbana" (Majjhima Nikaya 2-Att. 4.68).

Nibbana is meant specifically as pertains gnosis that which ends the identity of the mind (citta) with empirical phenomena. Doctrinally Nibbana is said of the mind which no "longer is coming (bhava) and going (vibhava)", but which has attained a status in perpetuity, whereby "liberation (vimutta) can be said".

It carries further connotations of stilling, cooling and peace. The realizing of nirvana is compared to the ending of avidya (ignorance) which perpetuates the will (cetana) into effecting the incarnation of mind into biological or other form passing on forever through life after life (samsara). Samsara is caused principally by craving and ignorance. Nirvana, then, is not a place nor a state, it is an absolute truth to be realized and a person can do so without dying. When a person who has realized nirvana dies, his death is referred as his parinirvana, his fully passing away, as his life was his last link to the cycle of death and rebirth (samsara) and he will not be reborn again. Buddhism holds that the ultimate goal and end of samsaric existence (of ever "becoming" and "dying" and never truly being) is realization of nirvana; what happens to a person after his parinirvana cannot be explained, as it is outside of all conceivable experience.

Nirvana and Samsara

In Mahayana Buddhism, calling nirvana the "opposite" of samsara or implying that it is apart from samsara is doctrinally problematic. According to early Mahayana Buddhism, they can be considered to be two aspects of the same perceived reality. By the time of Nagarjuna, there are teachings of the identity of nirvana and samsara. However, even here it is assumed that the natural man suffers from at the very least a confusion regarding the nature of samsara.

The Theravada school makes the antithesis of samsara and Nibbana the starting point of the entire quest for deliverance. Even more, it treats this antithesis as determinative of the final goal, which is precisely the transcendence of samsara and the attainment of liberation in Nibbana. Where Theravada differs significantly from the Mahayana schools, which also start with the duality of samsara and Nirvana, is in not regarding this polarity as a mere preparatory lesson tailored for those with blunt faculties, to be eventually superseded by some higher realization of non-duality. From the standpoint of the Pali Suttas, even for the Buddha and the Arahants suffering and its cessation, samsara and Nibbana, remain distinct.

In the experience of all, Nirvana is a state which all six bases (Eye, Ear, Nose, Tongue, Body and Mind) cannot feel.

It is probably best to understand the relationship between Nirvana and samsara in terms of the Buddha while on earth. Buddha was both in Samsara while having attained to Nirvana so that he was seen by all and simultaneously free from samsara.

Nirvana in Buddhist Commentaries

Sarvastivadin commentary, Abhidharma-mahavibhasa-sastra, gives the complete context of the possible meanings from its Sanskrit roots:

- Vana, implying the path of rebirth, + nir, meaning leaving off' or 'being away from the path of rebirth.'
- Vana, meaning 'stench', + nir, meaning 'freedom': 'freedom from the stench of distressing kamma.'
- Vana, meaning 'dense forests', + nir, meaning 'to get rid of' = 'to be permanently rid of the dense forest of the five aggregates (panca skandha), or the 'three roots of greed, hate and delusion (lobha, dosa, moha)' or 'three

characteristics of existence (impermanence, anitya; unsatisfactoriness, dukkha, soullessness, anatma).

- Vana, meaning 'weaving', + nir, meaning 'knot' = 'freedom from the knot of the distressful thread of kamma.'

Nirvana in the Mahaparinirvana Sutra

The nature of Nirvana assumes a differently aspected Mahayana focus in what alleges to be the final of all Mahayana Sutras, allegedly delivered by the Buddha on his last day of life on earth-the Mahaparinirvana Sutra or Nirvana Sutra. Here, as well as in a number of linked "tathagatagarbha" sutras, in which the Tathagatagarbha is equated with the Buddha's eternal Self or eternal nature, Nirvana is spoken of by the Mahayana Buddha in very "cataphatic", positive terms.

Nirvana, or "Great Nirvana", is indicated to be the sphere or domain (vishaya) of the True Self. It is seen as the state which constitutes the attainment of what is "Eternal, the Self, Bliss and the Pure". Maha-nirvana ("Great Nirvana") thus becomes equivalent to the ineffable, unshakeable, blissful, all-pervading and deathless Selfhood of the Buddha himself-a mystery which no words can adequately reach and which, according to the Nirvana Sutra, can only be fully known by an Awakened Being-a perfect Buddha-directly.

Strikingly, the Buddha of the Mahaparinirvana Sutra gives the following definition of the attributes of Nirvana, which includes the ultimate reality of the Self (not to be confused with the "worldly ego" of the 5 skandhas):

"The attributes of Nirvana are eightfold. What are these eight? Cessation [nirodha], loveliness/ wholesomeness [subha], Truth [satya], Reality [tattva], eternity [nitya], bliss [sukha], the Self [atman] and complete purity [parisuddhi]: that is Nirvana."

He further states: "Non-Self is Samsara [the cycle of rebirth]; the Self (atman) is Great Nirvana."

An important facet of Nirvana in general is that it is not something that comes about from a concatenation of causes, that springs into existence as a result of an act of creation or an agglomeration of causative factors: it was never created; it always was, is and will be. But due to the moral and mental darkness of ordinary, samsarically benighted sentient beings, it remains hidden from unawakened perception. The Buddha of the Mahaparinirvanasutra insists on its eternal nature and affirms its identity with the enduring, blissful Self, saying:

> *"It is not the case that the inherent nature of Nirvana did not primordially exist but now exists. If the inherent nature of Nirvana did not primordially exist but does now exist, then it would not be free from taints (asravas) nor would it be eternally (nitya) present in nature. Regardless of whether there are Buddhas or not, its intrinsic nature and attributes are eternally present... Because of the obscuring darkness of the mental afflictions (kilesas), beings do not see it. The Tathagata, endowed with omniscient awareness (sarvajna-jnana), lights the lamp of insight with his skill-in-means (upaya-kausalya) and causes Bodhisattvas to perceive the Eternal, Bliss, the Self and the Pure of Nirvana."*

Vitally, according to these Mahayana teachings, any being who has reached Nirvana is not blotted out or extinguished: there is the extinction of the impermanent and suffering-prone "worldly self" or ego (comprised of the five changeful skandhas), but not of the immortal "supramundane" Self of the indwelling Buddha Principle [Buddha-dhatu]. Spiritual death for such a Nirvanaed being becomes an utter impossibility. The Buddha states in the "Mahayana Mahaparinirvana Sutra" (Tibetan version): "Nirvana is deathless... Those who have passed into Nirvana are deathless. I say that anybody who is endowed with careful assiduity is not compounded and, even though they involve themselves in compounded things, they do not age, they do not die, they do not perish."

Paths to Nirvana in the Pali Canon

In the Visuddhimagga, Ch. I, v. 6 (Buddhaghosa & Nanamoli, 1999, pp. 6-7), Buddhaghosa identifies various options within the Pali canon for pursuing a path to Nirvana, including:

1. by insight (vipassana) alone
2. by jhana and understanding
3. by deeds, vision and righteousness

4. by virtue, consciousness and understanding
5. by virtue, understanding, concentration and effort
6. by the four foundations of mindfulness

Depending on one's analysis, each of these options could be seen as a reframing of the Buddha's Threefold Training of virtue, mental development and wisdom.

Three Jewels

The Three Jewels, also rendered as Three Treasures, Three Refuges or Triple Gem are the three things that Buddhists give themselves to and in return look toward for guidance, in the process known as taking refuge.

Taking refuge in the Three Jewels is central to Buddhist lay and monastic ordination ceremonies, as originated by Gautama Buddha.

Taking refuge in the Triple Gem is generally considered to make one officially a Buddhist.

Thus, in many Theravada Buddhist communities, the following Pali chant, the Vandana Ti-sarana is often recited by both monks and lay people:

- Buddham saranam gacchami

  I go for refuge in the Buddha
- Dhammam saranam gacchami

  I go for refuge in the Dharma
- Sangham saranam gacchami

  I go for refuge in the Sangha

The Mahayana Chinese/Japanese version differs only slightly from the Theravada:

I take refuge in the Buddha, wishing for all sentient beings to understand the great way and make the greatest vow.

I take refuge in the Dharma, wishing for all sentient beings to deeply delve into the Sutra Pitaka, gaining an ocean of knowledge.

I take refuge in the Sangha, wishing all sentient beings to lead the congregation in harmony, entirely without obstruction.

Importance of the Triple Gem

The Triple Gem is important and is one of the major practices of mental "reflection" in Buddhism, we reflect on the true qualities of the Buddha, Dharma and Sangha. These qualities are called the Mirror of the Dharma in the Mahaparinibbana Sutta and help us attain the true "mind like a mirror".

Reflection in the Mirror of the Dharma

The qualities of the Buddha, Dharma and Sangha are frequently repeated in the ancient texts. It is a Buddhist practise to reflect upon them.

- *The Buddha:* "The Blessed One is an Arahant, perfectly enlightened, accomplished in true knowledge and conduct, fortunate, knower of the world, unsurpassed leader of persons to be tamed, teacher of devas and humans, the Enlightened One, the Blessed One."

  In some traditions, the Buddha as refuge, is known as the historical Buddha and also 'the full development of mind', in other words, the full development of one's highest potential *i.e.* recognition of mind and the completion or full development of one's inherent qualities and activities.

- *The Dharma:* "The Dhamma is well expounded by the Blessed One, directly visible, immediate, inviting one to come and see, applicable, to be personally experienced by the wise."

  Refuge in the Dharma in the Vajrayana tradition includes reference not only to the words of the Buddha, but to the living experience of realization and teachings of fully realized practitioners. In Tibetan Buddhism, it includes both the Kangyur (the teaching of the Buddha) and the Tengyur (the commentaries by realized practioners) and in an intangible way also includes the living transmission of those masters, which can also be very inspiring.

- *The Sangha:* "The Sangha of the Blessed One's disciples is practising the good way, practising the straight way, practising the true way, practising the proper way; that is, the four pairs of persons, the eight types of individuals-

This Sangha of the Blessed One's disciples is worthy of gifts, worthy of hospitality, worthy of offerings, worthy of reverential salutation, the unsurpassed field of merit for the world."

In the Vajrayana, a more liberal definition of Sangha can include all practitioners who are actively using the Buddhas teachings to benefit themselves and/or others. It can be more strictly defined as the 'Realized Sangha' or 'Arya-Sangha', in other words, practitioners and historical students of the Buddha who have fully realized the nature of their mind, also known as realized Boddhisatvas; and 'Ordinary Sangha', which can loosely mean practitioners and students of the Buddha who are using the same methods and working towards the same goal.

In the Vajrayana traditions, there is another very important and expanded aspect of the Refuge, the refuge in the teacher. This can be understood on many levels including what is called the Three Roots-the Root of Blessing, Root of Methods and Root of Protection. Another way to understand this is as the Body (Sangha), Speech (Dharma) and Mind (Buddha) of the Buddha. The teacher has a prominent place in the Vajrayana, as without his personal permission and guidance, a practitioner cannot achieve proper spiritual progress.

Why is it Called the Triple Gem?

In Buddhism, the following three are called Gems (Ratna) as they are invaluable:

- Buddha, who, depending on one's interpretation, can mean the Historical Buddha, Shakyamuni, or the Buddha nature or ideal within all beings;
- Dharma, which is the Teachings of the Buddha.
- Sangha, The Community of those great people who have attained Enlightenment. So that those people (Sangha) will help you to attain Enlightenment.

The three gems are so called since amongst all gems, the Buddha gem and Dharma gem are considered incomparable in value as they are not material, so cannot be created, destroyed or changed in any way. Buddha's mind in his earth body or sambhogakaya is frequently associated with the greatest gem of all, the diamond. In the Anguttara Nikaya (3:25), Buddha talks about the diamond mind:

These three types of persons are found in the world: One with a mind like an open sore; one with a mind like a flash of lightning; one with a mind like a diamond.

- One who is irascible and very irritable, displaying anger, hatred and sulkiness; such a one is said to be a person with a mind like an open sore.
- One who understands the Four Noble Truths correctly is said to have a mind like a flash of lightning.
- One who has destroyed the mind-intoxicating defilements and realized the liberation of mind and the liberation by knowledge is said to have a mind like a diamond

With this we understand that to take refuge in the Buddha is to take refuge in the mind like a diamond, the hardest natural substance that can cut through all delusion.

The Three Gems when used in the process of taking refuge, become the Three Refuges.

The expression Three Gems are found in the earliest Buddhist literature of the Pali Canon, besides other works there is one sutta in the Sutta-nipata, called the Ratana-sutta which contains a series of verses on the Jewels in the Buddha, Dharma and Sangha. In the Ratana-sutta, all the qualities of the Sangha mentioned are attributes of the Buddha's enlightened disciples.

The Three Refuges occur very frequently in the ancient Buddhist Texts and here the Sangha is used more broadly to refer to either the Sangha of Bhikkhus, or the Sangha of Bhikkhunis. "I go to Master Gautama for refuge and to the Dhamma and to the Sangha of Bhikkhus."

Three Marks of Existence

After much meditation, the Buddha concluded that everything in the physical world (plus everything in the phenomenology of psychology) is marked by three characteristics, known as the three characteristics of existence, three signs of being or Dharma Seals.

Together the three characteristics of existence are called ti-lakkhana, in Pali; or tri-laksana, in Sanskrit.

- Dukkha (Sanskrit duhkha) or unsatisfactoriness. Nothing found in the physical world or even the psychological realm can bring lasting deep satisfaction.
- Anicca (Sanskrit anitya) or impermanence. This refers not only to the fact that all conditioned things eventually cease to exist, but also that all conditioned things are in a constant state of flux. (Visualize a leaf growing on a tree. It dies and falls off the tree but is soon replaced by a new leaf.)
- Anatta (Sanskrit anatman) impersonality, or non-Self. The human personality, "soul", or Self, is a conventional appellation applied to the assembly of physical and psychological components, each individually subject to constant flux; there is no central core (or essence); this is somewhat similar to a bundle theory of mind or soul.

There is often a fourth Dharma Seal mentioned:

- Nirvana is peace. Nirvana is the 'other shore' from Samsara.

By bringing the three (or four) seals into moment-to-moment experience through concentrated awareness, we are said to achieve Wisdom-the third of the three higher trainings-the way out of Samsara. In this way we can identify that, according to Sutra, the recipe (or formula) for leaving Samsara is achieved by a deep-rooted change to our Weltanschauung.

According to the Buddhist tradition, all phenomena (dharmas) are marked by three characteristics, sometimes referred to as the Dharma seals, that is dukkha (suffering), anicca (impermanence) and anatta (non-Self).

Dukkha

Whatever is impermanent is subject to change. Whatever is subject to change is subject to suffering. —*The Buddha*

Striving for what we desire, we may experience stress and suffering-dukkha. Getting what we desired, we may find delight and happiness. Soon after, the novelty may wear out and we may get bored with it. Boredom is a form of dissatisfaction (or suffering) and to escape from it, we divert ourselves from such boredom by indulging in a pursuit of new forms of pleasure. Sometimes not willing to relinquish objects that we are already disinterested in, we start to collect and amass possessions instead of sharing with others who may have better use in it than we do. Boredom is a result of change. Change of our interest in that object of desire that so captivated us in the first place.

If we do not get bored already, then change may instead occur in the object of desire. Silverware may become tarnished, a new dress worn thin or a gadget gone obsolete. Or it may become broken, causing us to grieve. In some cases it may get lost or stolen. In some cases, we may worry about such losses even before they happen. Husbands and wives worry about losing their spouses even though their partners are faithful. Unfortunately, sometimes our very worry and fear drives us to act irrationally, resulting in distrust and breaking up of the very relationship that we cherished so much.

While we like changes such as becoming an adult when we are in our teens, we dislike the change called aging. While we strive for change to become rich, we fear the change of retrenchment. We are selective in our attitude towards the transient nature of our very existence. Unfortunately, this transient nature is unselective. We can try to fight it, just as many have tried since beginningless time, only to have our efforts washed away through the passages of time. As a result, we continually experience dissatisfaction or suffering due to the very impermanence of compounded phenomena.

Only in the realm of Nirvana-so Mahayana Buddhism insists-can true and lasting happiness be found. Nirvana is the opposite of the conditional, the transitory and the painful (dukkha), so it does not result in disappointment or deterioration of the state of bliss. Nirvana is the refuge from the otherwise universal tyranny of change and suffering. In other schools of Buddhism, nirvana is not viewed as the goal, but merely as a projection from the state of samsara. According to these schools samsara (confusion) and nirvana (perfection) are two sides of the same coin that must be transcended through diligent practice of meditation.

Anicca

All compounded phenomena (things and experiences) are inconstant, unsteady and impermanent. (Practically) everything is made up of parts and is dependent on the right conditions for its existence. Everything is in constant flux and so conditions and the thing itself is constantly changing. Things are constantly coming into being and ceasing to be. Nothing lasts.

The important point here is that phenomena arise and cease according to (complex) conditions and not according to our whims and fancy. While we have limited ability to effect change to our possessions and surroundings, experience tells us that our feeble attempts are no guarantee that the results of our efforts will be to our likings. More often than not, the results fall short of our expectations.

In Mahayana Buddhism, a caveat is added: one should indeed always meditate on the impermanence and changefulness of compounded structures and phenomena, but one must guard against extending this to the realm of Nirvana, where impermanence holds no sway and eternity alone obtains. To see Nirvana or the Buddha (in his ultimate Dharmakaya nature) as impermanent would be to indulge in "perverted Dharma" and would be seriously to go astray, according to the Buddha's final Mahayana doctrines. Other schools of Buddhism, however, feel uneasy with such a teaching.

Anatta

In Indian philosophy, the concept of a Self is called atman (that is, "soul" or metaphysical Self), which refers to an unchanging, permanent essence conceived by virtue of existence. This concept and the related concept of Brahman, the Vedantic monistic ideal, which was regarded as an ultimate atman for all beings, were indispensable for mainstream Indian metaphysics, logic and science; for all apparent things there had to be an underlying and persistent reality, akin to a Platonic form. The Buddha rejected all concepts of atman, emphasizing not permanence, but changeability. He taught that all concepts of a substantial personal Self were incorrect and formed in the realm of ignorance.

However, in a number of major Mahayana sutras (*e.g.* the Mahaparinirvana Sutra, the Tathagatagarbha Sutra, the Srimala Sutra, among others), the Buddha is presented as clarifying this teaching by saying that, while the skandhas (constituents of the ordinary body and mind) are not the Self, there does truly exist an eternal, unchanging, blissful Buddha-essence in all sentient beings, which is the uncreated and deathless Buddha-nature ("Buddha-dhatu") or "True Self" of the Buddha himself. This immaculate Buddhic Self (atman) is in no way to be construed as a mundane, impermanent, suffering "ego", of which it is the diametrical opposite. On the other hand, this Buddha-essence or Buddha-nature is also often explained as the potential for achieving Buddhahood, rather than an existing phenomenon one can grasp onto as being me or Self.

It is the opposite of a personalised, samsaric "I" or "mine". The paradox is that as soon as the Buddhist practitioner tries to grasp at this inner Buddha potency and cling to it as though it were his or her ego writ large, it proves elusive. It does not "exist" in the time-space conditioned and finite mode in which mundane things are bodied forth. It is presented by the Buddha in the relevant sutras as ultimately inexplicable, primordially present Reality itself-the living potency for Buddhahood inside all beings. It is finally revealed (in the last of the Buddha's Mahayana sutras, the Nirvana Sutra) not as the circumscribed "non-Self", the clinging ego (which is indeed anatta/anatman), but as the ever-enduring, egoless Great Self or Dharmakaya of the Buddha.

The scriptural evidence of the Nikayas and Agamas is ambivalent with regard to the Buddha's reported views on the existence or otherwise of a permanent Self (atman/atta). Though he is clearly reported to have criticized many of the heterodox concepts concerning an eternal personal Self and to have denied the existence of an eternal Self with regards to any of the constituent elements (skandha) of a being, he is nevertheless not reported to have explicitly denied the existence of a non-personal, permanent Self, contrary to the popular, orthodox view of the Buddha's teachings. Moreover, when the Buddha predicates "anatman" (anatta) with regards to the constituents of a being, there is a grammatical ambivalence in the use of the term.

The most natural interpretation is that he is simply stating that "the constituents are not the Self" rather than "the constituents are devoid of Self". This ambivalence was to prove troublesome to Buddhists after the Buddha's passing. Some of the major schools of Buddhism that developed subsequently maintained the former interpretation, but other influential schools adopted the latter interpretation and took measures to establish their view as the orthodox Buddhist position.

One such proponent of this hard-line "non-Self" position was the monk Nagasena, who appears in the Questions of King Milinda, composed during the period of the Hellenistic Indo-Greek kingdom of the 2nd and 1st centuries BC. In this text, Nagasena demonstrates the concept of absolute 'non-Self' by likening human beings to a chariot and challenges the Greek king "Milinda" (Menander) to find the essence of the chariot. Nagasena states that just as a chariot is made up of a number of things, none of which are the essence of the chariot in isolation, without the other pieces, similarly no one part of a person is a permanent entity; we can be broken up into five constituents-body, sensations, ideation, mental formations and consciousness-the consciousness being closest to the permanent idea of 'Self', but is ever-changing with each new thought according to this viewpoint.

According to some thinkers both in the East and the West, the doctrine of "non-Self", may imply that Buddhism is a form of nihilism or something similar. However, as thinkers like Nagarjuna have clearly pointed out, Buddhism is not simply a rejection of the concept of existence (or of meaning, etc.) but of the hard and fast distinction between existence and non-existence, or rather between being and no-thingness.

Phenomena are not independent from causes and conditions and do not exist as isolated things as we perceive them to be. Philosophers such as Nagarjuna stress that the lack of a permanent, unchanging, substantial Self in beings and things does not mean that they do not experience growth and decay on the relative level. But on the ultimate level of analysis, one cannot distinguish an object from its causes and conditions, or even object and subject. (This is an idea appearing relatively recently in Western science.) Buddhism thus has much more in common with Western empiricism, pragmatism, anti-foundationalism and even poststructuralism than with nihilism.

In the Nikayas, the Buddha and his disciples are commonly found to ask in question or declare "Is that which is impermanent, subject to change, subject to suffering fit to be considered thus: 'This I am, this is mine, this is my self'?"

The question which the Buddha posts to his audience is whether compounded phenomena is fit to be considered as self, in which the audience agrees that it is unworthy to be considered so. And in relinquishing such an attachment to compounded phenomena, such a person gives up delight, desire and craving for compounded phenomena and is unbounded by its change. When completely free from attachments, craving or desire to the five aggregates, such a person experiences then transcends the very causes of suffering.

In this way, the insight wisdom or prajna of non-Self gives rise to cessation of suffering and not an intellectual debate over whether a self exists or not.

It is by realizing (not merely understanding intellectually, but making real in one's experience) the three marks of conditioned existence that one develops prajna, which is the antidote to the ignorance that lies at the root of all suffering. From the "tathagatagarbha-Mahayana" perspective (which diverges from the Theravadin understanding of Buddhism), however, a further step is required if full Buddhahood is to be attained: not only seeing what is impermanent, suffering and non-Self in the samsaric sphere, but equally recognising that which is truly Eternal, Blissful, Self and Pure in the transcendental realm-the realm of Mahaparinirvana.

Interpretations of the Three Marks by Various Schools

Some Buddhist traditions assert that Anatta pervades everything and is not limited to personality, or soul. These traditions assert that Nirvana also has the quality of Anatta, but that Nirvana (by definition) is the cessation of Dukkha and Anicca.

In Nagarjuna's MMK XXV:19, he says

There is not the slightest difference

Between Samsara and Nirvana

This verse points us to an interesting stress between dukkha and nirvana, through an argument based in anatta. This specific stress can be seen to be the key to (and possibly source for the development of) the deity yogas of vajrayana.

The sutra path enjoins us to identify the entire world (internally and externally) as samsara-a continual churning of suffering that nobody wants to be part of. Our practice is that of leaving the shores of samsara. On the other hand, we are told that unconditioned, enlightened activity is not actually different from samsara. Whereas the deity yoga of vajrayana enjoins us to identify the entire world as nirvana-a continual play of enlightening activity that everyone wishes to be a part of. Our practice here is that of arriving at the shores of nirvana.

At this level, the distinction between Sutra and Vajrayana remain that of view (departing vs. arriving), but basically the practitioner remains involved in undergoing a transformative development to his or her Weltanschauung and in this context, these practices remain rooted in psychological change, grounded in the development of Samatha, or training in concentration.

However, there are certain practices in Tantra which are not solely concerned with psychological change; these revolve around the basic idea that it is possible to induce deep levels of concentration through psycho-physical methods as a result of special exercises. The purpose remains the same (to achieve liberating view), but the method involves a 'short cut' for the training in Samatha.

Skandha

The five skandhas (Sanskrit) or khandhas (Pali) are the five "aggregates" which categorize or constitute all individual experience according to Buddhist phenomenology. An important corollary in Buddhism is that a "person" is made up of these five aggregates, beyond which there is no "self." In the Theravada tradition, suffering arises when one identifies with or otherwise clings to an aggregate; hence, suffering is extinguished by relinquishing attachments to aggregates. The Mahayana tradition further puts forth that ultimate freedom is realized by deeply penetrating the intrinsically empty nature of all aggregates.

Outside of Buddhist didactic contexts, "skandha" can mean mass, heap, bundle or tree trunk.

Definition

Buddhist doctrine describes five aggregates:

1. "form" or "matter" (Skt., Pali rupa): external and internal matter. Externally, rupa is the physical world. Internally, rupa includes the material body and the physical sense organs.
2. "sensation" or "feeling" (Skt., Pali vedana): sensing an object as either pleasant or unpleasant or neutral.
3. "perception" or "cognition" (Skt. samjna, Pali sanna): registers whether an object is recognized or not (for instance, the sound of a bell or the shape of a tree).
4. "mental formations" or "volition" (Skt. samskara, Pali sankhara): all types of mental habits, thoughts, ideas, opinions, compulsions and decisions triggered by an object.
5. "consciousness":
   - (a) In the Nikayas: cognizance.
   - (b) In the Abhidhamma: a series of rapidly changing interconnected discrete acts of cognizance.
   - (c) In Mahayana sources: the base that supports all experience.

In this scheme, form, the mental aggregates and consciousness are mutually dependent.

Other Buddhist literature has described the aggregates as arising in a linear or progressive fashion, from form to feeling to perception to mental formations to consciousness.

Theravada Perspectives

Bhikkhu Bodhi (2000b, p. 840) states that an examination of the aggregates has a "critical role" in the Buddha's teaching for multiple reasons, including:

1. *Understanding the Four Noble Truths*: The five aggregates are the "ultimate referent" in the Buddha's elaboration on suffering (dukkha) in his First Noble Truth and "since all four truths revolve around suffering, understanding the aggregates is essential for understanding the Four Noble Truths as a whole."
2. *Future Suffering's Cause*: The five aggregates are the substrata for clinging and thus "contribute to the causal origination of future suffering."
3. *Release*: Clinging must be removed from the five aggregates in order to achieve release.

Below, excerpts from the Pali literature will bear out Bhikkhu Bodhi's assessment.

Suffering's Ultimate Referent

In the Buddha's first discourse, the "Dhammacakka-ppavattana Sutta" ("The Setting in Motion the Wheel of Truth Discourse," SN 56:11), he provides a classic elaboration on the first of his Four Noble Truths, "The Truth of Suffering" (Dukkhasacca):

> *"The Noble Truth of Suffering (dukkha), monks, is this: Birth is suffering, aging is suffering, sickness is suffering, death is suffering, association with the unpleasant is suffering, dissociation from the pleasant is suffering, not to receive what one desires is suffering-in brief the five aggregates subject to grasping are suffering." [Boldface added.] (Trans. from the Pali by Piyadassi Thera, 1999.)*

According to Thanissaro (2002):

> *"Prior to the Buddha, the Pali word khandha had very ordinary meanings: A khandha could be a pile, a bundle, a heap, a mass. It could also be the trunk of a tree. In his first sermon, though, the Buddha gave it a new, psychological meaning, introducing the term 'clinging-khandhas' to summarize his analysis of the truth of stress and suffering. Throughout the remainder of his teaching career, he referred to these psychological khandhas time and again."*

In what way are the aggregates suffering? For this we can turn to Khandhavagga suttas.

Future Suffering's Cause

The Samyutta Nikaya contains a book entitled the "Khandhavagga" ("The Book of Aggregates") compiling over a hundred suttas related to the five aggregates. Typical of these suttas is the "Upadaparitassana Sutta" ("Agitation through Clinging Discourse," SN 22:7), which states in part:

> *"...[T]he instructed noble disciple... does not regard form [or other aggregates] as self, or self as possessing form, or form as in self, or self as in form. That form of his changes and alters. Despite the change and alteration of form, his consciousness does not become preoccupied with the change of form.... [T]hrough non-clinging he does not become agitated." (Trans. by Bodhi, 2000b, pp. 865-866.)*

Put another way, if we were to self-identify with an aggregate then we would cling (upadana) to such; and, given that all aggregates are impermanent (anicca), it would then be likely that at some level we would experience agitation (paritassati) or loss or grief or stress or suffering. Therefore, if we want to be free of suffering, it is wise to experience the aggregates clearly, without clinging or craving (tanha), as apart from any notion of self (anatta).

Many of the suttas in the Khandhavagga express the aggregates in the context of the following sequence:

1. An uninstructed worldling (assutava puthujjana)
    a. regards: form as self; self as possessing form; form as in self; self as in form.
    b. lives obsessed by the notions: I am form; and/or, form is mine
    c. this form changes
    d. with the changes of form, there arises dukkha
2. An instructed noble disciple (sutava ariyasavaka) does not regard form as self, etc. and thus, when form changes, dukkha does not arise.

Example of Aggregate-Clinging

To give a simplistic example, if one believes "this body is mine" or "I exist within this body," then as their body ages, becomes ill and approaches death, such a person will likely experience longing for youth or health or eternal life, will likely dread aging and sickness and death and will likely spend much time and energy lost in fears, fantasies and ultimately futile activities.

In the Nikayas, such is likened to shooting oneself with a second arrow, where the first arrow is a physical phenomenon (such as, in this case, a bodily manifestation associated with aging or illness or dying) and the second is the mental anguish of the undisciplined mind associated with the physical phenomenon.

On the other hand, one with a disciplined mind who is able to see this body as a set of aggregates will be free of such fear, frustration and time-consuming escapism.

But how does one become aware of and then let go of ones own identification with or clinging to the aggregates? Below is an excerpt from the classic Satipatthana Sutta that shows how traditional mindfulness practices can awaken understanding, release and wisdom.

Release Through Aggregate-contemplation

In the classic Theravada meditation reference, the "Satipathana Sutta" ("The Foundations of Mindfulness Discourse," MN 10), the Buddha provides four bases for establishing mindfulness: body (kaya), sensations (vedana), mind (citta) and mental objects (dhamma). When discussing mental objects as a basis for meditation, the Buddha identifies five objects, including the aggregates. Regarding meditation on the aggregates, the Buddha states:

> *"How, monks, does a monk live contemplating mental objects in the mental objects of the five aggregates of clinging?*
>
> *"Herein, monks, a monk thinks, 'Thus is material form; thus is the arising of material form; and thus is the disappearance of material form. Thus is feeling; thus is the arising of feeling; and thus is the disappearance of feeling. Thus is perception; thus is the arising of perception; and thus is the disappearance of perception. Thus are formations; thus is the arising of formations; and thus is the disappearance of formations. Thus is*

consciousness; thus is the arising of consciousness; and thus is the disappearance of consciousness.'

"...Or his mindfulness is established with the thought, 'Mental objects exist,' to the extent necessary just for knowledge and mindfulness and he lives detached and clings to nothing in the world. Thus also, monks, a monk lives contemplating mental objects in the mental objects of the five aggregates of clinging." (Nyanasatta, trans., 1994.)

Thus, through mindfulness contemplation, one sees an "aggregate as an aggregate"--sees it arising and dissipating. Such clear seeing creates a space between the aggregate and clinging, a space that will prevent or enervate the arising and propagation of clinging, thereby diminishing future suffering.

As clinging disappears, so too notions of a separate "self." In the Mahasunnata Sutta ("The Greater Discourse on Emptiness," MN 122), after reiterating the aforementioned aggregate-contemplation instructions (for instance, "Thus is form; thus is the arising of form; and, thus is the disappearance of form"), the Buddha states:

"When he [a monk] abides contemplating rise and fall in these five aggregates affected by clinging, the conceit 'I am' based on these five aggregates affected by clinging is abandoned in him...." (Nanamoli & Bodhi, 2001, p. 975.)

In a complementary fashion, in the Buddha's second discourse, the Anattalakkhana Sutta ("The Characteristic of Nonself," SN 22:59), the Buddha instructs:

"Monks, form is nonself. For if, monks, form were self, this form would not lead to affliction and it would be possible to [manipulate] form [in the following manner]: 'Let my form be thus; let my form not be thus....' [Identical statements are made regarding feeling, perception, volitional formations and consciousness.]

"...Seeing thus [for instance, through contemplation], monks, the instructed noble disciple becomes disenchanted with form [and the other aggregates].... Being disenchanted, he becomes dispassionate. Through dispassion [his mind] is liberated." (Bodhi, 2005, pp. 341-2.)

Mahayana Perspectives

In one of Mahayana Buddhism's most famous declarations, the aggregates are referenced:

"Form is emptiness, emptiness is form."

What does this mean? To what degree is it a departure from the aforementioned Theravada perspective? Moreover, more generally, how are the aggregates used in the Mahayana literature?

The Intrinsic Emptiness of all Things

The classic "Prajnaparamita Hridaya Sutra" ("Heart Sutra") begins:

The Bodhisattva Avalokita,
while moving in the deep course of Perfect Understanding,
shed light on the five skandhas
and found them equally empty [of self].
After this penetration, he overcame all pain.

From its very first verse, the Heart Sutra introduces an alternative practice and worldview to the Theravada perspective of the aggregates:

- *Prajnaparamita:* Whereas Theravada meditation practices with the aggregates generally use change-penetrating vipassana meditation, here the non-dualistic prajnaparamita practice is invoked.
- *Svabhava:* In Theravada texts, when "emptiness of self" is mentioned, the English word "self" is a translation of the Pali word "atta" (Sanskrit, "atman"); in the Heart Sutra, the English word "self" is a translation of the Sanskrit word "sva-bhava". According to Red Pine, "The 'self' (sva)... was more generalized in its application than 'ego' (atman) and referred not only to beings but to any inherent substance that could be identified as existing in time or space as a permanent or independent entity." (Italics added.)

In other words, whereas the Sutta Pitaka typically instructs one to apprehend the aggregates without clinging or self-identification, Prajnaparamita leads one to apprehend the aggregates as having no intrinsic reality. In the Heart Sutra's second verse, after rising from his aggregate meditation, Avalokiteshvara declares:

"Form is emptiness, emptiness is form,

form does not differ from emptiness, emptiness does not differ from form.

The same is true with feelings, perceptions, mental formations and consciousness."

Thich Nhat Hanh interprets this statement as:

"Form is the wave and emptiness is the water.... [W]ave is water, water is wave.... [T]hese five [aggregates] contain each other. Because one exists, everything exists."

Red Pine comments:

"That form is empty was one of the Buddha's earliest and most frequent pronouncements. But in the light of Prajnaparamita, form is not simply empty, it is so completely empty, it is emptiness itself, which turns out to be the same as form itself.... All separations are delusions. But if each of the skandhas is one with emptiness and emptiness is one with each of the skandhas, then everything occupies the same indivisible space, which is emptiness.... Everything is empty and empty is everything.

Tangibility and Transcendence

Commenting on the Heart Sutra, D.T. Suzuki notes:

"When the sutra says that the five Skandhas have the character of emptiness..., the sense is: no limiting qualities are to be attributed to the Absolute; while it is immanent in all concrete and particular objects, it is not in itself definable."

That is, from the Mahayana perspective, the aggregates convey the relative (or conventional) experience of the world by an individual, although Absolute truth is realized through them.

Vajrayana Perspectives

The Vajrayana tradition further develops the aggregates in terms of mahamudra epistemology and tantric reifications.

The Truth of our Insubstantiality

Referring to mahamudra teachings, Chogyam Trungpa (Trungpa, 2001, pp. 10-12; and, Trungpa, 2002, pp. 124, 133-4) identifies the form aggregate as the "solidification" of ignorance (Pali, avijja; Skt., avidya), allowing one to have the illusion of "possessing" ever dynamic and spacious wisdom (Pali, vijja; Skt. vidya) and thus being the basis for the creation of a dualistic relationship between "self" and "other."

According to Trungpa Rinpoche (1976, pp. 20-22), the five skandhas are "a set of Buddhist concepts which describe experience as a five-step process" and that "the whole development of the five skandhas...is an attempt on our part to shield ourselves from the truth of our insubstantiality," while "the practice of meditation is to see the transparency of this shield." (ibid, p.23)

Bardo Deity Manifestations

Trungpa Rinpoche writes (2001, p. 38):

"[S]ome of the details of tantric iconography are developed from abhidharma [that is, in this context, detailed analysis of the aggregates]. Different colours and feelings of this particular consciousness, that particular emotion, are manifested in a particular deity wearing such-and-such a costume, of certain particular colours, holding certain particular sceptres in his hand. Those details are very closely connected with the individualities of particular psychological processes."

Perhaps it is in this sense that the Tibetan Book of the Dead (Fremantle & Trungpa, 2003) makes the following associations between the aggregates and tantric deities during the bardo after death:

- "The blue light of the skandha of consciousness in its basic purity, the wisdom of the dharmadhatu, luminous, clear, sharp and brilliant, will come towards you from the heart of Vairocana and his consort and pierce you so that your eyes cannot bear it." (p. 63)
- "The white light of the skandha of form in its basic purity, the mirror-like wisdom, dazzling white, luminous and clear, will come towards you from the heart of Vajrasattva

and his consort and pierce you so that your eyes cannot bear to look at it." (p. 66)

- "The yellow light of the skandha of feeling in its basic purity, the wisdom of equality, brilliant yellow, adorned with discs of light, luminous and clear, unbearable to the eyes, will come towards you from the heart of Ratnasambhava and his consort and pierce your heart so that your eyes cannot bear to look at it." (p. 68)
- "The red light of the skandha of perception in its basic purity, the wisdom of discrimination, brilliant red, adorned with discs of light, luminous and clear, sharp and bright, will come from the heart of Amitabha and his consort and pierce your heart so that your eyes cannot bear to look at it. Do not be afraid of it." (p. 70)
- "The green light of the skandha of concept [samskara] in its basic purity, the action-accomplishing wisdom, brilliant green, luminous and clear, sharp and terrifying, adorned with discs of light, will come from the heart of Amoghasiddhi and his consort and pierce your heart so that your eyes cannot bear to look at it. Do not be afraid of it. It is the spontaneous play of your own mind, so rest in the supreme state free from activity and care, in which there is no near or far, love or hate." (p. 73)

Relation to other Buddhist Concepts

Other fundamental Buddhist concepts associated with the five skandhas include:

- *Samsara:* It is through the five skandhas that the world (samsara) is experienced and nothing is experienced apart from the five skandhas.
- *Three Characteristics:* It is through the five skandhas that impermanence (anicca) is experienced, that suffering (duhkha) arises and that "non-self" (anatta or anatman) can be realized.
- *Twelve Nidanas/Dependent Origination:* The Twelve Nidanas describe twelve phenomenal links by which suffering is perpetuated between and within lives. It is through the

five skandhas that clinging (upadana) occurs, a pivotal link in this endless chain of suffering.

- *Eighteen Dhatus:* The eighteen dhatus function through the five aggregates. The eighteen dhatus can be arranged into six triads, where each triad is composed of a sense organ, a sense object and sense consciousness. In regards to the aggregates:
    - o The first five sense organs (eye, ear, nose, tongue, body) are derivates of form. The sixth sense organ (mind) is part of consciousness.
    - o The first five sense objects (visible forms, sound, smell, taste, touch) are also derivatives of form. The sixth sense object (mental object) includes form, sensation, perception and mental formations.
    - o The six sense consciousness are the basis for consciousness.

Buddhist Cosmology

Buddhist cosmology is the description of the shape and evolution of the universe according to the canonical Buddhist scriptures and commentaries.

Introduction

The self-consistent Buddhist cosmology which is presented in commentaries and works of Abhidharma in both Theravada and Mahayana traditions, is the end-product of an analysis and reconciliation of cosmological comments found in the Buddhist sutra and vinaya traditions. No single sutra sets out the entire structure of the universe. However, in several sutras the Buddha describes other worlds and states of being and other sutras describe the origin and destruction of the universe.

The synthesis of these data into a single comprehensive system must have taken place early in the history of Buddhism, as the system described in the Pali Vibhajyavada tradition (represented by today's Theravadins) agrees, despite some trivial inconsistencies of nomenclature, with the Sarvastivada tradition which is preserved by Mahayana Buddhists.

The picture of the world presented in Buddhist cosmological descriptions cannot be taken as a literal description of the shape of the universe.

It is inconsistent and cannot be made consistent, with astronomical data that were already known in ancient India. However, it is not intended to be a description of how humans perceive their world; rather, it is the universe as seen through the divyacakrus, the "divine eye" by which a Buddha or an arhat who has cultivated this faculty can perceive all of the other worlds and the beings arising (being born) and passing away (dying) within them and can tell from what state they have been reborn and into what state they will be reborn.

Buddhist cosmology can accordingly be divided into two related kinds: spatial cosmology, which describes the arrangement of the various worlds within the universe and temporal cosmology, which describes how those worlds come into existence and how they pass away.

Spatial Cosmology

Spatial cosmology can also be divided into two branches. The vertical cosmology describes the arrangement of worlds in a vertical pattern, some being higher and some lower. The sahasra cosmology describes the grouping of these vertical worlds into sets of thousands, millions or billions.

Vertical Cosmology

In the vertical cosmology, the universe exists of many worlds-one might say "planes"-stacked one upon the next in layers. Each world corresponds to a mental state or a state of being. A world is not, however, a location so much as it is the beings which compose it; it is sustained by their karma and if the beings in a world all die or disappear, the world disappears too.

Likewise, a world comes into existence when the first being is born into it. The physical separation is not so important as the difference in mental state; humans and animals, though they partially share the same physical environments, still belong to different worlds because their minds perceive and react to those environments differently.

The vertical cosmology is divided into three realms, or dhatus, each corresponding to a different type of mentality. These three (Tridhatu) are the Arupyadhatu, the Rupadhatu and the Kamadhatu. This technical division does not correspond to the more informal categorization of the "six realms". In the latter scheme, all of the beings born in the Arupyadhatu and the Rupadhatu may be classified as "gods" or "deities" (deva), as can a considerable fraction of the beings born in the Kamadhatu, even though the deities of the Kamadhatu differ more from those of the Arupyadhatu than they do from humans.

It is to be understood that deva is an imprecise term referring to any being living in a longer-lived and generally more blissful state than humans. Most of them are not "gods" in the common sense of the term, having little or no concern with the human world and rarely if ever interacting with it; only the lowest deities of the Kamadhatu correspond to the gods described in many polytheistic religions.

The term "brahma" is used both as a name and as a generic term for one of the higher devas. In its broadest sense, it can refer to any of the inhabitants of the Arupyadhatu and the Rupadhatu. In more restricted senses, it can refer to an inhabitant of one of the nine lower worlds of the Rupadhatu, or in its narrowest sense, to the three lowest worlds of the Rupadhatu. A large number of devas use the name "Brahma", *e.g.* Brahma Sahampati, Brahma Sanatkumara, Baka Brahma, etc. It is not always clear which world they belong to, although it must always be one of the worlds of the Rupadhatu below the Suddhavasa worlds.

Arupyadhatu

The Arupyadhatu (Sanskrit) or Arupaloka (Pali) or "Formless realm" would have no place in a purely physical cosmology, as none of the beings inhabiting it has either shape or location; and correspondingly, the realm has no location either. This realm belongs to those devas who attained and remained in the Four Formless Absorptions of the arupadhyanas in a previous life and now enjoys the fruits (vipaka) of the good karma of that accomplishment. Bodhisattvas, however, are never born in the Arupyadhatu even when they have attained the arupadhyanas.

There are four types of Arupyadhatu devas, corresponding to the four types of arupadhyanas:

- Naivasamjnanasamjnayatana or Nevasannanasannayatana "Sphere of neither perception nor non-perception". In this sphere the formless beings have gone beyond a mere negation of perception and have attained a liminal state where they do not engage in "perception" (samjna, recognition of particulars by their marks) but are not wholly unconscious. This was the sphere reached by Udraka Ramaputra (Pali: Uddaka Ramaputta), the second of the Buddha's two teachers, who considered it equivalent to enlightenment.
- Akimcanyayatana or Akincannayatana "Sphere of Nothingness" (literally "lacking anything"). In this sphere formless beings dwell contemplating upon the thought that "there is no thing". This is considered a form of perception, though a very subtle one. This was the sphere reached by Arara Kalama, the first of the Buddha's two teachers; he considered it to be equivalent to enlightenment.
- Vijnananantyayatana or Vinnananancayatana "Sphere of Infinite Consciousness". In this sphere formless beings dwell meditating on their consciousness (vijnana) as infinitely pervasive.
- Akasanantyayatana or Akasanancayatana "Sphere of Infinite Space". In this sphere formless beings dwell meditating upon space or extension (akasa) as infinitely pervasive.

Rupadhatu

The Rupadhatu or "Form realm" is, as the name implies, the first of the physical realms; its inhabitants all have a location and bodies of a sort, though those bodies are composed of a subtle substance which is of itself invisible to the inhabitants of the Kamadhatu. According to the Janavasabha Sutta, when a brahma (a being from the Brahma-world of the Rupadhatu) wishes to visit a deva of the Trayastrinsa heaven (in the Kamadhatu), he has to assume a "grosser form" in order to be visible to them.

The beings of the Form realm are not subject to the extremes of pleasure and pain, or governed by desires for things pleasing to the senses, as the beings of the Kamadhatu are. The bodies of Form realm beings do not have sexual distinctions.

Like the beings of the Arupyadhatu, the dwellers in the Rupadhatu have minds corresponding to the dhyanas (Pali: jhanas). In their case it is the four lower dhyanas or rupadhyanas. However, although the beings of the Rupadhatu can be divided into four broad grades corresponding to these four dhyanas, each of them is subdivided into further grades, three for each of the four dhyanas and five for the Suddhavasa devas, for a total of seventeen grades (the Theravada tradition counts one less grade in the highest dhyana for a total of sixteen).

Physically, the Rupadhatu consists of a series of planes stacked on top of each other, each one in a series of steps half the size of the previous one as one descends. In part, this reflects the fact that the devas are also thought of as physically larger on the higher planes. The highest planes are also broader in extent than the ones lower down, as discussed in the section on Sahasra cosmology. The height of these planes is expressed in yojanas, a measurement of very uncertain length, but sometimes taken to be about 4,000 times the height of a man and so approximately 4.54 miles or 7.32 kilometers.

Suddhavasa Worlds

The Suddhavasa worlds, or "Pure Abodes", are distinct from the other worlds of the Rupadhatu in that they do not house beings who have been born there through ordinary merit or meditative attainments, but only those Anagamins ("Non-returners") who are already on the path to Arhat-hood and who will attain enlightenment directly from the Suddhavasa worlds without being reborn in a lower plane (Anagamins can also be born on lower planes).

Every Suddhavasa deva is therefore a protector of Buddhism. Because a Suddhavasa deva will never be reborn outside the Suddhavasa worlds, no Bodhisattva is ever born in these worlds, as a Bodhisattva must ultimately be reborn as a human being.

Since these devas rise from lower planes only due to the teaching of a Buddha, they can remain empty for very long periods if no Buddha arises. However, unlike the lower worlds, the Suddhavasa worlds are never destroyed by natural catastrophe. The Suddhavasa devas predict the coming of a Buddha and, taking the guise of Brahmins, reveal to human beings the signs by which a Buddha can be recognized. They also ensure that a Bodhisattva in his last life will see the four signs that will lead to his renunciation.

The five Suddhavasa worlds are:

- *Akanistha or Akanittha:* World of devas "equal in rank" (literally: having no one as the youngest). The highest of all the Rupadhatu worlds, it is often used to refer to the highest extreme of the universe. The current Sakra will eventually be born there. The duration of life in Akanistha is 16,000 kalpas (Vibhajyavada tradition). The height of this world is 167,772,160 yojanas above the Earth.
- *Sudarsana or Sudassi:* The "clear-seeing" devas live in a world similar to and friendly with the Akanistha world. The height of this world is 83,886,080 yojanas above the Earth.
- *Sudrsa or Sudassa:* The world of the "beautiful" devas are said to be the place of rebirth for five kinds of anagamins. The height of this world is 41,943,040 yojanas above the Earth.
- *Atapa or Atappa:* The world of the "untroubled" devas, whose company those of lower realms wish for. The height of this world is 20,971,520 yojanas above the Earth.
- *Avrha or Aviha:* The world of the "not falling" devas, perhaps the most common destination for reborn Anagamins. Many achieve arhatship directly in this world, but some pass away and are reborn in sequentially higher worlds of the Pure Abodes until they are at last reborn in the Akanistha world. These are called in Pali uddhatsotas, "those whose stream goes upward". The duration of life in Avaha is 1,000 kalpas (Vibhajyavada tradition). The height of this world is 10,485,760 yojanas above the Earth.

Brhatphala Worlds

The mental state of the devas of the Brhatphala worlds corresponds to the fourth dhyana and is characterized by equanimity (upeksa). The Brhatphala worlds form the upper limit to the destruction of the universe by wind at the end of a mahakalpa, that is, they are spared such destruction.

- *Asannasatta:* "Unconscious beings", devas who have attained a high dhyana (similar to that of the Formless Realm) and, wishing to avoid the perils of perception, have achieved a state of non-perception in which they endure for a time. After a while, however, perception arises again and they fall into a lower state.
- *Brhatphala or Vehapphala*: Devas "having great fruit". Their lifespan is 500 mahakalpas. (Vibhajyavada tradition). Some Anagamins are reborn here. The height of this world is 5,242,880 yojanas above the Earth.
- *Punyaprasava:* The world of the devas who are the "offspring of merit". The height of this world is 2,621,440 yojanas above the Earth.
- *Anabhraka:* The world of the "cloudless" devas. The height of this world is 1,310,720 yojanas above the Earth.

Subhakrtsna Worlds

The mental state of the devas of the Subhaktsna worlds corresponds to the third dhyana and is characterized by a quiet joy (sukha). These devas have bodies that radiate a steady light. The Subhakatsna worlds form the upper limit to the destruction of the universe by water at the end of a mahakalpa, that is, the flood of water does not rise high enough to reach them.

- *Subhakrtsna:* The world of devas of "total beauty". Their lifespan is 64 mahakalpas (some sources: 4 mahakalpas) according to the Vibhajyavada tradition. 64 mahakalpas is the interval between destructions of the universe by wind, including the Subhakstsna worlds. The height of this world is 655,360 yojanas above the Earth.
- *Apramanasubha:* The world of devas of "limitless beauty". Their lifespan is 32 mahakalpas (Vibhajyavada tradition).

They possess "faith, virtue, learning, munificence and wisdom". The height of this world is 327,680 yojanas above the Earth.

- *Parittasubha:* The world of devas of "limited beauty". Their lifespan is 16 mahakalpas. The height of this world is 163,840 yojanas above the Earth.

Abhasvara Worlds

The mental state of the devas of the Abhasvara worlds corresponds to the second dhyana and is characterized by delight (priti) as well as joy (sukha); the Abhasvara devas are said to shout aloud in their joy, crying aho sukham! ("Oh joy!"). These devas have bodies that emit flashing rays of light like lightning.

They are said to have similar bodies (to each other) but diverse perceptions. The Abhasvara worlds form the upper limit to the destruction of the universe by fire at the end of a mahakalpa, that is, the column of fire does not rise high enough to reach them. After the destruction of the world, at the beginning of the vivartakalpa, the worlds are first populated by beings reborn from the Abhasvara worlds.

- *Abhasvara or Abhassara:* The world of devas "possessing splendor". The lifespan of the Abhasvara devas is 8 mahakalpas (others: 2 mahakalpas). Eight mahakalpas is the interval between destructions of the universal by water, which includes the Abhasvara worlds. The height of this world is 81,920 yojanas above the Earth.
- *Apramanabha or Appamanabha:* The world of devas of "limitless light", a concept on which they meditate. Their lifespan is 4 mahakalpas. The height of this world is 40,960 yojanas above the Earth.
- *Parittabha or Parittabha:* The world of devas of "limited light". Their lifespan is 2 mahakalpas. The height of this world is 20,480 yojanas above the Earth.

Brahma Worlds

The mental state of the devas of the Brahma worlds corresponds to the first dhyana and is characterized by observation (vitarka) and reflection (vicara) as well as delight (priti) and joy (sukha). The Brahma worlds, together with the other lower worlds of the universe, are destroyed by fire at the end of a mahakalpa.

- Mahabrahma-the world of "Great Brahma", believed by many to be the creator of the world and having as his titles "Brahma, Great Brahma, the Conqueror, the Unconquered, the All-Seeing, All-Powerful, the Lord, the Maker and Creator, the Ruler, Appointer and Orderer, Father of All That Have Been and Shall Be." According to the Brahmajala Sutta (DN.1), a Mahabrahma is a being from the Abhasvara worlds who falls into a lower world through exhaustion of his merits and is reborn alone in the Brahma-world; forgetting his former existence, he imagines himself to have come into existence without cause. Note that even such a high-ranking deity has no intrinsic knowledge of the worlds above his own. Mahabrahma is 1 1/2 yojanas tall. His lifespan variously said to be 1 kalpa (Vibhajyavada tradition) or 1 1/2 kalpas long (Sarvastivada tradition), although it would seem that it could be no longer than 3/4 of a mahakalpa, *i.e.*, all of the mahakalpa except for the Sanvartasthayikalpa, because that is the total length of time between the rebuilding of the lower world and its destruction. It is unclear what period of time "kalpa" refers to in this case. The height of this world is 10,240 yojanas above the Earth.
- Brahmapurohita-the "Ministers of Brahma" are beings, also originally from the Abhasvara worlds, that are born as companions to Mahabrahma after he has spent some time alone. Since they arise subsequent to his thought of a desire for companions, he believes himself to be their creator and they likewise believe him to be their creator and lord. They are 1 yojana in height and their lifespan is variously said to be 1/2 of a kalpa (Vibhajyavada tradition) or a whole kalpa (Sarvastivada tradition). If they are later reborn in a lower world and come to recall some part of their last existence, they teach the doctrine of Brahma as creator as a revealed truth. The height of this world is 5,120 yojanas above the Earth.

- Brahmaparisadya-the "Councilors of Brahma" or the devas "belonging to the assembly of Brahma". They are also called Brahmakayika, but this name can be used for any of the inhabitants of the Brahma-worlds. They are half a yojana in height and their lifespan is variously said to be 1/3 of a kalpa (Vibhajyavada tradition) or 1/2 of a kalpa (Sarvastivada tradition). The height of this world is 2,560 yojanas above the Earth.

Kamadhatu

The beings born in the Kamadhatu differ in degree of happiness, but they are all, other than arhats and Buddhas, under the domination of Mara and are bound by desire, which causes them suffering.

Heavens

The following four worlds are bounded planes, each 80,000 yojanas square, which float in the air above the top of Mount Ṣumeru. Although all of the worlds inhabited by devas (that is, all the worlds down to the Caturmaharajikakayika world and sometimes including the Asuras) are sometimes called "heavens", in the western sense of the word the term best applies to the four worlds listed below:

- *Parinirmita-vasavartin*: The heaven of devas "with power over (others') creations". These devas do not create pleasing forms that they desire for themselves, but their desires are fulfilled by the acts of other devas who wish for their favor. The ruler of this world is called Vasavartin (Pali: Vasavatti), who has longer life, greater beauty, more power and happiness and more delightful sense-objects than the other devas of his world. This world is also the home of the devaputra (being of divine race) called Mara, who endeavors to keep all beings of the Kamadhatu in the grip of sensual pleasures. Mara is also sometimes called Vasavartin, but in general these two dwellers in this world are kept distinct. The beings of this world are 4,500 feet tall and live for 9,216,000,000 years (Sarvastivada tradition). The height of this world is 1,280 yojanas above the Earth.

- *Nirmanarati*: The world of devas "delighting in their creations". The devas of this world are capable of making any appearance to please themselves. The lord of this world is called Sunirmita (Pali Sunimmita); his wife is the rebirth of Visakha, formerly the chief of the upasikas (female lay devotees) of the Buddha. The beings of this world are 3,750 feet tall and live for 2,304,000,000 years (Sarvastivada tradition). The height of this world is 640 yojanas above the Earth.
- *Tusita*: The world of the "joyful" devas. This world is best known for being the world in which a Bodhisattva lives before being reborn in the world of humans. Until a few thousand years ago, the Bodhisattva of this world was Svetaketu (Pali: Setaketu), who was reborn as Siddhartha, who would become the Buddha Sakyamuni; since then the Bodhisattva has been Natha (or Nathadeva) who will be reborn as Ajita and will become the Buddha Maitreya (Pali Metteyya). While this Bodhisattva is the foremost of the dwellers in Turita, the ruler of this world is another deva called Santusita. The beings of this world are 3,000 feet tall and live for 576,000,000 years (Sarvastivada tradition). The height of this world is 320 yojanas above the Earth.
- *Yama*: Sometimes called the "heaven without fighting", because it is the lowest of the heavens to be physically separated from the tumults of the earthly world. Its ruler is the deva Suyama; according to some, his wife is the rebirth of Sirima, a courtesan of Rajagrha in the Buddha's time who was generous to the monks. The beings of this world are 2,250 feet tall and live for 144,000,000 years (Sarvastivada tradition). The height of this world is 160 yojanas above the Earth.

Worlds of Sumeru

The world-mountain of Sumeru is an immense, strangely shaped peak which arises in the centre of the world and around which the Sun and Moon revolve. Its base rests in a vast ocean and it is surrounded by several rings of lesser mountain ranges and oceans. The three worlds listed below are all located on or around Sumeru: the Trayastrinsa devas live on its peak, the Caturmaharajikakayika devas live on its slopes and the Asuras live in the ocean at its base. Sumeru and its surrounding oceans and mountains are the home not just of these deities, but also vast assemblies of beings of popular mythology who only rarely intrude on the human world.

- *Trayastrimsa*: The world "of the Thirty-three (devas)" is a wide flat space on the top of Mount Sumeru, filled with the gardens and palaces of the devas. Its ruler is Sakra devanam indra, "lord of the devas". Besides the eponymous Thirty-three devas, many other devas and supernatural beings dwell here, including the attendants of the devas and many apsarases (nymphs). The beings of this world are 1,500 feet tall and live for 36,000,000 years (Sarvastivada tradition) or 3/4 of a yojana tall and live for 30,000,000 years (Vibhajyavada tradition). The height of this world is 80 yojanas above the Earth.
- *Caturmaharajikakayika*: The world "of the Four Great Kings" is found on the lower slopes of Mount Sumeru, though some of its inhabitants live in the air around the mountain. Its rulers are the four Great Kings of the name, Virushaka, Virupakna and their leader Vaisravasa. The devas who guide the Sun and Moon are also considered part of this world, as are the retinues of the four kings, composed of Kumbhashas (dwarfs), Gandharvas (fairies), Nagas (dragons) and Yakhas (goblins). The beings of this world are 750 feet tall and live for 9,000,000 years (Sarvastivada tradition) or 90,000 years (Vibhajyavada tradition). The height of this world is from sea level up to 40 yojanas above the Earth.
- *Asura*: The world of the Asuras is the space at the foot of Mount Sumeru, much of which is a deep ocean. It is not the Asuras' original home, but the place they found themselves after they were hurled, drunken, from Trayastrinsa where they had formerly lived. The Asuras are always fighting to regain their lost kingdom on the top of Mount Sumeru, but are unable to break the guard of

the Four Great Kings. The Asuras are divided into many groups and have no single ruler, but among their leaders are Vemacitrin (Pali: Vepacitti) and Rahu.

Earthly Realms

- *Manusyaloka*: This is the world of humans and human-like beings who live on the surface of the earth. The mountain-rings that engird Sumeru are surrounded by a vast ocean, which fills most of the world. The ocean is in turn surrounded by a circular mountain wall called Cakravara which marks the horizontal limit of the world. In this ocean there are four continents which are, relatively speaking, small islands in it. Because of the immenseness of the ocean, they cannot be reached from each other by ordinary sailing vessels, although in the past, when the cakravartin kings ruled, communication between the continents was possible by means of the treasure called the cakraratna (Pali cakkaratana), which a cakravartin and his retinue could use to fly through the air between the continents. The four continents are:
    - o Jambudvipa or Jambudipa is located in the south and is the dwelling of ordinary human beings. It is said to be shaped "like a cart", or rather a blunt-nosed triangle with the point facing south. (This description probably echoes the shape of the coastline of southern India.) It is 10,000 yojanas in extent (Vibhajyavada tradition) or has a perimeter of 6,000 yojanas (Sarvastivada tradition) to which can be added the southern coast of only 3 1/2 yojanas' length. The continent takes its name from a giant Jambu tree (Syzygium cumini), 100 yojanas tall, which grows in the middle of the continent. Every continent has one of these giant trees. All Buddhas appear in Jambudvipa. The people here are five to six feet tall and their length of life varies between 80,000 and 10 years.
    - o Purvavideha or Pubbavideha is located in the east and is shaped like a semicircle with the flat side pointing westward (*i.e.*, towards Sumeru). It is 7,000 yojanas in

extent (Vibhajyavada tradition) or has a perimeter of 6,350 yojanas of which the flat side is 2,000 yojanas long (Sarvastivada tradition). Its tree is the acacia. The people here are about 12 feet tall and they live for 250 years.

- o Aparagodaniya or Aparagoyana is located in the west and is shaped like a circle with a circumference of about 7,500 yojanas (Sarvastivada tradition). The tree of this continent is a giant Kadambu tree. The human inhabitants of this continent do not live in houses but sleep on the ground. They are about 24 feet tall and they live for 500 years.
- o Uttarakuru is located in the north and is shaped like a square. It has a perimter of 8,000 yojanas, being 2,000 yojanas on each side. This continent's tree is called a kalpavkkha (Pali: kapparukkha) or kalpa-tree, because it lasts for the entire kalpa. The inhabitants of Uttarakuru are said to be extraordinarily wealthy. They do not need to labor for a living, as their food grows by itself and they have no private property. They have cities built in the air. They are about 48 feet tall and live for 1,000 years and they are under the protection of Vaisravana.

- *Tiryagyoni-loka*: This world comprises all members of the animal kingdom that are capable of feeling suffering, from the smallest insect to the elephant.
- *Pretaloka*: The pretas, or "hungry ghosts", are mostly dwellers on earth, though due to their mental state they perceive it very differently from humans. They live for the most part in desert and waste places.

Narakas

Naraka or Niraya is the name given to one of the worlds of greatest suffering, usually translated into English as "hell" or "purgatory". As with the other realms, a being is born into one of these worlds as a result of his karma and resides there for a finite length of time until his karma has achieved its full result, after which he will be reborn in one of the higher worlds as the result of an earlier karma that had not yet ripened. The mentality of a being in the hells corresponds to states of extreme fear and helpless anguish in humans. Physically, Naraka is thought of as a series of layers extending below Jambudvipa into the earth. There are several schemes for counting these Narakas and enumerating their torments. One of the more common is that of the Eight Cold Narakas and Eight Hot Narakas.

Cold Narakas

- Arbuda-the "blister" Naraka
- Nirarbuda-the "burst blister" Naraka
- Atata-the Naraka of shivering
- Hahava-the Naraka of lamentation
- Huhuva-the Naraka of chattering teeth
- Utpala-the "blue lotus" Naraka
- Padma-the "lotus" Naraka
- Mahapadma-the "great lotus" Naraka

Each lifetime in these Narakas is twenty times the length of the one before it.

Hot Narakas

- Sanjiva-the "reviving" Naraka. Life in this Naraka is 162×10^{10} years long.
- Kalasutra-the "black thread" Naraka. Life in this Naraka is 1296×10^{10} years long.
- Samghata-the "crushing" Naraka. Life in this Naraka is $10{,}368 \times 10^{10}$ years long.
- Raurava-the "screaming" Naraka. Life in this Naraka is $82{,}944 \times 10^{10}$ years long.
- Maharaurava-the "great screaming" Naraka. Life in this Naraka is $663{,}552 \times 10^{10}$ years long.
- Tapana-the "heating" Naraka. Life in this Naraka is $5{,}308{,}416 \times 10^{10}$ years long.
- Pratapana-the "great heating" Naraka. Life in this Naraka is $42{,}467{,}328 \times 10^{10}$ years long.

- Avici-the "uninterrupted" Naraka. Life in this Naraka is $339{,}738{,}624 \times 10^{10}$ years long.

The Foundations of the Earth

All of the structures of the earth, Sumeru and the rest, extend downward to a depth of 80,000 yojanas below sea level-the same as the height of Sumeru above sea level. Below this is a layer of "golden earth", a substance compact and firm enough to support the weight of Sumeru. It is 320,000 yojanas in depth and so extends to 400,000 yojanas below sea level. The layer of golden earth in turn rests upon a layer of water, which is 8,000,000 yojanas in depth, going down to 8,400,000 yojanas below sea level. Below the layer of water is a "circle of wind", which is 16,000,000 yojanas in depth and also much broader in extent, supporting 1,000 different worlds upon it.

Sahasra Cosmology

While the vertical cosmology describes the arrangement of the worlds vertically, the sahasra (Sanskrit: "thousand") cosmology describes how they are grouped horizontally. The four heavens of the Kamadhatu, as mentioned, occupy a limited space no bigger than the top of Mount Sumeru. The three Brahma-worlds, however, stretch out as far as the mountain-wall of Cakravana, filling the entire sky. This whole group of worlds, from Mahabrahma down to the foundations of water, constitutes a single world-system. It corresponds to the extent of the universe that is destroyed by fire at the end of one mahakalpa.

Above Mahabrahma are the Abhasvara worlds. These are not only higher but also wider in extent; they cover 1,000 separate world-systems, each with its own Sumeru, Cakravana, Sun, Moon and four continents. This system of 1,000 worlds is called a sahasra-cunika-lokadhatu, or "small chiliocosm". It corresponds to the extent of the universe that is destroyed by water at the end of 8 mahakalpas.

Above the Abhasvara worlds are the Subhakstsna worlds, which cover 1,000 chiliocosms, or 1,000,000 world-systems. This larger system is called a dvisahasra-madhyama-lokadhatu, or "medium dichiliocosm". It corresponds to the extent of the universe that is destroyed by wind at the end of 64 mahakalpas. Likewise, above the Subhakhtsna worlds, the Suddhavasa and Brhatphala worlds cover 1,000 dichiliocosms, or 1,000,000,000 world-systems.

This largest grouping is called a trisahasra-mahasahasra-lokadhatu or "great trichiliocosm".

Temporal Cosmology

Buddhist temporal cosmology describes how the universe comes into being and is dissolved. Like other Indian cosmologies, it assumes an infinite span of time and is cyclical.

This does not mean that the same events occur in identical form with each cycle, but merely that, as with the cycles of day and night or summer and winter, certain natural events occur over and over to give some structure to time.

The basic unit of time measurement is the mahakalpa or "Great Eon". The exact length of this time in human years is never defined exactly, but it is meant to be very long, to be measured in billions of years if not longer.

A mahakalpa is divided into four kalpas or "eons", each distinguished from the others by the stage of evolution of the universe during that kalpa. The four kalpas are:

- Vivartakalpa "Eon of evolution"-during this kalpa the universe comes into existence.
- Vivartasthayikalpa "Eon of evolution-duration"-during this kalpa the universe remains in existence in a steady state.
- Samvartakalpa "Eon of dissolution"-during this kalpa the universe dissolves.
- Samvartasthayikalpa "Eon of dissolution-duration"-during this kalpa the universe remains in a state of emptiness.

Each one of these kalpas is divided into twenty antarakalpas (Pali antarakappa, "inside eons") each of about the same length. For the Sarvartasthayikalpa this division is merely nominal, as nothing changes from one antarakalpa to the next; but for the other three kalpas it marks an interior cycle within the kalpa.

Vivartakalpa

The Vivartakalpa begins with the arising of the primordial wind, which begins the process of building up the structures of the universe that had been destroyed at the end of the last mahakalpa. As the extent of the destruction can vary, the nature of this evolution can vary as well, but it always takes the form of beings from a higher world being born into a lower world.

The example of a Mahabrahma being the rebirth of a deceased Abhasvara deva is just one instance of this, which continues throughout the Vivartakalpa until all the worlds are filled from the Brahmaloka down to Naraka. During the Vivartakalpa the first humans appear; they are not like present-day humans, but are beings shining in their own light, capable of moving through the air without mechanical aid, living for a very long time and not requiring sustenance; they are more like a type of lower deity than present-day humans are.

Over time, they acquire a taste for physical nutriment and as they consume it, their bodies become heavier and more like human bodies; they lose their ability to shine and begin to acquire differences in their appearance and their length of life decreases. They differentiate into two sexes and begin to become sexually active. Then greed, theft and violence arise among them and they establish social distinctions and government and elect a king to rule them, called Mahasammata, "the great appointed one". Some of them begin to hunt and eat the flesh of animals, which have by now come into existence. These developments are described in the Agganna Sutta (DN.27).

Vivartasthayikalpa

First Antarakalpa: The Vivartasthayikalpa begins when the first being is born into Naraka, thus filling the entire universe with beings. During the first antarakalpa of this eon, human lives are declining from a vast but unspecified number of years (but at least several tens of thousands of years) toward the modern lifespan of less than 100 years. At the beginning of the antarakalpa, people are still generally happy. They live under the rule of a universal monarch or "wheel-turning king" (cakravartin), who conquer. The

Mahasudassana-sutta (DN.17) tells of the life of a cakravartin king, Mahasudassana (Sanskrit: Mahasudarsana) who lived for 336,000 years.

The Cakkavatti-sihanada-sutta (DN.26) tells of a later dynasty of cakravartins, Darhanemi and five of his descendants, who had a lifespan of over 80,000 years. The seventh of this line of cakravartins broke with the traditions of his forefathers, refusing to abdicate his position at a certain age, pass the throne on to his son and enter the life of a sramara. As a result of his subsequent misrule, poverty increased; as a result of poverty, theft began; as a result of theft, capital punishment was instituted; and as a result of this contempt for life, murders and other crimes became rampant.

The human lifespan now quickly decreased from 80,000 to 100 years, apparently decreasing by about half with each generation (this is perhaps not to be taken literally), while with each generation other crimes and evils increased: lying, adultery, evil speech, greed and hatred, wrong views, incest and other sorts of sexual abnormalities, disrespect for parents and elders.

During this period, according to the Mahapadana-sutta (DN.14) three of the four Buddhas of this antarakalpa lived: Krakucchanda Buddha (Pali: Kakusandha), at the time when the lifespan was 40,000 years; Kanakamuni Buddha (Pali: Konagamana) when the lifespan was 30,000 years; and Kasyapa Buddha (Pali: Kassapa) when the lifespan was 20,000 years.

Our present time is taken to be toward the end of the first antarakalpa of this Vivartasthayikalpa, when the lifespan is less than 100 years, after the life of Sakyamuni Buddha, who lived to the age of 80.

The remainder of the antarakalpa is prophesied to be miserable: lifespans will continue to decrease and all the evil tendencies of the past will reach their ultimate in destructiveness. People will live no longer than ten years and will marry at five; foods will be poor and tasteless; no form of morality will be acknowledged. The most contemptuous and hateful people will become the rulers. Incest will be rampant. Hatred between people, even members of the same family, will grow until people think of each other as hunters do of their prey. Eventually a great war will ensue, in which the most hostile and aggressive will arm themselves and go out to kill each other. The less aggressive will hide in forests and other secret places while the war rages. This war marks the end of the first antarakalpa.

Second Antarakalpa: At the end of the war, the survivors will emerge from their hiding places and repent their evil habits. As they begin to do good, their lifespan increases and the health and welfare of the human race will also increase with it. After a long time, the descendants of those with a 10-year lifespan will live for 80,000 years and at that time there will be a cakravartin king named Sarkha. During his reign, the current bodhisattva in the Tunita heaven will descend and be reborn under the name of Ajita. He will enter the life of a sramara and will gain perfect enlightenment as a Buddha; and he will then be known by the name of Maitreya.

After Maitreya's time, the world will again worsen and the lifespan will gradually decrease from 80,000 years to 10 years again, each antarakalpa being separated from the next by devastating war, with peaks of high civilization and morality in the middle. After the 19th antarakalpa, the lifespan will increase to 80,000 and then not decrease, because the Vivartasthayikalpa will have come to an end.

Sarvartakalpa

The Sarvartakalpa begins when beings cease to be born in Naraka. This cessation of birth then proceeds in reverse order up the vertical cosmology, *i.e.* pretas then cease to be born, then animals, then humans and so on up to the realms of the deities. When these worlds as far as the Brahmaloka are devoid of inhabitants, a great fire consumes the entire physical structure of the world. It burns all the worlds below the Abhasvara worlds. When they are destroyed, the Sarvartasthayikalpa begins.

Sarvartasthayikalpa

There is nothing to say about the Sarvartasthayikalpa, since nothing happens in it below the Abhasvara worlds. It ends when the primordial wind begins to blow and build the structure of the worlds up again.

Other Destructions: The destruction by fire is the normal type of destruction that occurs at the end of the Sarvartakalpa. But every eighth mahakalpa, after seven destructions by fire, there is a destruction by water. This is more devastating, as it eliminates not just the Brahma worlds but also the Abhasvara worlds.

Every sixty-fourth mahakalpa, after 56 destructions by fire and 7 destructions by water, there is a destruction by wind. This is the most devastating of all, as it also destroys the Subhakhtsna worlds. The higher worlds are never destroyed.

Dharma

Dharma or Dhamma in Buddhism has two primary meanings:

- the teachings of the Buddha which lead to enlightenment
- the constituent factors of the experienced world

In East Asia, the character for Dharma is pronounced fa in Mandarin and ho in Japanese. The Tibetan translation of this term is chos (cho).

Buddha's Teachings

What is called Buddhism in the west has been referred to in India (the teachings' place of origin) and the east generally for many centuries as buddha-dharma. This term has no sectarian connotations but simply means "Path of Awakening" and thus conforms to a universal understanding of dharma.

The status of dharma is regarded variably by different traditions. Some regard it as an ultimate and transcendent truth which is utterly beyond worldly things, somewhat like the Christian logos.

Others, who regard the Buddha as simply an enlightened human being, see dharma as the 84,000 different teachings that the Buddha gave to various types of people based on their needs. The teachings are expedient means of raising doubt in the hearer's own cherished beliefs and view of life; when doubt has opened the door to the truth, the teaching can be put aside.

"Dharma" usually refers inclusively not just to the sayings of the Buddha but to the later traditions of interpretation and addition that the various schools of Buddhism have developed to help explain and expand upon the Buddha's teachings. For others still, they see the dharma as referring to the "truth" or ultimate reality or "the way things are".

The dharma is one of the Three Jewels of Buddhism of which practitioners of Buddhism seek refuge in (what one relies on for his/her lasting happiness).

The three jewels of Buddhism are the Buddha (mind's perfection of enlightenment), the dharma (teachings and methods) and the Sangha (awakened beings who provide guidance and support).

Buddha's Dharma Body

The qualities of the Dharma (Law, truth) is the same as the qualities of the Buddha and forms his "truth body" or "Dhamma Kaya": In the Samyutta Nikaya, Vakkali Sutta, Buddha said to his disciple Vakkali that,

"Yo kho Vakkali dhammam passati so mam passati"

Vakkali, whoever sees Dhamma, sees me [the Buddha]

Another reference from the Agganna Sutta of the Digha Nikaya, says to his disciple Vasettha:

"Tathagatassa h'etam Vasettha adivacanam Dhamma-kayo iti pi...":

O Vasettha! The Word of Dhammakaya is indeed the name of the Tathagata

Qualities of Buddha Dharma

The Teaching of the Buddha also has six supreme qualities:

1. *Svakkhato:* The Dhamma is not a speculative philosophy, but is the Universal Law found through enlightenment and is preached precisely. Therefore it is excellent in the beginning (sila-Sanskrit sila-moral principles), excellent in the middle (samadhi-concentration) and excellent in the end (panna-Sanskrit prajna... Wisdom),
2. *Sanditthiko*: The Dhamma can be tested by practice and therefore he who follows it will see the result by himself through his own experience.

3. *Akaliko:* The Dhamma is able to bestow timeless and immediate results here and now, for which there is no need to wait until the future or next existence.
4. *Ehipassiko*: The Dhamma welcomes all beings to put it to the test and come see for themselves.
5. *Opanayiko*: The Dhamma is capable of being entered upon and therefore it is worthy to be followed as a part of one's life.
6. *Paccattam Veditabbo Vinnuhi*: The Dhamma can be perfectly realized only by the noble disciples (Ariyas) who have matured and enlightened enough in supreme wisdom.

Knowing these attributes, Buddhists believe that they will attain the greatest peace and happiness through the practice of the Dhamma. Each person is therefore fully responsible for himself to put it in the real practice.

Here the Buddha is compared to an experienced and skilful doctor and the Dhamma to proper medicine. However efficient the doctor or wonderful the medicine may be, the patients cannot be cured unless they take the medicine properly. So the practice of the Dhamma is the only way to attain the final deliverance of Nibbana.

These teachings ranged from understanding karma (Pali: kamma) (cause and effect) and developing good impressions in one's mind, to reach full enlightenment by recognizing the nature of mind.

Dharmas in Buddhist Phenomenology

Other uses include dharma, normally spelled with a small "d" (to differentiate), which refers to a phenomenon or constituent factor of human experience.

This was gradually expanded into a classification of constituents of the entire material and mental world. Rejecting the substantial existence of permanent entities which are qualified by possibly changing qualities, Buddhist Abhidharma philosophy, which enumerated seventy-five dharmas, came to propound that these "constituent factors" are the only type of entity that truly exists.

This notion is of particular importance for the analysis of human experience: Rather than assuming that mental states inhere in a cognizing subject, or a soul-substance, Buddhist philosophers largely propose that mental states alone exist as "momentary elements of consciousness" and that a subjective perceiver is assumed. One of the central tenets of Buddhism, is the denial of a separate permanent "I" and is outlined in the three marks of existence. The three signs: 1. Dukkha (Pali: Dukkha)-Suffering, 2. Anitya (Pali: Anicca)-Change/Impermanence, 3. Anatman (Pali: Anatta)-Non-self. At the heart of Buddhism, is the denial of a "self" or "I" (and hence the delusion) as a separate self-existing entity.

Later, Buddhist philosophers like Nagarjuna would question whether the dharmas (momentary elements of consciousness) truly have a separate existence of their own. (*i.e.* Do they exist apart from anything else?) Rejecting any inherent reality to the dharmas, he asked (rhetorically):

> *When all dharmas are empty, what is endless? What has an end?*
>
> *What is endless and with an end? What is not endless and not with an end?*
>
> *What is it? What is other? What is permanent? What is impermanent?*
>
> *What is impermanent and permanent? What is neither?*
>
> *Auspicious is the pacification of phenomenal metastasis, the pacification of all apprehending;*
>
> *There is no dharma whatsoever taught by the Buddha to whomever, whenever, wherever.--Mulamadhyama-kakarika, nirvanaparikna, 25:22-24*

Dharma as Righteousness

According to S. N. Goenka, teacher of Vipassana Meditation, the original meaning of dhamma is "dhareti ti dhamma', or "that which is contained". Dharma in the Buddhist scriptures has a variety of meanings, including "phenomenon" and "nature" or "characteristic". Dharma also means 'mental contents' and is paired with citta, which means heart/mind. The pairing is paralleled with the pairing of kaya (body) and vedana (feelings or sensations, that which arise within the body but experienced through the mind), in major sutras such as the Mahasatipatthana sutra.

Dharma is also used to refer to the teachings of the Buddha, not in the context of the words of one man, even an enlightened man, but as a reflection of natural law which was re-discovered by this man and shared with the world. A person who lives their life with an understanding of this natural law, is a "dhammic" person, which is often translated as "righteous".

7

Social Structure in Buddhism India

The Clans and Nations

It is much the same with the clans. We have a good deal of information, which is, however, at the best only fragmentary, about three or four of them. Of the rest we have little more than the bare names.

More details are given, very naturally, of the Sakiya clan than of the others. The general position of their country is intimated by the distances given from other places. It must have been just on the border of Nepalese and English territory, as is now finally settled by the recent discoveries of the tope or burial-mound put up by the Sakiyas over the portion they retained of the relics from the Buddha's funeral pyre, and of Asoka's inscription, in situ, recording his visit to the Lumbini garden in which the Buddha was born. Which of the numerous ruins in the immediate vicinity of these discoveries are those of Kapilavastu, the chief town of the clan, and which are the remains of the other townships belonging to them, will be one of the questions to be solved by future exploration.

It was at the last-mentioned place that the mother of the Buddha was born. And the name of her father is expressly given as Añjana the Sakiyan. When, therefore, we find in much later records the statements that she was of Koliyan family; and that Prince Devadaha, after whom the town was so named, was a

Koliyan chief, the explanation may well be that the Koliyans were a sort of subordinate subdivision of the Sakiya clan.

The existence of so considerable a number of market towns implies, in an agricultural community, a rather extensive territory. Buddhaghosa has preserved for us an old tradition that the Buddha had eighty thousand families of relatives on the father's side and the same on the mother's side. Allowing six or seven to a family, including the dependents, this would make a total of about a million persons in the Sakiya territory. And though the figure is purely traditional, and at best a round number (and not uninfluenced by the mystic value attached to it), it is, perhaps, not so very far from what we might expect.

The administrative and judicial business of the clan was carried out in public assembly, at which young and old were alike present, in their common Mote Hall (santhagara) at Kapilavastu. It was at such a parliament, or palaver, that King Pasenadi's proposition was discussed. When Ambalaha goes to Kapilavastu on business, he goes to the Mote Hall where the Sakiyas were then in session. And it is to the Mote Hall of the Mallas that Ananda goes to announce the death of the Buddha, they being then in session there to consider that very matter.

A single chief-how, and for what period chosen, we do not know-was elected as office-holder, presiding over the sessions, and, if no sessions were sitting, over the State. He bore the title of raja, which must have meant something like the Roman consul, or the Greek archon. We hear nowhere of such a triumvirate as bore corresponding office among the Licchavis, nor of such acts of kingly sovereignty as are ascribed to the real kings mentioned above. But we hear at one time that Bhaddiya, a young cousin of the Buddha's, was the raja; and in another passage, Suddhodana, the Buddha's father (who is elsewhere spoken of as a simple citizen, Suddhodana the Sakiyan), is called the raja.

A new Mote Hall, built at Kapilavastu, was finished whilst the Buddha was staying at the Nigrodharama (the pleasaunce under the Banyan Grove) in the Great Wood (the Mahavana) near by. There was a residence there, provided by the community, for recluses of all schools. Gautama was asked to inaugurate the new hall, and he did so by a series of ethical discourses, lasting through the night, delivered by himself, Ananda, and Moggallana. They are preserved for us in full at M. 1. 353, foll., and S. 4. 182, foll.

Besides this Mote Hall at the principal town we hear of others at some of the other towns above referred to. And no doubt all the more important places had such a hall, or pavilion, covered with a roof, but with no walls, in which to conduct their business. And the local affairs of each village were carried on in open assembly of the householders, held in the groves which, then as now, formed so distinctive a feature of each village in the long and level alluvial plain. It was no doubt in this plain, stretching about fifty miles from east to west, and thirty or forty miles to the southward from the foot of Himalaya Hills, that the majority of the clan were resident.

The clan subsisted on the produce of their rice-fields and their cattle. The villages were grouped round the rice-fields, and the cattle wandered through the outlying forest, over which the peasantry, all Sakiyas by birth, had rights of common. There were artisans, probably not Sakiyas, in each village; and men of certain special trades of a higher standing; the carpenters, smiths, and potters for instance, had villages of their own. So also had the Brahmins, whose services were in request at every domestic event. Khomadussa, for instance, was a Brahmin settlement. There were a few shops in the bazaars, but we do not hear of any merchants and bankers such as are mentioned as dwelling at the great capitals of the adjoining kingdoms. The villages were separated one from another by forest jungle, the remains of the Great Wood (the Maha Vana), portions of which are so frequently mentioned as still surviving throughout the clanships, and which must originally (not so very long, probably, before the time under discussion) have stretched over practically the whole level country between the foot of the mountains and the Great River, the Ganges. After the destruction of the clans by the neighbouring monarchies this jungle again spread over the country. From the fourth century onwards, down to our own days, the forest covered over the remains of the ancient civilisation.

This jungle was infested from time to time by robbers, sometimes runaway slaves. But we hear of no crime, and there was not probably very much, in the villages themselves-each of them a tiny self-governed republic. The Koliyan central authorities were served by a special body of peons, or police, distinguished, as by a kind of uniform, from which they took their name, by a special headdress. These particular men had a bad reputation for extortion and violence. The Mallas had similar officials, and it is not improbable that each of the clans had a somewhat similar set of subordinate servants.

A late tradition tells us how the criminal law was administered in the adjoining powerful confederate clan of the Vajjians, by a succession of regularly appointed officers,-"Justices, lawyers, rehearsers of the law-maxims, the council of representatives of the eight clans, the general, the vice-consul, and the consul himself." Each of these could acquit the accused. But if they considered him guilty, each had to refer the case to the next in order above them, the consul finally awarding the penalty according to the Book of Precedents. We hear of no such intermediate officials in the smaller clans; and even among the Vajjians (who, by the by, are all called "rajas" in this passage), it is not likely that so complicated a procedure was actually followed. But a book of legal precedents is referred to elsewhere, and tables of the law also. It is therefore not improbable that written notes on the subject were actually in use.

The names of other clans, besides the Sakiyas, are:

1. The Bhaggas of Sumsumara Hill.
2. The Buhs of Allakappa.
3. Kalamas of Kesaputta.
4. The Koliyas of Rama-gama.
5. The Mallas of Kusinara.
6. The Mallas of Pava.
7. The Moriyas of Pipphalivana.
8. The Videhas of Mithila.
9. The Licchavis of Vesali.

There are several other names of tribes of which it is not yet known whether they were clans or under monarchical government.

We have only one instance of any tribe, once under a monarchy, reverting to the independent state. And whenever the supreme power in a clan became hereditary, the result seems always to have been an absolute monarchy, without legal limitations of any kind.

The political divisions of India at or shortly before the time when Buddhism arose are well exemplified by the stock list of the Sixteen Great Countries, the Sixteen Powers, which is found in several places in the books. It is interesting to notice that the names are names, not of countries, but of peoples, as we might say Italians or Turks. This shows that the main idea in the minds of those who drew up, or used, this old list was still tribal and not geographical. The list is as follows: 1. Anga, 2. Magadha, 3. Kasi, 4. Kosala, 5. Vajji, 6. Malla, 7. Ceti, 8. Vamsa, 9. Kuru, 10. Pañcala, 11. Maccha, 12. Surasena, 13. Assaka, 14. Avanti, 15. Gandhara, 16. Kamboja

1. The Angas dwelt in the country to the east of Magadha, having their capital at Champa, near the modern Bhagalpur. Its boundaries are unknown. In the Buddha's time it was subject to Magadha, and we never hear of its having regained independence. But in former times it was independent, and there are traditions of wars between these neighbouring countries. The Anga raja in the Buddha's time was simply a wealthy nobleman, and we only know of him as the grantor of a pension to a particular Brahmin.
2. The Magadhas, as is well known, occupied the district now called Behar. It was probably then bounded to the north by the Ganges, to the east by the river Champa, on the south by the Vindhya Mountains, and on the west by the river Sona. In the Buddha's time (that is, inclusive of Anga) it is said to have had eighty thousand villages and to have been three hundred leagues (about twenty-three hundred miles) in circumference.
3. The Kasis are of course the people settled in the district round Benares. In the time of the Buddha this famous old kingdom of the Bharatas had fallen to so low a political level that the revenues of the township had become a bone of con-tension between Kosala and Magadha, and the

kingdom itself was incorporated into Kosala. Its mention in this list is historically important, as we must conclude that the memory of it as an independent state was still fresh in men's minds. This is confirmed by the very frequent mention of it as such in the Jatakas, where it is said to have been over two thousand miles in circuit. But it never regained independence; and its boundaries are unknown.

4. The Kosalas were the ruling clan in the kingdom whose capital was Savatthi, in what is now Nepal, seventy miles north-west of the modern Gorakhpur. It included Benares and Saketa; and probably had the Ganges for its southern boundary, the Gandhak for its eastern boundary, and the mountains for its northern boundary. The Sakiyas already acknowledged, in the seventh century BC, the suzerainty of Kosala.

   It was the rapid rise of this kingdom of Kosala, and the inevitable struggle in the immediate future between it and Magadha, which was the leading point in the politics of the Buddha's time. These hardy mountaineers had swept into their net all the tribes between the mountains and the Ganges. Their progress was arrested on the east by the free clans. And the struggle between Kosala and Magadha for the paramount power in all India was, in fact, probably decided when the powerful confederation of the Licchavis became arrayed on the side of Magadha. Several successful invasions of Kasi by the Kosalans under their kings, Vanka, Dabbasena, and Kansa, are referred to a date before the Buddha's time. And the final conquest would seem to be ascribed to Kansa, as the epithet "Conqueror of Benares" is a standing addition to his name.

5. The Vajjians included eight confederate clans, of whom the Licchavis and the Videhans were the most important. It is very interesting to notice that while tradition makes Videha a kingdom in earlier times, it describes it in the Buddha's time as a republic. Its size, as a separate kingdom, is said to have been three hundred leagues (about twenty-three hundred miles) in circumference. Its capital, Mithila, was about thirty-five miles north-west from Vesali, the

capital of the Licchavis. There it was that the great King Janaka ruled a little while before the rise of Buddhism. And it is probable that the modern town of Janak-pur preserves in its name a memory of this famous Rajput scholar and philosopher of olden time.

6. The Mallas of Kusinara and Pava were also independent clans, whose territory, if we may trust the Chinese pilgrims, was on the mountain slopes to the east of the Sakiya land, and to the north of the Vajjian confederation. But some would place it south of the Sakiyas and east of the Vajjians.

7. The Cetis were probably the same tribe as that called Cedi in older documents, and had two distinct settlements. One, probably the older, was in the mountains, in what is now called Nepal. The other, probably a later colony, was near Kosambi to the east and has been even confused with the land of the Vamsa, from which this list makes them distinct.

8. Vamsa is the country of the Vacchas, of which Kosambi, properly only the name of the capital, is the more familiar name. It lay immediately to the north of Avanti, and along the banks of the Jumna.

9. The Kurus occupied the country of which Indraprastha, close to the modern Delhi, was the capital; and had the Panchalas to the east, and the Matsyas to the south. Tradition gives the kingdom a circumference of two thousand miles. They had very little political importance in the Buddha's time. It was at Kammassa-dhamma in the Kuru country that several of the most important Suttantas-the Maha Satipalahana, for instance, and the Maha Nidana-were delivered. And Ramahapala was a Kuru noble.

10. The two Pañcalas occupied the country to the east of the Kurus, between the mountains and the Ganges. Their capitals were Kampilla and Kanoj.

11. The Macchas, or Matsyas, were to the south of the Kurus and west of the Jumna, which separated them from the Southern Pañcalas.

12. The Surasenas, whose capital was Madhura, were

immediately south-west of the Macchas, and west of the Jumna.

13. The Assakas had, in the Buddha's time, a settlement on the banks of the Godhavari. Their capital was Potana, or Potali. The country is mentioned with Avanti in the same way as Anga is with Magadha, and its position on this list, between Surasena and Avanti, makes it probable that, when the list was drawn up, its position was immediately north-west of Avanti. In that case the settlement on the Godhavari was a later colony; and this is confirmed by the fact that there is no mention of Potana (or Potali) there. The name of the tribe is also ambiguous. Sanskrit authors speak both of Asmaka and of Asvaka. Each of these would be Assaka, both in the local vernacular and in Pali. And either there were two distinct tribes so called, or the Sanskrit form Asvaka is a wrong reading, or a blunder in the Sanskritisation of Assaka.
14. Avanti, the capital of which was Ujjeni, was ruled over by King Carva Pajjota (Pajjota the Fierce). The country, much of which is rich land, had been colonised or conquered by Aryan tribes who came down the Indian valley, and turned west from the Gulf of Kach. It was called Avanti at least as late as the second century AD, but from the seventh or eighth century onwards it was called Malava.
15. Gandhara, modern Kandahar, was the district of Eastern Afghanistan, and it probably included the north-west of the Panjab. Its capital was Takkasila. The King of Gandhara in the Buddha's time, Pukkusati, is said to have sent an embassy and a letter to King Bimbisara of Magadha.
16. Kamboja was the adjoining country in the extreme north-west, with Dvaraka as its capital.

From the political point of view this list is curious. Some names we should expect to find-Sivi, for instance, and Madda and Sovira, and Udyana and Virata-are not there. The Mallas and the Cetis occupy a position much more important than they actually held in the early years of Buddhism. Vesali, soon to become a "Magadha town," is still independent. And Anga and Kasi, then incorporated in neighbouring kingdoms, arc apparently looked upon as of equal rank with the others. It is evident that this was an old list, corresponding to a state of things existent some time before, and handed on by tradition in the Buddhist schools. But this only adds to its interest and importance.

Geographically also the list is very suggestive. No place south of Avanti (about 23° N.) occurs in it; and it is only at one place that the list goes even so far to the south as that. Not only is the whole of South India and Ceylon ignored in it, but there is also no mention of Orissa, of Bengal east of the Ganges, or even of the Dekkan. The horizon of those who drew up the list is strictly bounded on the north by the Himalayas, and on the south (except at this one point) by the Vindhya range, on the west by the mountains beyond the Indus, and on the east by the Ganges as it turns to the south.

The books in which the list has been preserved have preserved also abundant evidence of a further stage of political movement. And in geographical knowledge they look at things from an advanced point of view. They know a very little farther south at the one point where the old list goes farthest in that direction.

The expression Dakkhinapatha which occurs in an isolated passage in one of our oldest documents cannot indeed possibly mean the whole country comprised in our modern phrase the Dekkan. But it is used, in the very passage in question, as descriptive of a remote settlement or colony on the banks of the upper Godhavari. The expression does not occur in any one of the Four Nikayas. When it appears again, in a later stage, it seems still to refer only, in a vague way, to the same limited district, on the banks of the Godhavari. And it is coupled with Avanti, the Avanti of the ancient list.

The expression, in its form, is curious. It means "the Southern Road," a strange name to apply to any fixed locality. Already in a Vedic hymn though it is one of the latest, we hear of a banished man going along the "path of the South." No doubt at different times different points on that path had been reached. In the Buddha's time the most southerly town is given (at S. N. 1011) as Patilahana, the place afterwards called Paithana, and Baithana by the Greeks (73° 2 E. by 21° 42' N.). And the extreme southerly point reached at all is the hermitage on the Godhavari, about 20° N. One place still farther south may possibly be referred to incidentally as known in the Buddha's time. A teacher of olden time named Tagara-sikhin, is several times mentioned. Sikhin is otherwise known as a name, and the distinctive epithet Tagara may possibly be local, and mean "of Tagara," the modern Ter, 76° 12' E. by 18°, 19' N. But the point is very doubtful, the place is not mentioned elsewhere, and I think another explanation of the name is more likely.

Besides this extension in the Dekkan, the Nikayas speak also of sea voyages out of sight of land and they mention the Kalinga forest, and the settlement on the coast there, with its capital Dantapura. The Vinaya has a probable reference to Bharu-kaccha, and the Udana one to Supparaka. These points, taken together (and no doubt others can be traced), show a marked advance in geographical knowledge. But it is suggestive to notice that the advance is limited, and that there is still no reference whatever either to South India or to Ceylon, which play so great a part in the story of the Ramayana.

These geographical considerations are of very considerable importance for the history of later Vedic and early Sanskrit literature. They go far to confirm Professor Bhandarkar's recent views as to the wholesale recasting of Brahmin literature in the Gupta period. If Apastamba, for instance, as Hofrath Dr. Bühler thought, and Hiranya-Kesin, wrote in the south, below the Godhavari, then they must be later than the books whose evidence we have been considering.

The consideration of this question has been hindered by a generally accepted hypothesis which does not fit the facts. It is supposed that the course of Aryan migration lay along the valleys of the Ganges and the Jumna. It cannot have been so simple. We must postulate at least two other lines of equal importance-one down the Indus, round the Gulf of Cutch, and so up to Avanti; and another along the foot of the mountains from Kashmir, by way of Kosala, to the Sakiya country, and so on through Tirhut to Magadha and Anga. There is a great deal more evidence available, both in literature and in the conclusions to be drawn from language, as to tribal migration in India than has yet been collected or analysed. Mr. Grierson, for instance, has only just recently pointed out the important fact that, even now, the dialects of Rajasthan have a close resemblance to the dialects spoken along the Himalayas not only in Nepal but as far west, at least, as Chamba. This would tend to show that their ancestors must have been living close together when they began their wanderings to the east and the south respectively. Both started from the Northern Panjab, and probably neither migration followed the Ganges route.

These children of hillmen tended to cleave to the hills; and, like mountaineers all the world over, were generally distinguished by a sturdy independence, both in politics and religion. Widely separated, they were always sympathetic; and any forward movement, such as Buddhism, readily found supporters among them.

Another point on which this geographical evidence throws light is the date of the colonisation of Ceylon. That cannot have taken place in any considerable degree before the period in which the Nikayas were composed. We know it had become a well-established fact at the time of Asoka. It must have happened, therefore, between these two dates; and no doubt nearer to the earlier of the two. The Ceylon chronicles, therefore, in dating the first colony in the very year of the Buddha's death (a wrong synchronism which is the cause of much confusion in their early chronology) must be in error.

It would be of great assistance on several questions if we could form some conclusion as to the number of inhabitants in Northern India in the seventh century, BC; though any such conclusion would necessarily be of the vaguest description. To judge from the small numbers of the great cities, and from the wide extent of forest and wilderness, mentioned in the books, it cannot have been very-large. Perhaps the whole territory may have contained fifteen to twenty millions. In the fourth century, BC, the confederation formed to oppose Alexander was able to muster an army of four hundred thousand. And in the third century, BC, Megasthenes describes the army of Magadha as then consisting, in peace time, of two hundred thousand foot, three hundred elephants, and ten thousand chariots.

The following is a list of the principal cities existing in India in the seventh century BC

Ayojjha (from which the Anglo-Indian word Oudh is derived) was a town in Kosala on the river Sarayu. The city owes all its fame to the fact that the author of the Ramayana makes it the capital at the date of the events in his story. It is not even mentioned in the Mahabharata; and was quite unimportant in the Buddha's time. There is another Ayojjha in the extreme west; and a third is said (wrongly, I think) to have been situate on the Ganges.

Baranasi (Benares) on the north bank of the Ganges, at the junction between it and the river Barana. The city proper included the land between the Barana and a stream called the Asi, as its name suggests. Its extent, including the suburbs, is often stated to have been, at the time when it was the capital of an independent kingdom (that is, some time before the rise of Buddhism) twelve leagues, or about eighty-five miles. Seeing that Megasthenes gives the circuit of the walls of Pataliputta, where he himself lived, as 220 stadia (or about twenty-five miles), this tradition as to the size of the city, or rather county, Benares at the height of its prosperity seems by no means devoid of credit. Its Town Hall was then no longer used as a parliament chamber for the transaction of public business. Public discussions on religious and philosophical questions were carried on in it.

Champa, on the river of the same name, was the ancient capital of Anga. Its site has been identified by Cunningham with the modern villages of similar names twenty-four miles east of Bhagalpur; and is stated to have been sixty leagues from Mithila. It was celebrated for its beautiful lake, named after Queen Gaggara, who had it excavated. On its banks was a grove of Champaka trees, well known for the fragrant odour of their beautiful white flowers. And there, in the Buddha's time, wandering teachers were wont to lodge. The Indian colonists in Cochin China named one of the most important of their settlements after this famous old town. And the Champa in Anga was again, in its turn, so named after the still older Champa in Kashmir.

Kampilla, the capital of the Northern Pañcalas. It was on the northern bank of the Ganges, about long. 79° W., but its exact site has not yet been decided with certainty. Kosambi, the capital of the Vatsas or Vamsas. It was on the Jumna, and thirty leagues, say 230 miles, by river from Benares. It was the most important entrepót for both goods and passengers coming to Kosala and Magadha from the south and west. In the Sutta Nipata (1010-1013) the whole route is given from a place south of Ujjen, through Koshambi to Kusinara, with the stopping-places on the way. The route from Koshambi to Rajagaha was down the river. In the Buddha's time there were already four distinct establishments of his Order in the suburbs of Koshambi-the Badarika, Kukkuna, and Ghosita Parks, and the Mango Grove of Pavariya.] The Buddha was often there, at one or other of these residences; and many of his discourses there have been handed down in the books.

Madhura, on the Jumna, the capital of the Surasenas. It is tempting to identify it with the site of the modern Mathura, in spite of the difference in spelling. Very ancient remains have been found there. The king of Madhura in the Buddha's time bore the title of Avanti-putto, and was therefore related to the royal family at Ujjeni. Madhura was visited by the Buddha, and was the residence of Maha Kaccana, one of his most influential disciples, to whom tradition attributes the first grammatical treatment of the Pali language, and after whom the oldest Pali grammar is accordingly named. As Madhura is mentioned in the Milinda (331) as one of the most famous places in India, whereas in the Buddha's time it is barely mentioned, the time of its greatest growth must have been between these dates. It was sufficiently famous for the other Madhura, in Tinnevelly, first mentioned in the Mahavansa, to be named after it. A third Madhura, in the extreme north, is mentioned at Jat. 4. 79, and Peta Vatthu Vamana, 111. Mithila, the capital of Videha, and the capital therefore of the kings Janaka and Makhadeva, was in the district now called Tirhut. Its size is frequently given as seven leagues, about fifty miles, in circumference.

Rajagaha, the capital of Magadha, the modern Rajgir. There were two distinct towns; the older one, a hill fortress, more properly Giribbaja, was very ancient, and is said to have been laid out by Maha Govinda the architect. The later town, at the foot of the hills, was built by Bimbisara, the contemporary of the Buddha, and is

Rajagaha proper. It was at the height of its prosperity during, and immediately after, the Buddha's time. But it was abandoned by Sisuńaga, who transferred the capital to Vesali; his son Kakasoka transferring it to Pataliputta, near the site of the modern Patna.

The fortifications of both Giribbaja and Rajagaha are still extant, 4½ and 3 miles respectively in circumference; the most southerly point of the walls of Giribbaja, the "Mountain Stronghold," being one mile north of the most northerly point of the walls of the new town of Rajagaha, the "King's House." The stone walls of Giribbaja are the oldest extant stone buildings in India.

Roruka, or in later times Roruva, the capital of Sovira, from which the modern name Surat is derived, was an important centre of the coasting trade. Caravans arrived there from all parts of India, even from Magadha. As Ophir is spelt by Josephus and in the Septuagint Sophir, and the names of the ivory, apes, and peacocks imported thence into Palestine are Indian names, it is not improbable that Roruka was the seaport to which the authors of the Hebrew chronicles supposed that Solomon's vessels had traded. For though the more precise name of the port was Roruka, we know from such expressions as that used in the Milinda, p. 29, that the Indians talked about sailing to Sovira. The exact site has not yet been rediscovered, but it was almost certainly on the Gulf of Kach, somewhere near the modern Kharragoa. When its prosperity declined, its place was taken by Bharukaccha, the modern Bharoch, or by Supparaka, both on the opposite, the southern, side of the Kathiawad peninsula.

Sagala. There were three cities of this name. But the two in the far East were doubtless named after the famous Sagala in the extreme north-west, which offered so brave a resistance to Alexander, and where King Milanda afterwards reigned. It lay about 32° N. by 74° E., and was the capital of the Maddas. Cunningham thought he had found the ruins of it; but no excavations have been carried out, and the exact site is still therefore uncertain.

Saketa, the site of which has been indentified with the ruins, as yet unexplored, at Sujan Kot, on the Sai River, in the Unao district of the modern province of Audh. In ancient times it was an important city in Kosala, and sometimes the capital. In the Buddha's time the capital was Savatthi. Saketa is often supposed to be the same as Ayojjha (Oudh), but both cities are mentioned as existing in the Buddha's time. They were possibly adjoining, like London and Westminster. But it is Saketa, and not Ayojjha, that is called one of the six great cities of India. The Añjana Wood near by Saketa is the place at which many of the Buddhist Suttas are said to have been spoken. The distance from Saketa northwards, to Savatthi was six leagues, about forty-five miles, and could be covered in one day with seven relays of horses. But there was a broad river on the way, only to be crossed by ferry; and there are constant references to the dangers of the journey on foot.

Savatthi, or Sravasti, was the capital of Northern Kosala, the residence of King Pasenadi, and one of the six great cities in India during the lifetime of the Buddha. Archaeologists differ as to its position; and the decision of this vexed point is one of the first importance for the early history of India, as there must be many inscriptions there. It was six leagues north of Saketa, forty-five leagues north-west of Rajagaha, more than one hundred north-east of Supparaka, thirty leagues from Sankassa and on the bank of the Achiravati.

Ujjeni, the capital of Avanti, the Greek Ozene, about 77° E. and 23° N. There Kaccana, one of the leading disciples of the Buddha, and also Asoka's son Mahinda, the famous apostle to Ceylon, were born. In later times there was a famous monastery there called the Southern Mount; and in earlier times the capital had been Mahissati. Vedisa, where the famous Bhilsa Topes were lately found, and Erakaccha, another well-known site, were in the vicinity. Vedisa was fifty leagues from Pataliputta.

This was the capital of the Licchavi clan, already closely related by marriage to the kings of Magadha, and the ancestors of the kings of Nepal, of the Mauryas, and of the dynasty of the Guptas. It was the headquarters of the powerful Vajjian confederacy, afterwards defeated, but not broken up, by Ajatasattu. It was the only great city in all the territories of the free clans who formed so important a factor in the social and political life of the sixth century BC It must have been a great and flourishing place.

But though different guesses have been made as to its site, no one of them has yet been proved to be true by excavation. It was somewhere in Tirhut; and just three leagues, or, say, twenty-five miles, north of the Ganges, reckoned from a spot on the bank of that river, five leagues, say thirty-eight miles, from Rajagaha. Behind it lay the Great Forest, the Mahavana, which stretched northwards to the Himalayas. In that wood a hermitage had been built by the community for the Buddha, and there many of his discourses were delivered. And in an adjoining suburb, the founder of the Jains, who was closely related to some of the leading chiefs, was born. We hear of its three walls, each of them a gavuta, a cow's call, distant from the next; and of the 7707 rajas, that is Licchavi chiefs, who dwelt there; and of the sacred pool in which they received their consecration. There were many shrines of pre-Buddhistic worship in and around the city, and the discovery and excavation of the site is most desirable.

The same may indeed be said of all these ancient cities. Not one of them has been properly excavated. The archeeology of India is, at present, an almost unworked field.

The Village

In the Buddha's time and in that portion of North India where the Buddhist influence was most early felt-that is to say in the districts including and adjoining those now called the United Provinces and Behar-the social conditions were, on the whole, simple. But there are several points of great interest on which they differed from those of the same districts now, and from those of related tribes in Europe then.

Divergent theories have been propounded to explain these differences. The influence of food and climate is assigned a paramount importance. Vegetarian diet is supposed to explain the physical and mental degeneracy proved by the presumed absence of political movements and ardent patriotism. Or the enervating and tropical heat of the sultry plains is supposed to explain at once the want of political vigour and the bad philosophy. Or the overwhelming mental effect of the mighty powers of nature-the vivid storms of thunder and lightning, the irresistible rays of the scorching sun, the depressing majesty of the great mountains-are called upon as a sufficient explanation of the inferiority of the Indian peoples. Or the contact with aboriginal tribes in a semi-savage state of development, the frequent intermarriages, and the consequent adoption of foolish and harmful superstitions, are put forward as the reasons for whatever we find strange in their life and thought.

It may be doubted whether our knowledge of the state of things in the seventh century BC, either on the shores of the Mediterranean on the one hand, or in the Ganges Valley on the other, is sufficiently clear and precise to justify our taking for granted the then inferiority of the Indians. In some respects it would seem to be the other way. In intellectual vigour, at least, the Indians were not wanting. That Europeans should believe, as a matter of course, in the vast superiority of Europeans, not only now, but always, is psychologically interesting. It is so like the opinion of the ancient Greeks about barbarians, and of the modern Chinese about foreigners. But the reasons given are vague, and will scarcely bear examination. I recollect hearing Professor Buhler at the Oriental Congress in Paris, in 1897, when the argument of climate was adduced, entering an emphatic caution. As Inspector of Schools in India for many years, he knew the climate well; and observed that exaggerated estimates of its baneful influence had been most often advanced by those who had never been in India. Those who had lived there knew the great amount of energy and work, both physical and intellectual, that was not only possible, but habitual, to both Europeans and the natives of India. I can fully confirm this. The climate has its positive advantages. All the other most ancient civilisations (in Egypt for instance, in Mesopotamia, and in China) grew up, under somewhat similar outward conditions, in warm and fertile river valleys. And climate varies greatly even in India. We must not forget that the Sakiya country, at least, in which Buddhism arose, stretchcd up into the lower slopes of the Himalayas. And in the seventh century BC the most powerful kingdom was the Northern Kosala, whose capital lay under the hills, and whose power mainly depended on the mountaineers drawn from its vicinity.

It is probable that economic conditions and social institutions were a more important factor in Indian life than geographical position. Now the social structure of India was based upon the village. We do not as yet know all the details of its organisation; and no doubt different villages, in different districts, varied one from another in the customs of land-tenure and in the rights of individual householders as against the community.

It is a common error, vitiating all conclusions as to the early history of India, to suppose that the tribes with whom the Aryans, in their gradual conquest of India, came into contact, were savages. Some were so. There were hill tribes, gypsies, bands of hunters in the woods. But there were also settled communities with highly developed social organisation, wealthy enough to excite the cupidity of the invaders, and in many cases too much addicted to the activities of peace to be able to offer, whenever it came to a fight, a prolonged resistance. But they were strong enough to retain, in some cases, a qualified independence, and in others to impose upon the new nation that issued from the struggle many of their own ideas, many of the details of their own institutions.

And in many cases it never came to a struggle at all. The country was immense. Compared with its wide expanse the tribes and clans were few. Often separated one from the other by broad rivers and impenetrable forest, there must have been ample opportunity for independent growth, and for the interaction of peaceful contact.

These circumstances will explain the divergency in the village arrangements. But in some respects they were all similar. We nowhere hear of isolated houses. The houses were all together, in a group, separated only by narrow lanes. Immediately adjoining was the sacred grove of trees of the primeval forest, left standing when the forest clearing had been made. Beyond this was the wide expanse of cultivated field, usually rice-field. And each village had grazing ground for the cattle, and a considerable stretch of jungle, where the villagers had common rights of waste and wood.

The cattle belonged severally to the householders of the village. But no one had separate pasture. After the crop was cut the cattle roamed over the field. When the crops were growing they were sent all together, under the charge of a herdsman, hired by the village collectively, to the village grazing grounds beyond the field. The herdsman was an important personage, and is described as "knowing the general appearance of each one of his charge and the marks upon it, skilled to remove flies' eggs from their hide and to make sores heal over, accustomed to keep a good fire going with smoke to keep the gnats away, knowing where the fords are and the drinking places, clever in choosing pasture, leaving milk in the udders, and with a proper respect for the leaders of the herd."

The fields were all cultivated at the same time, the irrigation channels being laid by the community, and the supply of water regulated by rule, under the supervision of the headman. No individual or corporate proprietor needed to fence his portion of the fields. There was a common fence; and the whole field, with its rows of boundaries, which were also the water channels, bore the appearance of the patched robe of a member of the Buddhist Order. As a general rule the great field was divided into plots corresponding in number to that of the heads of houses in the villages; and each family took the produce of its share. But there was no such proprietary right, as against the community, as we are accustomed to in England. We hear of no instance of a shareholder selling or mortgaging his share of the village field to an outsider; and it was impossible for him to do so, at least without the consent of the village council. We have three instances of sales of land in the books. But in one case it was forest land cleared by the proprietor or his ancestors. A very old text apparently implies that a piece of ground was given as a sacrificial fee. But it is at once added that the earth itself said, and Mother Earth was a most dread divinity,-"No mortal must give me away!"

Neither had any individual the right of bequest, even to the extent of deciding the shares of his own family. All such matters were settled by custom, by the general sense of the community as to what was right and proper. And the general sense did not recognise the right of primogeniture. Very often a family, on the death of a householder, would go on as before under the superintendence of the eldest son. If the property were divided, the land was equally divided among the sons. And though the eldest son received an extra share (differing in different places and times) in the personal property, that also was otherwise divided equally. We find in the earliest law book, that of Gautama, a statement that the youngest son also, as in the analogous English law of gavelkind, received an extra share; but in the later law books this disappears. The women, too, had their personal property, chiefly jewellery and clothes; and the daughters inherited from the mother. They had no need of a separate share of the land, as they had the advantage of the produce falling to the share of their husbands and brothers.

No individual could acquire, either by purchase or inheritance, any exclusive right in any portion of the common grassland or woodland. Great importance was attached to these rights of pasture and forestry. The priests claimed to be able, as one result of performing a particular sacrifice (with six hundred victims!), to ensure that a wide tract of such land should be provided. And it is often made a special point, in describing the grant of a village to a priest, that it contained such common. What happened in such a case was that the king granted, not the land (he had no property in the land), but the tithe due, by custom, to the government as yearly tax. The peasantry were ousted from no one of their rights. Their position was indeed improved. For, paying only the same tax as before, they thus acquired the protection of a strong influence, which would not fail, on occasion, to be exerted on their behalf.

Not that they were usually without some such protection. It was through the village headman that all government business was carried on, and he had both opportunity and power to represent their case to the higher officials. From the fact that the appointment of this officer is not claimed for the king until the later law books it is almost certain that, in earlier times, the appointment was either hereditary, or conferred by the village council itself.

This village headman had, no doubt, to prepare the road, and provide food, on the occasion of a royal person or high official visiting his village. But we find no mention of corvée, forced labour (raja-kariya) at this period. And even in the law books which refer to a later date, this is mentioned as a service due from artisans and mechanics, and not from villagers.

On the other hand villagers are described as uniting, of their own accord, to build Mote-halls and Rest-houses and reservoirs, to mend the roads between their own and adjacent villages, and even to lay out parks. And it is interesting to find that women are proud to bear a part in such works of public utility.

The economic conditions in such villages were simple. None of the householders could have been what would now be called rich. On the other hand there was a sufficiency for their simple needs, there was security, there was independence. There were no landlords, and no paupers. There was little if any crime. What crime there was in the country (of which later) was nearly all outside the villages. When the central power was strong enough, as it usually was, to put down dacoity, the people, to quote the quaint words of an old Suttanta, "pleased one with another and happy, dancing their children in their hands, dwelt with open doors."

The only serious inroad upon that happiness seems to have been famine resulting from drought. It is true that Megasthenes, long ambassador at the court of Magadha, says that, owing to irrigation, famines were quite unknown. But we have too many references to times of scarcity, and that, too, in the very districts adjacent to Patna where Megasthenes lived, to accept his statement as accurate for the time we are discussing. As those references refer, however, to a date two centuries earlier, it is possible (but not, I think, very probable) that things, in this respect, had improved in the interval between the times referred to in our records, and that of Megasthenes. We shall see below, in the chapter on Chandragupta, that his statements often require correction. And this is, more probably, merely another instance of a similar kind.

It was under some such economic conditions as these that the great bulk-say at least 70-80 per cent.-of the people lived. In the books, ancient and modern, a few of the remaining few are so much more constantly mentioned (precisely because they differ from the mass, and the mass is taken for granted as understood) that the impression given to the reader fs apt to be entirely misleading. These others-priests and kings, outcasts and jugglers, soldiers, citizens, and mendicant thinkers-played their part, and an important part. But the peoples of India, then much more even than now, were, first and foremost, village folk. In the whole vast territory from Kandahar nearly to Calcutta, and from the Himalayas southwards to the Run of Kach, we find mentioned barely a score of towns of any considerable size. It will have been seen, however, that the mass of the people, the villagers, occupied a social grade quite different from, and far above, our village folk. They held it degradation, to which only dire misfortune would drive them, to work for hire. They were proud of their standing, their family, and their village. And they were governed by headmen of their own class and village, very probably selected by themselves, in accordance with their own customs and ideals.

Social Grades

Perhaps the most important of these in their own eyes were the customs as to the holding and distribution of lands and property. But those as to religion on the one hand, and as to connubium and commensality on the other, had probably a greater effect on their real well-being and national progress.

We have learnt in recent years that among primitive peoples all over the world there exist restrictions as to the connubium (the right of intermarriage), and as to commensality (the right of eating together). Customs of endogamy and exogamy, that is, of choosing a husband or wife outside a limited circle of relationship, and inside a wider circle, were universal. A man, for instance, may not marry in his own family, he may marry within his own clan, he may not marry outside the clan. Among different tribes the limits drawn were subject to different customs, were not the same in detail. But the limits were always there. There were customs of eating together at sacred tribal feasts from which foreigners were excluded; customs of not eating together with persons outside certain limits of relationship, except under special circumstances; customs by which an outsider could, by eating with men of a tribe, acquire certain rights of relationship with that tribe. Here again the details differ. But the existence of such restrictions as to commensality was once universal.

In India also in the seventh century BC such customs were prevalent, and prevalent in widely different forms among the different tribes,-Aryan, Dravidian, Kolarian, and others,-which made up the mixed population. We have unfortunately only Aryan records. And they, of course, take all the customs for granted, being addressed to people who knew all about them. We have therefore to depend on hints; and the hints given have not, as yet, been all collected and sifted. But a considerable number, and those of great importance, have been already observed; so that we are able to draw out some principal points in a sketch that requires future filling in.

The basis of the social distinctions was relationship; or, as the Aryans, proud of their lighter colour, put it colour. Their books constantly repeat a phrase as being common amongst the people,-and it was certainly common at least among the Aryan sections of the people,-which divided all the world, as they knew it, into four social grades, called Colours. At the head were the Kshatriyas, the nobles, who claimed descent from the leaders of the Aryan tribes in their invasion of the continent. They were most particular as to the purity of their descent through seven generations, both on the father's and the mother's side; and are described as "fair in colour, fine in presence, stately to behold." Then came the Brahmins, claiming descent from the sacrificing priests, and though the majority of them followed then other pursuits, they were equally with the nobles distinguished by high birth and clear complexion. Below these were the peasantry, the people, the Vaishyas or Vessas. And last of all came the Sudras, which included the bulk of the people of non-Aryan descent, who worked for hire, were engaged in handicraft or service, and were darker in colour.

In a general way this classification corresponded to the actual facts of life. But there were insensible gradations within the borders of each of the four Colours, and the borders themselves were both variable and undefined.

And this enumeration of the populace was not complete. Below all four, that is below the Sudras, we have mention of other "low tribes" and "low trades"-hina-jatiyo and hina-sippani. Among the first we are told of workers in rushes, bird-catchers, and cart-makers-aboriginal tribesmen who were hereditary craftsmen in these three ways. Among the latter-mat-makers, barbers, potters, weavers, and leather-workers-it is implied that there was no hard and fast line, determined by birth. People could, and did, change their vocations by adopting one or other of these "low trades." Thus at Jat. 5. 290, foll., a love-lorn Kshatriya works successively (without any dishonour or penalty) as a potter, basket-maker, reed-worker, garland-maker, and cook. Also at Jat. 6. 372, a sethi works as a tailor and as a potter, and still retains the respect of his high-born relations.

Finally we hear in both Jain and Buddhist books of aboriginal tribes, Chandalas and Pukkusas, who were more despised even than these low tribes and trades.

Besides the above, who were all freemen, there were also slaves: individuals had been captured in predatory raids and reduced to slavery, or had been deprived of their freedom as a judicial punishment; or had submitted to slavery of their own accord. Children born to such slaves were also slaves; and the emancipation of slaves is often referred to. But we hear nothing of such later developments of slavery as rendered the Greek mines, the Roman latifundia, or the plantations of Christian slave-owners, scenes of misery and oppression. For the most part the slaves were household servants, and not badly treated; and their numbers seem to have been insignificant.

Such were the divisions of the people. The three upper classes had originally been one; for the nobles and priests were merely those members of the third class, the Vessas, who had raised themselves into a higher social rank. And though more difficult probably than it had been, it was still possible for analogous changes to take place. Poor men could become nobles, and both could become Brahmins.

We have numerous instances in the books, some of them unconsciously preserved even in the later priestly books which are otherwise under the spell of the caste theory. And though each case is then referred to as if it were exceptional, the fact no less remains that the line between the "Colours" was not yet strictly drawn. The members of the higher Colours were not even all of them white. Some, no doubt, of the Kshatriyas were descended from the chiefs and nobles of the Dravidian and Kolarian tribes who had preserved, by conquest or by treaty, their independence or their social rank. And others of the same tribes were, from time to time, acquiring political importance, and with it an entry into a higher social grade.

That there was altogether a much freer possibility of change among the social ranks than is usually supposed is shown by the following instances of occupation]:

1. A Kshatriya, a king's son, apprentices himself successively, in pursuance of a love affair, to a potter, a basket-maker, a florist, and a cook, without a word being added as to loss of caste when his action becomes known.
2. Another prince resigns his share in the kingdom in favour of his sister, and turns trader.
3. A third prince goes to live with a merchant and earns his living "by his hands."
4. A noble takes service, for a salary, as an archer.
5. A Brahmin takes to trade to make money to give away.
6. Two other Brahmins live by trade without any such excuse.
7. A Brahmin takes the post of an assistant to an archer, who had himself been previously a weaver.

8, 9. Brahmins live as hunters and trappers.

10. A Brahmin is a wheelwright.

Brahmins are also frequently mentioned as engaged in agriculture, and as hiring themselves out as cowherds and even goatherds. These are all instances from the Jatakas. And a fortiori-unless it be maintained that Buddhism brought about a great change in this respect-the statt of things must have been even more lax at the time when Buddhism arose.

The customs of connubium were by no means co-extensive with the four Colours, They depended among the Aryans on a quite different idea, that of the group of agnates (the Gotta); and among the other people either on the tribe, or on the village. No instance is known of the two parties to a marriage belonging by birth to the same village. On the other hand, there were numerous instances of irregular unions. And in some cases the offspring of such unions took rank even as nobles (Kshatriyas) or as Brahmins.

As to customs of eating or not eating together, the books contain only a few hints. We have clear instances of a Brahmin eating with a Kshatriya, another of a Brahmin eating the food of a Chandala, and repenting of doing so. The whole episode of the marriage of the Sakiya maiden to Pasenadi, King of Kosala, turns on the belief that a Kshatriya will not eat, even with his own daughter, if she be slave-born. And we hear of sending people to Coventry (as we should say) for breach of such customs. Thus at J. 4. 388, Brahmins are deprived, by their brother Brahmins, of their status as Brahmins, for drinking water mixed with the rice water a Chandala had used. And in an older document, one of the Dialogues, we are told how this was done. Three Brahmins "for some offence or other, outlaw a Brahmin, shaving him and cutting him dead by pouring ashes over him, thus banishing him from the land and from the township." And the passage goes on to state that if Kshatriyas had done this to a Kshatriya the Brahmins would still admit him to connubium, and allow him to eat with them at their sacred feasts. It then adds that "whosoever are in bondage to the notions of birth or of lineage, or to the pride of social position or connection by marriage, they are far from the best wisdom and righteousness." We see, therefore, that the whole passage is tinged with Buddhist views. But it is none the less good evidence that at the time when it was written such customs, and such pride of birth, were recognised as a factor in the social life of the people.

Again at Jat. 5. 280, we have, as the central incident of a popular story, the detail, given quite as a matter of course, that a Brahmin takes, as his only wife, the discarded consort of a Kshatriya. The people laugh at him, it is true, but not because he is acting in any way unworthy of its social standing, only because he is old and ugly.

There are also numerous instances, even in the priestly manuals of custom, of unions between men and women of all degrees of social importance. These are not only between men of rank and girls of a lower social grade, but also between men of a lower, and women of a higher, position; and we ought not to be in the least surprised to find such cases mentioned in the books. Even without them we should know, from the existing facts, what must have happened. It is generally admitted that there are now no pure Aryans left in India. Had the actual custom been as strict as the Brahmin theory this would not be so. Just as in England we find

Iberians, Kelts, Angles, Saxons, Danes, and Normans now fused, in spite of theoretical restrictions on intermarriage, into one nation, so in Northern India the ancient distinctions, Aryan, Kolarian, and Dravidian, cannot, at the time of the rise of Buddhism, any longer be recognised. Long before the priestly theory of caste had been brought into any sort of working order, a fusion, sufficient at least to obliterate completely the old landmarks, was an accomplished fact; and the modern divisions, though race has also its share in them, use different names, and are based on different ideas.

We may remark incidentally that there can have been no such physical repulsion as obtains between the advanced and savage races of to-day-a repulsion arising partly from great difference in customs and in intellectual culture, but still more largely dependent on difference of colour. On the other hand, though the fact of frequent intermarriage is undoubted; though the great chasm between the proudest Kshatriya on the one hand and the lowest Chandala on the other was bridged over by a number of almost imperceptible stages, and the boundaries between these stages were constantly being overstepped, still there were also real obstacles to unequal unions. Though the lines of demarcation were not yet drawn hard and fast, we still have to suppose, not a state of society where there were no lines of demarcation at all, but a constant struggle between attracting and repelling forces.

It will sound most amazing to those familiar with Brahmin pretensions (either in modern times in India, or in priestly books such as Manu and the epics) to hear Brahmins spoken of as "low-born." Yet that precisely is an epithet applied to them in comparison with the kings and nobles. And it ought to open our eyes as to their relative importance in these early times.

The fact is that the claim of the priests to social superiority had nowhere in North India been then, as yet, accepted by the people. Even such books of the priests themselves as are pre-Buddhistic imply this earlier, and not the later, state of things with which we are so much familiar. They claim for the northwestern, as distinct from the easterly, provinces a most strict adherence to ancient custom. The ideal land is, to them, that of the Kurus and Panchalas, not that of the Kasis and Kosalas. But nowhere do they put forward in their earlier books those arrogant claims, as against the Kshatriyas, which are a distinctive feature of the later literature. The kings are their patrons to whom they look up, from whom they hope to receive approval and rewards. And it was not till the time we are now discussing that they put forward claims, which we find still vigorously disputed by all Kshatriyas-and by no means only by those of noble birth (a small minority of the whole) who happen also to be Buddhists.

We find, for instance, that the Jain books take it throughout as a matter of course, that the priests, as regards social standing, are below the nobles. This was the natural relation between the two, as we find throughout the world. Certain priests, in India as elsewhere, had very high social rank-Pokkharasadi and Sonadana for instance. They were somewhat like the great abbots and bishops in our Middle Ages. But as a class, and as a whole, the priests looked up to the nobles, and were considered to be socially beneath them.

Restrictions as to marriage and as to eating together, such as then existed in North India, existed also everywhere throughout the world, among peoples of a similar stage of culture. They are, it is true, the key to the origin of the later Indian caste system. But that system involves much more than these restrictions. And it is no more accurate to speak of caste at the Buddha's time in India, than it would be to speak of it as an established institution, at the same time, in Italy or Greece. There is no word even for caste. The words often wrongly rendered by that modern expression (itself derived from a Portuguese word) have something to do with the question, but do not mean caste.

The Colours (Varna) were not castes. No one of them had any of the distinctive marks of a caste, as the term is now used, and as it always has been used since it was first introduced by Europeans, and there was neither connubium nor commensality between the members of each. Jati is "birth"; and pride of birth may have had to do with the subsequent building up of caste prejudices; but it exists in Europe today, and is an idea very different from that of caste. Kula is "family" or "clan" according to the context. And though the medieval caste system had much to do with families and clans, it is only misleading to confuse terms which are so essentially different, or to read back a medieval idea into these ancient documents. The caste system, in any proper or exact use of the term, did not exist till long afterwards.

Economic Conditions

There has been as yet no attempt to reconstruct a picture of the economic conditions at any period in the early history of India. Professor Zimmer, Dr. Fick, and Professor Hopkins have dealt incidentally with some of the points on the basis respectively of the Vedas, the Jatakas, and the Epics. But generally speaking the books on India have been so exclusively concerned with questions of religion and philosphy, of literature and language, that we seem apt to forget that the very necessities of life, here as elsewhere, must have led the people to occupy their time very much, not to say mostly, with other matters than those, with the earning of their daily bread, with the accumulation and distribution of wealth. The following remarks will be chiefly based on Mrs. Rhys-Davids's articles on this important subject in the Economic Journal, for 1901, and in the Journal of the Royal Asiatic Society, for 1901.

When the King of Magadha, the famous (and infamous) Ajatasattu, made his only call upon the Buddha, he is said to have put a puzzle to the teacher to test him-a puzzle characteristic of the King's state of mind. It is this:

> *"What in the world is the good of your renunciation, of joining an Order like yours? Other people (and here he gives a list), by following ordinary crafts, get something out of them. They can make themselves comfortable in this world, and keep their families in comfort. Can you, Sir, declare to me any such immediate fruit, visible in this world, of the life of a recluse?"*

The list referred to is suggestive. In the view of the King the best examples of such crafts were the following: 1. Elephant-riders. 2. Cavalry. 3. Charioteers. 4. Archers. 5-13. Nine different grades of army folk. 14. Slaves. 15. Cooks. 16. Barbers. 17. Bath-attendants. 18. Confectioners. 19. Garland-makers. 20. Washermen. 21. Weavers. 22. Basket-makers. 23. Potters. 24. Clerks. 25. Accountants.

These are just the sort of people employed about a camp or a palace. King-like, the King considers chiefly those who minister to a king, and are dependent upon him. In the answer he is most politely reminded of the peasant, of the tax-payer, on whom both he and his depended. And it is evident enough from other passages that the King's list is far from exhaustive.

There is mention, in other documents of the same age, of guilds of work-people; and the number of these guilds is often given afterwards as eighteen.

Four of these are mentioned by name. But a list of the whole eighteen has unfortunately not yet been found. It would probably have included the following:

1. The workers in wood. They were not only carpenters and cabinet-makers, but also wheel-wrights; and the builders of houses, and of ships, and of vehicles of all sorts (863).
2. The workers in metal. They made any iron implements-weapons of all kinds, ploughshares, axes, hoes, saws, and knives. But they also did finer work-made needles, for instance, of great lightness and sharpness, or gold and (less often) silver work of great delicacy and beauty (864).
3. The workers in stone. They made flights of steps, leading up into a house or down into a reservoir; faced the reservoir; laid foundations for the woodwork of which the upper part of the houses was built; carved pillars and bas-reliefs; and even did finer work such as making a crystal bowl, or a stone coffer (864). Beautiful examples of these two last were found in the Sakiya Tope.
4. The weavers. They not only made the cloths which the people wrapped round themselves as dress, but manufactured fine muslin for export, and worked costly and dainty fabrics of silk cloth and fur into rugs, blankets, coverlets, and carpets.
5. Leather workers, who made the numerous sorts of foot-covering and sandals worn by the people mostly in cold weather; and also the embroidered and costly articles of the same kind mentioned in the books (865).
6. Potters, who made all sorts of dishes and bowls for domestic use; and often hawked their goods about for sale.

7. Ivory workers, who made a number of small articles in ivory for ordinary use, and also costly carvings and ornaments such as those for which India is still famous (864).
8. Dyers, who coloured the clothes made by the weavers (864).
9. Jewellers, some of whose handiwork has survived, and is also so often represented in bas-reliefs that we know fairly well the shape and size of the ornaments they made.
10. The fisher folk. They fished only in the rivers. There is no mention of sea-fishing known to me.
11. The butchers, whose shops and slaughterhouses are several times mentioned (873).
12. Hunters and trappers, mentioned in various passages as bringing the animal and vegetable products of the woods, and also venison and game, for sale on carts into the city (873). It is doubtful whether they were formed into guilds. But their industry was certainly a very important one. The large stretches of forest, open to all, separating most of the settlements; the absence of any custom of breeding cattle for the meat-market; the large demand for ivory, fur, sinews, creepers, and all the other produce of the woods; and the congeniality of the occupation, all tended to encourage the hunters. And there is no reason to suppose that the very ancient instinct of the chase was confined to the so-called savages. The kings and nobles also, whether Aryan by blood or not, seem to have taken pleasure in it, quite apart from the economic question of food supply. But men of good birth followed it as a trade; and when Brahmins did so (868) they are represented as doing so for profit.
13. The cooks and confectioners, a numerous class, probably formed a guild. But there is no passage saying that they did.
14. The barbers and shampooers had their guilds. They dealt in perfumes, and were especially skilled in arranging the elaborate turbans worn by the wealthier classes.

15. The garland-makers and flower-sellers (866).
16. Sailors, occupied for the most part in the traffic up and down the great rivers, but also going to sea. In some of our earliest documents we hear of sea voyages out of sight of land; and in the later documents, such as the Jatakas, the mention of such voyages is frequent (872). So the earlier documents speak of voyages lasting six months made in ships (nava, perhaps, "boats") which could be drawn up on shore in the winter, And later texts, of about the third century BC, speak of voyages down the Ganges from Benares to the mouth of the river and thence across the Indian Ocean to the opposite coast of Burma; and even from Bharukaccha (the modern Baroch) round Cape Comorin to the same destination (871). It is clear, therefore, that during the whole of this period the occupation of sailor was neither unfrequent nor unimportant.
17. The rush-workers and basket-makers (868).
18. Painters (865). They were mostly house-painters. The woodwork of the houses was often covered with fine chunam plaster and decorated with painting. But they also painted frescoes. These passages tell us of pleasure-houses, adorned with painted figures and patterns, belonging to the kings of Magadha and Kosala; and such frescoes were no doubt similar in character to, but of course in an earlier style than, the well-known ancient frescoes of the seventh and eighth centuries AD on the Ajanta Caves, and of the fifth century on the Sigiri Rock in Ceylon.

It is doubtful with regard to two or three in this list whether they were organised in guilds (seniyo, puga). But it is certain that these were among the most important branches of handicraft apart from agriculture; and most of them had, no doubt, their guilds not unlike the medieval guilds in Europe. It is through their guilds that the king summons the people on important occasions (865). The Aldermen or Presidents (pamukha) of such guilds are sometimes described as quite important persons, wealthy, favourites at the court. The guilds are said to have had powers of arbitration between the members of the guild and their wives.

And disputes between one guild and another were in the jurisdiction of the maha-sethi, the Lord High Treasurer, who acted as a sort of chief Alderman over the Aldermen of the guilds (865).

Besides the peasantry and the handicraftsmen there were merchants who conveyed their goods either up and down the great rivers, or along the coasts in boats; or right across country in carts travelling in caravans. These caravans, long lines of small two-wheeled carts, each drawn by two bullocks, were a distinctive feature of the times. There were no made roads and no bridges. The carts struggled along, slowly, through the forests, along the tracks from village to village kept open by the peasants. The pace never exceeded two miles an hour. Smaller streams were crossed by gullies leading down to fords, the larger ones by cart ferries. There were taxes and octroi duties at each different country entered (875); and a heavy item in the cost was the hire of volunteer police who let themselves out in bands to protect caravans against robbers on the way (866). The cost of such carriage must have been great; so great that only the more costly goods could bear it.

The enormous traffic of today in the carriage of passengers, food-stuffs, and fuel was non-existent. Silks, muslins, the finer sorts of cloth and cutlery and armour, brocades, embroideries and rugs, perfumes and drugs, ivory and ivory work, jewellery and gold (seldom silver),-these were the main articles in which the merchant dealt.

The older system of traffic by barter had entirely passed away never to return. The later system of a currency of standard and token coins issued and regulated by government authority had not yet arisen. Transactions were carried on, values estimated, and bargains struck in terms of the kahapana, a square copper coin weighing about 146 grains, and guaranteed as to weight and fineness by punch-marks made by private individuals. Whether these punch-marks are the tokens of merchants, or of guilds, or simply of the bullion dealer, is not certain (874).

No silver coins were used (877). There were half and quarter kahapanas, and probably no other sort. The references to gold coins are late and doubtful; and no such coins have been found. Some thin gold films with punch marks on them were found in the Sakiya Tope, but these are too flimsy to have been used in circulation as coins (878). It is interesting to notice that Alexander, when in India, struck a half kahapana copper piece, square (in imitation of the Indian money), and not round like the Greek coins of the time. It is only in later times that we hear (as for instance in Manu, 8. 401) of any market price being fixed by government regulation. In the sixth century BC there is only an official called the Valuer, whose duty it was to settle the prices of goods ordered for the palace-which is a very different thing (875). And there are many instances, incidentally given, of the prices of commodities fixed, at different times and places, by the haggling of the market (875). These are all collected together in the article referred to (at pp. 882, foll.); and the general result seems to be that though the kahapana would be worth, at the present value of copper, only five sixths of a penny, its purchasing power then was about equivalent to the purchasing power of a shilling now.

.Besides the coins, there was a very considerable use of instruments of credit. The great merchants in the few large towns gave letters of credit on one another. And there is constant reference to promissory notes (879). The rates of interest are unfortunately never stated. But interest itself is mentioned very early; and the law books give the rate of interest current at a somewhat later date for loans on personal security as about eighteen per cent. per annum (881).

There were no banking facilities. Money was hoarded either in the house, or buried in jars in the ground, or deposited with a friend, a written record of the transaction being kept (881).

The details of prices above referred to enable us to draw some conclusion as to the spending power of the poor, of the man of the middle classes, and of the wealthy merchants and nobles respectively. Of want, as known in our great cities, there is no evidence. It is put down as the direst misfortune known that a free man had to work for hire. And there was plenty of land to be had for the trouble of clearing it, not far from the settled districts.

On the other hand, the number of those who could be considered wealthy from the standards of those times (and of course still more so from our own) was very limited. We hear of about a score of monarchs, whose wealth consisted mainly of the land tax, supplemented by other dues and perquisites; of a considerable number of wealthy nobles, and some priests, to whom grants had been made of the tithe arising out of certain parishes or counties or who had inherited similar rights from their forefathers; of about a dozen millionaire merchants in Takkasila, Savatthi, Benares, Rajagaha, Vesali, Koshambi, and the seaports (882), and of a considerable number of lesser merchants and middlemen, all in the few towns. But these were the exceptions. There were no landlords. And the great mass of the people were well-to-do peasantry, or handicrafts-men, mostly with land of their own, both classes ruled over by local headmen of their own selection.

Before closing this summary of the most important economic conditions in Northern India in the sixth century BC it may be well to bring together the few notices we have in the books about the trade routes. There is nothing about them in the pre-Buddhistic literature. In the oldest Pali books we have accounts of the journeys of the wandering teachers; and as, especially for longer journeys, they will generally have followed already established routes, this is incidental evidence of such as were then in use by traders. Later on, we have accounts of routes actually followed by merchants, either on boats, or with their caravans of bullock carts. We can thus draw up provisionally the following list:

1. North to South-west. Savatthi to Patilahana (Paithan) and back. The principal stopping places are given (beginning from the south) as Mahissati, Ujjeni, Gonaddha, Vedisa, Koshambi, and Saketa.
2. North to South-east. Savatthi to Rajagaha. It is curious that the route between these two ancient cities is never, so far as I know, direct, but always along the foot of the mountains to a point north of Vesali, and only then turning south to the Ganges. By taking this circuitous road the rivers were crossed at places close to the hills where the fords were more easy to pass. But political considerations may also have had their weight in the original choice of this route, still followed when they were no longer of much weight. The stopping places were (beginning at Savatthi), Setavya,

Kapilavastu, Kusinara, Pava, Hatthi-gama, Veshali, Pataliputra, and Nalanda. The road probably went on to Gaya, and there met another route from the coast, possibly at Tamralipti, to Benares.

3. East to West. The main route was along the great rivers, along which boats plied for hire. We even hear of express boats. Upwards the rivers were used along the Ganges as far west as Sahajati, and along the Jumna as far west as Koshambi. Downwards, in later times at least, the boats went right down to the mouths of the Ganges, and thence either across or along the coast to Burma. In the early books we hear only of the traffic downward as far as Magadha, that is, to take the farthest point, Champa. Upwards it went thence to Koshambi, where it met the traffic from the south (Route 1), and was continued by cart to the south-west and north-west.

Besides the above we are told of traders going from Videha to Gandhara, from Magadha to Sovira, from Bharukaccha round the coast to Burma, from Benares down the river to its mouth and thence on to Burma, from Champa to the same destination. In crossing the desert west of Rajputana the caravans are said to travel only in the night, and to be guided by a "land-pilot," who, just as one does on the ocean, kept the right route by observing the stars. The whole description of this journey is too vividly accurate to life to be an invention. So we may accept it as evidence not only that there was a trade route over the desert, but also that pilots, guiding ships or caravans by the stars only, were well known.

In the solitary instance of a trading journey to Babylon (Baveru) we are told that it was by sea, but the port of departure is not mentioned. There is one story, the worldwide story of the Sirens, who are located in Tambapanai-dipa, a sort of fairy land, which is probably meant for Ceylon. Lanka does not occur. Traffic with China is first mentioned in the Milinda (pp. 127, 327, 359), which is some centuries later.

8

Brahminical Religious Text and Caste System

Varna Ashram and Hindu Scriptures

Introduction: The 'Varna' popularly known as the 'Caste system' is perhaps the most explosive topics in Hinduism, which so often gives handle to Non-Hindus to bash Hinduism. Popular misconceptions say that the Vedic religion encourages division of human beings based on one's birth. As a result, some people have been kept backward and uneducated while others have abused this misconceptions and misinformation for personal gains. Much of this misconception can be attributed to the use of the words 'Varna' and 'Jati' interchangeably. A closer analysis will reveal just how wrong these misconceptions are.

Caste: "The word caste is not a word that is indigenous to India. It originates in the Portuguese word casta which means race, breed, race or lineage. However, during the 19th century, the term caste increasingly took on the connotations of the word race. Thus, from the very beginning of western contact with the subcontinent European constructions have been imposed on Indian systems and institutions. The caste system had been a fascination of the British since their arrival in India.

Coming from a society that was divided by class, the British attempted to equate the caste system to the class system. As late as 1937 Professor T. C. Hodson stated that: "Class and caste stand to each other in the relation of family to species. The general classification is by classes, the detailed one by castes. The former represents the external, the latter the internal view of the social organization."

The difficulty with definitions such as this is that class is based on political and economic factors, caste is not. Caste was seen as the essence of Indian society, the system through which it was possible to classify all of the various groups of indigenous people according to their ability, as reflected by caste, to be of service to the British. It was not until 1872 that a planned comprehensive census was attempted. This was done under the direction of Henry Beverely, Inspector General of Registration in Bengal. The census went well beyond counting heads or even enquiring into sex ratios or general living conditions. Among the many questions were enquiries regarding nationality, race, tribe, religion and caste." (from The Indian Caste System and the British, by Kevin Hobson).

Varna: The root word for Varna is 'Vri' which means one's occupation. The Varna Dharma was based on division of labour. This division was solely based on the attitude of an individual and his/her propensity for performing certain duties according to Gunas (qualities). There are three Gunas-Sattva (white), Rajas (red), and Tamas (black).

Jati: The Root word for 'jati' is 'jan', which means Birth.

The Issue: The issue of Varna Dharma is highly misunderstood. There are many issues and reasons for the decline of Varna Dharma. A key point in the Varna Dharma is the definition and Gunas associated with various classes of Varnas. This paper deals with following two main issues;

- Definition and duties of the Varna Dharma
- Basis of division-Gunas or birth

Supremacy of Vedas

First part in the understanding of Varna Dharma is to accept supremacy of Vedas in all the Hindu scriptures. As Swami Vivekananda said "The Vedas are our only authority, thus says the Shukla Yajur Veda (XXVI, 2). The Smritis, Puranas, Tantras-all these are acceptable as far as they agree the Vedas; and wherever they are contradictory, they are to be rejected as unreliable".

Even Manu Smriti declares that the Vedas are the supreme authority. The knowledge of the sacred law is prescribed for those who are not given to the acquisition of wealth and to the gratification of their desires; to those who seek the knowledge of the sacred law the supreme authority the revelation (Sruti).

What Constitutes Vedic Knowledge

The second part in the understanding of Varna Dharma is what constitutes Vedic knowledge.

Nirukta says on this topic; "He, who reads the Vedas even with proper accents, but does not know their meanings, is like a tree weighed down by its fruit, branches, leaves and flowers, or like a beast of burden carrying on its back grain which it can not eat. But he, who understands their meanings and acts up to their teachings by avoiding sin and leading a virtuous life, enjoys perfect happiness in this world, and eternal bliss hereafter in consequence thereof", Nirukta 1, 18. Once supremacy of Vedas and the meanings of Vedic education are understood, all the doubts about Varna Dharma will evaporate. There is no division in Vedic knowledge. The division is in our ignorance.

Origin of Varnas

The first reference to the origin of Varna Dharma comes from the Rig Veda and subsequently explained in the Gita and Smritis (*e.g.* Manu, Prashar etc.).

Rigveda: The Purusa Sukta has the first reference to the origin of four groups. The Brahmana (spiritual wisdom and splendour) was His Mouth; the Kshatriya (administrative and military prowess) His Arms became. His Thighs the Vaishya (commercial and business enterprise) was; of His Feet the Sudra (productive and sustaining force) was born. (by Swami Krishnananda The Divine Life Society Sivananda Ashram, Rishikesh, India)

Gita: The Gita elaborates on the origin of Varnas. "The fourfold order was created by Me according to the divisions of quality (Guna) and work (karma); though I am its creator, know Me to be incapable of action or change." (from The Bhagawad Gita by S. Radhakrishnan)

Definition and Duties of Varnas

Brahman (the Supreme Reality) is not known to those who are possessed of avarice, delusion, fear, egotism, lust, anger, and sin or possessed of (unable to bear) heat and cold, hunger and thirst, or mental resolve and indecision, or pride of birth in a Brahmin (priest) family, or vanity in having read a mass of books on Mukti (liberation or salvation).

Gita: "There is no being on earth, or again in heaven among the gods, that is liberated from the three qualities (Sattva, Rajas, and Tamas) born of Nature." "Of Brahmans, Kshatriyas and Vaishyas, as also the Sudras, O Arjuna, the duties are distributed according to the qualities born of their own nature."

"Serenity, self-restraint, austerity, purity, forgiveness and also uprightness, knowledge, realization and belief in God are the duties of the Brahmans, born of their own nature."

"Prowess, splendour, firmness, dexterity and also not fleeing from battle, generosity and lordliness are the duties of Kshatriyas, born of their own nature."

"Agriculture, cattle-rearing and trade are the duties of the Vaishya merchant class), born of their own nature; and action consisting of service is the duty of the Sudras, born of their own nature." (All meanings from Srimad Bhagawad Gita by Swami Chinmayananda)

Varna by Birth: The next issue in the Varna system is to understand the order and how to belong to one Varna. Is it by birth or by 'guna'.

Channdogaya Upanishad: The following story (Channdogaya Upanishad, 4.1.4) reveals that Brahminhood does not depend on birth but on character and Gunas.

"Satyakama, the son of Jabala, addressed his mother and said "I wish to become a brahmacharin, mother. Of what family am I?" She said to him: I do not know, my child, of what family thou art. In my youth, when I had to move about much as a servant, I conceived thee. So I do not know of what family thou art. I am Jabala by name. Thou art Satyakama. Say that thouart Satyakama Jabala."

He going to Gautama, the son of Haridrumat, said to him: I wish to become a brahmacharin with thee, Sire. May I come to you?

He said to him, "Of what family art thou, my friend?"

He replied: "I do not know, Sire, of what family I am. I asked my mother, and she answered: "In my youth, when I had to move about much as a servant, I conceived thee. So I do not know of what family thou art. I am Jabala by name. Thou art Satyakama.' I am therefore Satyakama Jabala, Sire."

He said to him" "No one but a true Brahmin would speak out. Go and fetch fuel, I shall initiate thee. Thou has not swerved from the truth."

Vajra Suchikopanishad: I now proceed to declare the vajrasuuchi-the weapon that is the destroyer of ignorance-which condemns the ignorant and praises the man of divine vision.

There are four castes-the Brahman, the Kshatriya, the vaishya, and the shudra. Even the smritis declare in accordance with the words of the Vedas that the Brahman alone is the most important of them.

Then this needs to be examined. What is meant by the Brahman? Is it a jiva ? Is it a body ? Is it a class? It is Gyana? Is it karma? Or is it a doer of Dharma?

To begin with: is jiva the Brahman? No. Since the jiva is the same in the many past and future bodies (of all persons), and since the jiva is the same in all of the many bodies obtained through the force of karma, there jiva is not the Brahman. Then is the body the Brahman? No. Since the body, as it is made up of the five elements, is the same for all people down to chandalas, etc., since old age and death, dharma and adharma are found to be common to them all, since there is no absolute distinction that the Brahmans are white-coloured, the Kshatriyas red, the vaishyas yellow, and the shudras dark, and since in burning the corpse of his father, etc., the stain of the murder of a Brahman, etc., will accrue to the son, etc., therefore the body is not the Brahman.

Then is a class the Brahman? No. Since many rishis have sprung from other castes and orders of creation-Rishyashringa was born of deer; kaushika, of kusha grass; jaambuka of a jackal; Valmiki of valmika (an ant-hill); Vyasa of a fisherman's daughter; Gautama, of the posteriors of a hare; Vashishtha of Urvasi (a celestial nymph in the court of Indra); and agastya of a water-pot; thus have we heard. Of these, many rishis outside the caste have stood first among the teachers of divine wisdom; therefore a class is not the Brahman.

Is Gyana the Brahman? No. Since there were many Kshatriyas and others well versed in the cognition of divine Truth, therefore Gyana is not the Brahman.

Then is karma the Brahman? No. Since the prarabdha, sanchita, aagami karmas are the same for all beings, and since all people perform their actions impelled by karma, therefore karma is not the Brahman.

Then is the doer of dharma (virtuous actions) the Brahman? No. Since there are many Kshatriyas, etc., who are givers of gold, therefore a doer of virtuous actions is not the Brahman.

Who indeed then is Brahman ? Whoever he may be, he who has directly realised his aatmaa and who is directly cognizant, like the myrobalan in his palm, of his aatmaa, that is without a second, that is devoid of class and actions, that is free from the faults of the six stains (hunger, thirst, grief, confusion, old age, and death) and the six changes (birth, existence etc.), that is of the nature of truth, knowledge, bliss and eternity, that is without any change in itself, that is the substratum of all the kalpas, that exists penetrating all things that pervades everything within and without as aakaash, that is of nature of undivided bliss, that cannot be reasoned about and that is known only by direct cognition. He who by the reason of having obtained his wishes is devoid of the faults of thirst after worldly objects and passions, who is the possessor of the qualifications beginning with saama (dama, uparati, titikshaa, samadhana, sraddha), who is free from emotion, malice, thirst after worldly objects, desire, delusion, etc., whose mind is untouched by pride, egoism, etc., who possesses all these qualities and means-he only is the Brahman. Such is the opinion of the veda, the smritis, the itihasa, and the puranas. Otherwise one cannot obtain the status of a Brahman. One should meditate on his aatma as sachchidananda, and the non-dual Brahman. Yea, one should meditate on his aatma as the sachchidananda Brahman. Such is the Upanishad.

Right to Study Vedas

Contrary to existing view everyone irrespective of caste or sex, has right to read the Veda or hear it read.

Yajur Veda: "As I have given this Word (*i.e.* the four Vedas) which is the word of salvation for all making-Brahmans, Kshatriyas, Vaishyas, Sudras, women, servants, aye, even the lowest of the low, so shoul you all do, *i.e.* teach and preach Veda. Let all men therefore read and recite, teach, and preach the Veda and thereby acquire true knowledge, practice virtue, shun vice, and consequently being freed from all sorrow and pain, enjoy true happiness." 26,2 (translated from Sayarth Prakash, Ch 3, page 78).

Atharva Veda: "Just as boys acquire sound knowledge and culture by the practice of Brahmacharya and then marry girls of their own choice, who are young, well educated, loving and of like temperament, so should a girl practice Brahmacharya, study the Veda and other sciences and there by perfect her knowledge, refine her character, give her hand to a man of her own choice, who is young, learned and loving." (Xl, xvi, 3, 18.)

Brahma-Sutras: "Apasudradhikaranam: Topic 9 (Sutras 34-38) The right of the Sudras to the study of Vedas discussed Sugasya tadanadarasravanat tadadravanat suchyate hi I.3.34 (97) Suk: grief; Asya: his; Tat: that, namely that grief; Anadarasravanat: from hearing his (the Rishi's) disrespectful speech; Tada: then; Adravanat: because of going to him i.e, to Raikva; Suchyate: is referred to; Hi: because. (King Janasruti) was in grief on hearing some contemptuous words used about him by the sage in the form of a swan; owing to his approaching Raikva, overwhelming with that grief, Raikva called him Sudra; for it (the grief) is pointed at by Raikva.

The Purvapakshin says: The Sudras also have got bodies and desires. Hence they are also entitled. Raikva refers to Janasruti who wishes to learn from him by the name of Sudra. "Fie, necklace and carriage be thine, O Sudra, together with the cows" Chh. Up.

IV-2 & 3. But when he appears a second time, Raikva accepts his presents and teaches him. Smriti speaks of Vidura and others who were born from Sudra mothers as possessing highest knowledge. Therefore the Sudra has a claim to Brahma Vidya or knowledge of Brahman. This Sutra refutes the view and denies the right to the study of the Vedas for Sudra. The word 'Sudra' does not denote a Sudra by birth which is its conventional meaning, because Janasruti was a Kshatriya king. Here we will have to take the etymological meaning of the word which is, "He rushed into grief (Sukam abhi dudrava) or as "grief rushed on him" or as "he in his grief rushed to Raikva". The following Sutra also intimates that he was a Kshatriya.

Kshatriyatva: the state of his being a Kshatriya; Avagateh: on account of being known or understood; Cha: and; Uttaratra: latter on in a subsequent part of the text; Chaitrarathena: with Chaitraratha; Lingat: because of the indicatory sign or the inferential mark.

And because the Kshatriyahood (of Janasruti) is known from the inferential mark (supplied by his being mentioned) later on with Chaitraratha (who was a Kshatriya himself).

An argument in support of Sutra 34 is given. Janasruti is mentioned with the Kshatriya Chaitraratha Abhipratarin in connection with the same Vidya. Hence we can infer that Janasruti also was a Kshatriya because, as a rule, equals are mentioned together with equals. Hence the Sudras are not qualified for the knowledge of Brahman.

Samskaraparamarsat tadabhavabhilapacca (I.3.36) (99) Samskara: the purificatory ceremonies, the investiture with sacred thread; Paramarsat: because of the reference; Tat: that ceremony; Abhava: absence; Abhilapat: because of the declaration; Cha: and. Because purificatory ceremonies are mentioned (in the case of the twice-born) and their absence is declared (in the case of the Sudra).

The discussion on the privilege of Brahma Vidya on the part of Sudras is continued. In different places of the Vidyas the Upanayana ceremony is referred to. The Upanayana ceremony is declared by the scriptures to be a necessary condition for the study of all kinds of knowledge or Vidya. We read in Prasna Up. I-1

"Devoted to Brahman, firm in Brahman, seeking for the highest Brahman they, carrying fuel in their hands, approached the venerable Pippalada, thinking that he would teach them all that." Upanayana ceremony is meant for the higher castes. With reference to the Sudras on the other hand, the absence of ceremonies is frequently mentioned in the scriptures. "In the Sudra there is not any sin by eating prohibited food, and he is not fit for any ceremony" Manu X-12-6. A Sudra by birth cannot have Upanayana and other Samskaras without which the Vedas cannot be studied. Hence the Sudras are not entitled to the study of the Vedas. The next Sutra further strengthens the view that a Sudra can have no Samskara.

And on account of the prohibition in Smriti of (the Sudras) hearing, studying and understanding (the Veda) and performing Vedic rites (they are not entitled to the knowledge of Brahman).

Note: Sutras 34-38 of Brahma-Sutras disqualify the Sudras for the Knowledge of Brahman (Supreme Reality) through the study of the Vedas. But it is possible for them to attain that Knowledge through the Puranas and the epics (Ramayana and the Mahabharata)."

"Wherever it is declared (in the books of Rishis) that the Sudras are debarred from the study of the Veda, the prohibition simply amounts to this that he, that does not learn anything even after a good deal of teaching, being ignorant and destitute of understanding, is called a Sudra. It is useless for him to learn and for others to teach him any longer." Satyarth Prakash, chapter 3, 78.

Inter Movement in Varna

Can people by their actions move from one Varna to another? The answer is YES, which is another argument in favour of Varna not based on birth.

Gita: "By following his qualities of work, every man can become perfect. Now please hear from Me how this can be done. (By A. C Bhaktivedanta Swami Prabhupada)."

From Whom is the evolution of all beings, by Whom all this is pervaded, worshipping Him with one's own duty, man attains Perfection. (by Swami Chinmayananda)

Better is one's own duty (though) destitute of merits, than the duty of another wellperformed. He who does the duty ordained by his own nature incurs no sin. (by Swami Chinmayananda)

One should not give up the work suited to one's nature, O Son of Kunti (Arjuna), though it may be defective, for all enterprises are clouded by defects as fire by smoke. (The Bhagavadgita by S. Radhakrishnan).

Apastamba Sutras: "A low Class man may, by leading a virtuous life, rise to the level of a higher Class man and should be ranked as such. In like manner a high Class man can by leading a sinful life, sink down to the level of a Class lower than his, and should be considered as such." (Translation from Stayarth Prakash, chapter 4, page 100)

Manu Smriti

The scriptures are quoted out of context as if they are stand alone political statements. Manu Smriti is not very entertaining for Sudras is true, only when not understood properly. People take pride in quoting from Manu Smriti to show their knowledge and understanding, and also to put down Varna Dharma. A careful reading will give a different picture. Manu Smriti is very infamous for treatment of Sudras by popular belief. There are shlokas in Manu Smriti that debars a Sudra from learning any Vedic knowledge when read in isolation and not as one part of a scripture. The maximum damage to Varna Dharma was caused by piece meal acquisition and application of knowledge. Manu Smriti deals with all the four Varnas and not only Sudras. The first issue with Manu Smriti is what Vedic knowledge is and what different Varnas are.

Definitions and Duties of Varna: "The study of true sciences, the practice of Brahmacharya, the performance of Homa, the acceptance of truth and rejection of untruth, the dissemination of true knowledge, leading a virtuous life as enjoined by the Veda, the performance of seasonal Homa, the reproduction of good children, faithful discharge of the Five Great Daily Duties, and doing such other good works as are productive of beneficial results to the community, such as developing technical arts, association with the good and the learned, truthfulness in word, deed and thought, and devotion to public good and like, all these things go to make a Brahma.

To Brahmans he assigned teaching and studying (the Veda), sacrificing for their own benefit and for others, giving and accepting (of alms).

Inter Movement of Varnas: "As the son of a Sudra may attain the rank of a Brahmin if he were to possess his qualifications, character and accomplishments, and as the son of a Brahmin may become a Sudra, if he sinks to his level in his character, inclinations and manners, even so must it be with him who springs from a Kshatriya; even so with him who is born of a Vaishya.

In other words, a person should be ranked with the Class whose qualifications, accomplishments, and character he possesses.

> *"A Dwija as well his children who, instead of studying the Veda, wastes his time in doing other things soon goes down to the level of a Shudra." Manu Smriti 2, 168*
>
> *"A twice-born man who, not having studied the Veda, applies himself to other (and worldly study), soon falls, even while living, to the condition of a Sudra and his descendants (after him)." Manu Smriti 2, 168.*

Special Treatment for Brahmans!: It is true that not very complementary and rude things were said about Sudras in Manu Smriti. But as shown in Manu Smriti (discussed in the definition section) that the position of Brahmin's was full of responsibility and not privileges. In (a case of) theft the guilt of a Sudra shall be eightfold, that of a Vaishya sixteen fold, that of a Kshatriya two-and-thirty fold, 8,337

That of a Brahmana sixty-fourfold, or quite a hundredfold, or (even) twice four-and-sixtyfold; (each of them) knowing the nature of the offence. 8,338 Guna or Birth-The Deciding Factor.

> *"A Brahmana who departs from the rule of conduct, does not reap the fruit of the Veda, but he who duly follows it, will obtain the full reward. (Manu Smriti 1,109)."*
>
> *"Declares out Manu: Take the jewel of a woman for your wife, though she be of inferior descent. Learn supreme knowledge*

with service even from the man of low birth; and even from the Chandala, learn by serving him the way to salvation."

Is Breakdown in Varna Unexpected?

Prashar Smriti: Smriti created by sage Parashar and known by his name as 'Parashar Smriti, is the most benevolent for the modern Kali Yuga. Parashar has himself said:

Krite Tu Manavo Dharmastretayaam Gautamo Smritah ||

Dwapare Shankhalikhitaa Kalau Parasharah Smritah ||

Meaning-Manu Smriti was most relevant in Satya Yuga. In Treta, Smriti created by Gautam had most relevance whereas in Dwapar, Shankh's Smriti was mostly recognized. But in Kali Yuga, it is Parashar Smriti that by and large shows the way to the ignorant people.

Sri Ramacharitamanasa: Sri Ramacharitamanasa, Uttar-kanda, verses 97-98, explains very clearly that what happened and happening to Varna Dharma.

"No one follows the duties of one's own caste, and the four Dharms or stages of life also disappear. Every man and woman takes delight in revolting against the Vedas. The Brahmans sell the Vedas; the kings bleed their subjects; no one respects the injunction of the Vedas. The right course for every individual is that which one takes a fancy to; a man of erudition is he who plays the braggart.

Whoever launches spurious undertakings and is given over to hypocrisy, him does everyone call a saint. He alone is clever, who robs another of his wealth; he who puts up false appearances is an ardent follower of established usage. He who is given to lying and is clever at joking is spoken of as a man of parts in the Kali age. He alone who is a reprobate and has abandoned the path of the Vedas is a man of wisdom and dispassion in the Kali age. He alone who has grown big nails and long locks of matted hair is a renowned ascetic in the Kali age. (1-4)"

What went Wrong?: Swami Dayananda Saraswati (founder of Arya Samaj) has discussed this issue (downfall of Varna Dharma) very nicely in Satyarth Prakash and it states as:

"When the Brahmans became destitute of knowledge, there could be no talk of the ignorance of the Kshatriyas, Vaishyas and Shudras. Even the ancient practice of the study of the Vedas and other Shastras with their meanings died away. The Brahmans only learnt the Vedas by note-just enough to enable them to earn their livelihood. Even that much they did teach to the Kshatriyas, and others.

As the ignorant became the teachers of the people, deceitfulness, fraud, hypocrisy, and irreligion began to increase among them. The Brahmans thought that they should make some arrangement for their livelihood. They held a council among themselves and agreed to preach to the Kshatriyas and others: "We alone are the object of worship to you. You could never enter Heaven or obtain salvation except by serving us. Should you not serve us, you shall fall into an awful Hell."

The Vedas, and the Shastras written by the Vedic sages and seers have declared men of learning and as Brahmans and worthy of respect; but here they, who were ignorant, lascivious, deceitful, licentious, lazy and irreligious, declared themselves as Brahmans and worthy of homage. But how could the sterling virtues of the righteous, learned and truth-loving Brahmans be found in them. When the Kshatriyas and others became absolutely destitute of Sanskrit learning, whatever cock and bull stories the Brahmans concocted, the simpletons believed. They ensnared all in their net of hypocrisy, brought them under thorough control and began to teach:-"Whatever a Brahman declares is as infallible as words falling from Divine lips."

Conclusions: The most important issue in the understanding of Varna Dharma is to understand the definitions of the various Varnas as explained in Hindu scriptures. The rules of the groups prescribe the duties to society. The duties for various Varnas were based on the 'guna' of an individual and were dependent on the capacities of individuals. Therefore the division of labour, which broadly falls into 'the four orders of human beings' is based upon "guna and karma" of each individual.

"The complete definition of the Varna not only removes our present misunderstanding but also provides us with some data to understand its true significance. Not by mere birth is man

a Brahmana (Brahmin); by cultivating good intentions and noble thoughts alone can we ever aspire to Brahmana-hood; nor can we pose as Brahmana merely because of our external physical marks, or bodily actions in the outer world. The definition insists that he alone is a Brahmana, whose thoughts are as much Sattvik, as his actions are. A Kshatriya is one who is Rajasik in his thoughts and actions. A Sudra is not only one whose thoughts are Tamasik, but he who lives a life of low endeavours, for satisfying his base animal passions and flesh-appetites. The scientific attitude in which this definition has been declared, is clear from the exhaustive implications of the statement: "According to the differentiation of 'guna' and 'karma'."

As discussed earlier, there was no exclusion of any Varna to read Vedic Knowledge in the Veda. Later on restriction were put on people because of with Tamsic Guna. There was a structured and step-wise approach to learning which everyone was supposed to follow.

All Dwij's were following that system of learning. No Vedic knowledge was given even to Dwij's who do not follow the process of learning. With time this (not learning Vedas) became a rule in the society which led to consolidation of Vedic knowledge in very few peoples hand. If a tumbler is full of dirt, grease and other impurities, then it is an unfit receptacle for holding pure water. The mind is the container and if it is filled with Tamasic qualities, then it is an unfit receptacle for receiving pure spiritual knowledge.

"It is written in Chhandogya Upanishad that Gragee and other women of yore have read the Veda, and even Janshruti, a Sudra by birth, has studied the Veda under Raikyamuni" Satyarth Prakash, chapter 11.

Brahma Sutras and Manu Smriti discuss that Sudras can not study Veda. But the important issue is to know who Sudra is. Why he can not study the Vedas.

As explained in the section on "Inter-movement in Varna Dharma" section, when Sudra can become a Brahman then he has all the right to study the Veda. The restriction placed on the study of Vedas is because of absence of the process (character, capability, and/or prerequisite) to study the Vedas.

The issue is not whether Varna Dharma is based on birth or not, nor whether Brahmans are higher Varna than any other. These may be important but not sufficient. If Sudras are not Sudra by birth then Brahmans are not Brahmans by birth alone too. This must be an important aspect in the equation in any meaningful discussion about Varna Dharma.

There was no pecking order (higher or lower) in the society according to scriptures. Individuals were identified by their knowledge. The reverence given to a person in society (based on his knowledge) was a responsibility and not a privilege. All men are not equally wise or equally intelligent. Each one is trying to grapple with problems of life with whatever degree of wisdom each possesses. Hinduism provides for the highly evolved as well as those not so evolved or least evolved and even those not at all evolved in distinct categories of Brahimn, Kshatriya, Vaishya and Sudra with distinct Svadharma (assigned duties) suited to their individual state of evolution.

Realisation is not dependent on birth or book-learning as has been repeatedly demonstrated in the lives of saints, from the very earliest times to our own day (Comments by Swami Madhavananda, Advaita Ashrama).

> *"Who are Rishis? Vatsyayana says, He who has attained through proper means the direct realization of Dharma, he alone can be a Rishi even if he is a Mlechcha by birth"*

Many great Rishis were born in lower castes (*e.g.*) Vashishtha was the son of a prostitute; VYASA was born of a fisher woman; PARASARA's mother was a chandala; Nammalwar was a Sudra. Similarly Valmiki, Vishvamitra, Agastya were Brahmins inspite of their non-Brahmin origin. Swami Vivekananda is one of the most revered Hindu worldwide and was a non Brahmin. All these Hindus prove that birth was not a major player in attaining Brahminhood. It is the intellectual and spiritual level that differentiates people.

Swami Sivananda (The Divine Life Society, Rishikesh), in his commentary on Gita,Ch.18, verses 41,and 45 says: "Mankind is organised into the four castes and each man`s life is divided into four stages, according to the nature of the Gunas and the degree of growth or evolution. This is the division of labour for which each caste is fitted according to its own nature.

The duty prescribed is your sole support, each devoted to his own duty in accordance with his own nature or caste, and the highest service you can render to the Supreme is to carry it out wholeheartedly, without expectation of fruits, with the attitude of dedication to the Lord. The caste system is, indeed, a splendid thing. It is quite flawless. But the defect came in from somewhere else. The classes gradually neglected their duties. The test of ability and character slowly vanished. Birth became the chief consideration in determining castes. All castes fell from their ideals and forgot all about their duties."

Scriptures treated all the Varnas as same and none was higher than the other. And nobody belongs to any Varna by birth. Vajra Suchikopanishad clearly states that one cannot be a Brahmin either by its being, birth, physical equipment of body and colour or by wisdom and knowledge or by religious action even The basis of Varna was guna and not birth. Vajra suchikopanishad of Sama Veda defines the word Brahmin in most unambiguous terms thus: One is a Brahmin not because of his birth or caste or heredity or colour or profession or acquisition of worldly knowledge or mere observation of social and moral codes, but because of his spiritual knowledge, his abidance in the Supreme Reality, his state of self-realization.

This is the conclusion of all Veda, Srutis, Puranas, Itihasas and of all great men of India.

According to 'Guru Bala Prabodhika' a commentary on Amara Kosa, the ancient Sanskrit lexicon, a Brahmin is one who knows Brahman (Supreme God), not one who is borne into a caste. (Brahmin Parabrahmani nishtatwat Brahmana).

One of the main reasons for confusion about Varnas is that there is a vast amount of scriptures in the Hindu Dharma. People do not always know the order of the scriptures. Even when the order is known, the scriptures are not easily interpreted since all scriptures are written in Sanskrit. Even the people who can interpret the scriptures not necessarily understand them. The confusion is not what is written originally in Sanskrit but in the misunderstanding of the Sanskrit translations. The first issue in understanding of Varna Dharma is to understand the order of the scriptures. The Vedas are the ultimate authority in Hindu Dharma. The second issue is to understand that Varna Ashram is evolutionary in nature.

A key issue in understanding of Varna lies in knowledge of Sanskrit. There was and is no misunderstanding about Varnas as written in Sanskrit. The Varna Ashram started falling apart when the original Sanskrit work is translated in to English, especially by the people who do not have command over both languages (Sanskrit and English) and with limited knowledge about the scriptures.

There are many words and terms in Sanskrit which have no equivalent in English language-Dharma and Varna are two examples. The closest meaning in English is a force fit and not necessarily the right choice. The right approach in understanding Vedic concepts starts with learning of Sanskrit. As Swami Sivananda said "Varnasrama pertains to body alone, but not to the pure, allpervading, immortal soul or Atman. Attain Knowledge of the Self and become an Ativarnasrami like Lord Dattatreya. Hear what he says:-

Mahadadi jagat sarvam
Na kinchit pratibhati me
Brahmaiva kevalam sarvam
Katham varnasramasthitih
"The whole world, from Mahat downwards, does not shine in Me. Everything is Brahman only. Where then is Varnasrama?"

Vedic Vocations

Rather coincidentally, at the dawn of civilization, as the people gathered and lived in clans or tribes (Visha), they collectively-irrespective of their undertakings within Visha (such as in agriculture, woodworking, trade and other vocations)-came to be known as the Vaishya (meaning-belonging to Visha).

To meet the liturgical needs of the society, the Vaishya-from among themselves-would select, on the basis of skills in elocution, the Brahmins (students or orators of the Vedas-compiled knowledge). Similarly, for administrative purposes, Vaishya with qualities of leadership would be selected as Kshatriya (sovereign, tribal chieftain, administrator of Kshatar-dominion or tribal area / town). Furthermore, a Visha (tribe)-in addition to having the Vaishyas (including Brahmins, Kshatriya, cowherders and woodworkers etc.)-also embodied people known as Shudra (meaning-not of tribe) representing all the newcomers (immigrants) to that particular tribe. They included persons from other tribes (such as the vanquished foes and the migrants) and the children born out of inter-tribal unions.

Being somewhat new into that tribe and encountering unfamiliar rules, regulations and customs, a Shudra was limited in his vocational options and was generally relegated to providing service and assistance to members of the host tribe. But over time, like a modern day immigrant, he would surpass the tribal or social barriers so as to fully assimilate in that society and pursue other professions. Thus, all the responsibilities related to a Visha could be grouped into four sub-categories: Brahmin, Kshatriya, Vaishya and Shudra; the duties and skills involved with each of them are indicated in the following Sections.

Note also that, in old times, there was no concept of money or cash. People produced things and bartered (traded) them for other goods and services. A producer or trader belonging to Vaishya would include people such as farmer producing grains and milk etc., blacksmith (Lohar) making iron implements, leather-worker (Charmar or Chamar, charm meaning leather) manufacturing shoes, and so on.

Thus, for subsistence, a Brahmin would do worship (puja) in a 'Vaishya' farmer's house and get grains and milk in return. Similarly, a Chamar would exchange shoes for food items from a farmer, iron implements from a Lohar, and so on. Similarly, a 'Shudra' servant might work or help in a farmer's field for food in return. If he were to help a Lohar, then Lohar would provide him with food items. Moreover, all these people would give a share of their goods (produce) and services to the Kshatriya (tribal chief) for administration of Visha (tribe or society). Society was basically managed through bartering system.

Background and Discussion

Various Social and Cultural Issues: The ancient society recognized the importance of all. Irrespective of one's skill or background, there was a place for him / her to participate actively and make useful contribution. The ceremonial rites, though conducted by the learned priest, were open to all. People used prayers for atonement and benediction for all. Everyone sent their "heroes" (sons) to the battles for Visha or to protect and assist the Sovereign. A number of important aspects of the ancient society can be further clarified by considering the following passages (with references to one God or BRAHMAN+, and manifesting as Agni, Indra or Savitar) from Vedas& (ancient Hindu texts).

From the Rigveda:

"What God shall we adore with our oblation?...He is the God of gods and none beside Him...O Father, thou Creator of Heaven and Earth, by eternal Law ruling-protect us...O Almighty, the Lord of beings, you alone pervade all the created beings..." (Book 10, Hymn: 121.8-10)/p. 98

"We all possess various thoughts and plans and diverse are the callings of men. The carpenter seeks out that which is cracked, the physician the ailing, the priest the worshipper......." (Book 9, Hymn 112.1)/p. 84

"I am a bard, my father is a physician, my mother's job is to grind the corn......" (Book 9, Hymn 112.3)/p. 84

"The man who has awakened to the knowledge, becomes perfect. Let him speak for us to the gods..." (Book 5, Hymn 65.1)/p. 49

"May they, our Fathers who in their skill belong to the lowest order, attain higher one, those of midmost may attain the highest. May they who have attained a life of spirit, the knower of sacrifice, the guileless, help us when called upon...." (Book 10, Hymn 15.1-2)/p. 87

"Let gods lead us, let there be a stable union of the wife and husband... May authority be ever yours (i.e., wife's) in speech. Happy be you and prosper with your children, and be ever watchful to rule the household. Unite yourself with this man your husband. So authority will be yours in speech.. May the kinsman of the bride thrive well.." (Book 10, Hymn 85.26-28)/ p. 94

"May the gods grant riches to the men more liberal than the terrifying..." (Book 1, Hymn 185.9)/p. 26

From the Yajurveda:

"May gods anoint this man to be without rival, for mighty rule, for mighty dominion and for great splendour. This man, son of such a person, such a woman, of such a clan, is anointed king, O you subjects... He is your lord...He is also sovereign of our learned Brahmins...Let all men protect him." (Kanda 1, Prapathaka 8, Hymn i.8.10.c)/p. 54

"O Agni, may all mortals seek your friendship, the guide of all. May all solicit you for glory, riches and fame. May all of us prosper as you do." (Kanda 1, Prapathaka 3, Hymn i.4.46.a-c)/p. 64

"O Agni, grant glory to our Brahmins, set luster in our Kshatriyas, luster in our Vaishyas, luster in our Shudras.." (Kanda 5, Prapathaka 7, Hymn v.7.6.d)/ p. 102

"O god Savitar.. strengthen the life of subjects, strengthen the subjects..." (Kanda 1, Prapathaka 3, Hymn i.3.6.m-n)/p. 34

"O Agni...each fault done in a village or in forest, in society or mind, each sinful act that we have committed to Shudra or Vaishya or by preventing a religious act, even of that sin, you are the expiation..." (Kanda 1, Prapathaka 8, Hymn i.8.3.d) / p. 111

"He who knows well both knowledge and Nescience simultaneously, overcoming death by knowledge attains life immortal." (Isa Upanishad-verse 11) / p. 159

From the Samveda:

"May our subjects be rich and strong with the favour of Indra. May we be wealthy in food, rejoice with them..." (Part Second, Book 4, Ch. 1, Hymn 14) / p. 74

From the Bhagawad Gita:

As a part of God's creation (work), the four vocations are subgrouped according to people's guna (skills) and karma (assignments). Know that all work is for Him, even though He is beyond work, in Eternity. (Ch. 4-verse 13)

Ignorant men, but not the wise, say that Sankhya (variously as: Jnana Yoga, Sanyasa or Surrender, Path of Vision or Wisdom) and Yoga (variously as: Karma Yoga, Tyaga or Renunciation, Path of Action, Bhakti or devotional service, Japaa or Silence, Dhayana or Contemplation/Meditation, Brahamcharya or Austerity, Vaanprastha or Hermitlike) are different paths; but he who gives his self (soul) to one reaches the end of two. (Ch. 5-verse 4)

Even if the greatest sinner worships God with all his soul, he must be considered righteous because of his righteous will. (Ch. 9-verse 30)

And he shall soon become pure and reach everlasting peace. For this is His covenant that he who adores Him is not lost. (Ch. 9-verse 31)

God is one in all, but it seems as if he were many; He (as Vishnu / preserver) supports all beings: from Him (as Rudra/destroyer) ensues end, and from Him (as Brahma / creator) ensues beginning. (Ch. 13-verse 16)

The duties involving Brahmin, Kshatriya, Vaishya and Shudra are grouped according to people's abilities and skills. (Ch. 18-verse 41)

The skills for a Brahmin involve serenity, self-harmony, austerity and purity, loving-forgiveness and righteousness; vision, wisdom and faith. (Ch. 18- verse 42)

The qualities needed according to Kshatriya are: a heroic mind, splendor or inner fire, constancy, resourcefulness, courage in battle, generosity and noble leadership. (Ch. 18-verse 43)

Trade, agriculture and rearing of cattle may be tackled by Vaishya; and the background (tenure) of a Shudra is also suited to providing support. (Ch. 18-verse 44)

People attain perfection when they find joy in their work. Hear how a person attains perfection and finds joy in his work. (Ch. 18-verse 45)

A person achieves perfection when his work is-performed with pure feeling of-worship of God, from whom all things come and who is in all. (Ch. 18-verse 46)

The words of vision and wisdom have been conveyed. Ponder them in the silence of your soul, and then in freedom do your will. (Ch. 18-verse 63)

Hindu Dharma (Hinduism): Hinduism is religion based on the Vedas, and also known as the Sanatan Dharma (eternal religion) or Vedic Dharma.

In the Vedas, god Bhaga was the bestower of auspicious blessings. It soon became the power of goodness, and he who possessed this power was called Bhagvan. The religion associated with Bhagvan (or Bhagvat) was called Bhagvata Dharma.

Likewise, Indu (Soma-juice or nectar) used to be offered to God as libation in Vedic yajnas (worships), and consumed afterwards by people (Hindu) for health, life, prosperity and progeny. Hindu means as someone propitiated by Indu (the Vedic libation). Note, H--in Hindu, and pronounced as in hut--implies auspiciousness or delight.

Religion belonging to Hindu is called Hindu Dharma.

In response to the misconception that the word Hindu originated as some foreigners stepped into India, note that no one from outside could have come to India and started calling the locals Hindu suddenly if such a word (in Sanskrit--not those foreigners' language) had not already existed there. 'Hindu' also is not related to 'Sindhu'--a word with similar ending and meaning ocean or river, especially in the west of India.

The words Sindhu (ocean or river) and Hindu (expiated by Indu) are linguistically and phonetically different, and Hindu is not derived from Sindhu. Note that Vedic Sanskrit did use the letters (sounds) 's' and 'dh' and therefore would not replace them with 'h' and 'd', respectively, transforming Sindhu into Hindu. In addition, the ancient Greeks reaching India (circa Alexander the great) could have easily pronounced Sindhu without changing it to Hindu by dropping S in favour of H since they were used to pronounce Sigma (an alphabet in Greek, their mother-toungue) which is syllabically somewhat similar to Sindhu.

Furthermore, Muslims entering India for the first time and speaking Arabic or Persian—languages having alphabets Sad and Sin etc. for 's' sounds—would not have to substitute H for S in Sindhu (and thus make it Hindu) to pronounce or use it in their own languages. The word Hindu—not specific to any particular region or area—was already in use when these foreigners arrived in India, and they did not invent it from Sindhu accidentally or due to necessity.

Women's Issues: It seems from the above that the ancient society was quite considerate and respectful to those (both men and women) engaged in various vocations, and people were free to make choices or changes in their careers or skills if the opportunity existed. Vedic prayers also indicate that the women had considerable say in selecting their marriage partners, and were espoused to live in monogamous relationships while enjoying same rights as their husbands. Furthermore, in the Vedas there is little evidence of child marriages, dowry system and the practice of suttee or sati (self-immolation of a woman upon her husband's death).

Similarly, there is no indication of any stigma relating to widowhood or the remarriage of a widow. Note also that the well-educated, scholarly and charismatic women of yore, who also participated in many philosophical debates with men, included Gargi (the daughter of Vachaknu-from the Brihadaranyaka Upanishad) and Vidyottama (wife of the famed poet and writer, Kaalidasa, who started his life as a humble and menial worker in the woods). It is clear that the women or the lowly and humble in the society were neither ignored nor abandoned.

Listed below are a few examples of multi-vocational families and people changing their occupations and life styles.

(a) As indicated in the above, from the Rigveda, the mother of a bard (probably of the scriptures) was working in corn-grinding (an activity usually for a Shudra).

(b) Majority of the Rishis (sages) were both Brahmin and Kshatriya so as to manage their Aashramas (hermitages) effectively.

(c) In the Chandogya Upanishad, Satyakama (the illegitimate, varnasankra, son of a Shudra woman who did not even remember who her son's father was) went on to be accepted and educated for Brahmin work (the Gita: Ch. 18-verse 42). This shows that the people (including the Shudra and of unknown lineage) had the choice of pursuing any occupation (even that of a Brahmin).

(d) Valmiki (given to chanda-meaning impetuosity-in his early days) started life as a robber. But later in life, after performing penance, he studied to become a Brahmin. He went on to become a great Rishi (sage) and wrote the Ramayana in Sanskrit. Thus, going from being a chandaal (meaning-cruel and brutal person) to a great human being not only demonstrates his personal endeavour, but also that the society was quite accepting of such a process and its outcome. In general, as indicated here and in the Vedic passages, the concept of untouchability (with respect to the Shudra or any one else as a dalit / untouchable) did not exist. Any shunning or condemnation of a person was due mainly to his / her engaging in an activity not useful or acceptable to the society. Above all, it is also clear that any type of socially stigmatic situation could be easily improved through penance and by changing one's behaviour. Incidentally, this type of humane rehabilitation of criminals and sinners is a sign of civilized people long ago; and this humane practice exists even today in various countries claiming to be modern and civilized.

(e) In one of the stories from the Ramayana, Rishi Vishvamitra is said to have conducted Yajna (worship) at which the officiating priest was a once Kshatriya and the Yajamaan (worshipper) a Chandaal.

(f) In the Mahabharata, Satyavati (a Shudra-girl whose father was a fisherman), when presented with a marriage proposal from king Shantanu, married him only after he accepted her pre-nuptial agreement. Her own children, in stead of another older heir to the throne, went on to inherit the Kshatriya kingdom as was demanded in the pre-nuptial agreement. This indicates that the intercaste marriages and exchanges were quite prevalent; and that the women and Shudras could make free choices even when there was royalty involved.

(g) *Matrimonial and Vocational Choices:* The evolution of society and customs was mainly due to the individual and collective needs and choices (as indicated also in some of the above Vedic quotes on marriage, vocational activities etc.). In addition, the role and influence of various espoused or suggested proclamations such as involving the varnashrama dharma (casteo-monastic orders) etc.-based on non-scriptural (non-Vedic) writings (such as Manusmriti etc. accredited to Manu et al.)-on the development and progress of society at large (across-the-board) was rather insignificant.

The ancient society (generally modest and homogeneous economically) did not restrict the cross-caste matrimonial and occupational choices. In spite of the socially liberal conditions, though, the change in vocation did not always lead to significant economic gains. In addition, some vocations (*e.g.*, Vaishya and Shudra) were inherently conducive for their young to quickly and easily engage in the family business / profession and settle down (socially and economically) early in life. Consequently, the children from these families found the other vocations (such as the Brahmins and, to some extent, the Kshatriya) to be less rewarding and not worth the preparatory effort, which included living and training (and paying the teacher through labour) for decades in hermitages in harsh and forest-like conditions where the knowledge exchange between the guru and the pupils was usually in the oral tradition since the written manuscripts (on papyrus etc.) were scarce.

On the other hand, the children from the Brahmins and the Kshatriyas families were predisposed (through the natural and continuous exposure to the family business) and were readily inducted by their parents into their traditional professions. Over time, this type of selecting the professions inadvertently gave rise to the tradition of vocation based families all around even though the society had not sought such an outcome. Note that the society in this respect remained flexible and allowed people (including the Shudra, who also engaged in menial and ignoble pursuits) the freedom of choice in their undertakings.

In a similar and related context, it was deemed vocationally advantageous and convenient for a couple to marry if they both had the same background, because they would then be able to get involved in their family occupation quickly and easily without facing any uncertainty or requiring any additional apprenticeship. Moreover, the bride or the groom in this type of wedding arrangement would be less likely to encounter any unexpected, unfamiliar, inhospitable and unwanted post-marital social situations. Note also that, in addition to the weddings involving same type of families, the marriages among people from vastly different backgrounds also frequently took place (as in the case of Satyavati and Shantanu) and the society posed no restrictions.

Thus it was basically an arbitrary social custom which arose over time as a matter of convenience whereby the people stuck to their family professions and also married within same type of families (vocations). Note, the lack of relevant information available in print etc. probably also led to the guru-pupil based disciplic tradition for knowledge/spirituality which would otherwise be not as crucial. In any case, people (of any caste) desiring to not follow these customs or to break away from them simply should go on their own-without any fear of repercussions from the state, society or religion-to learn and pursue new vocations; and in the process they would also be able to find compatible and willing marriage partners for themselves within the society at large. Moreover (as regards to the Gita: Ch. 5-V. 18, Ch. 6-V. 9, Ch. 9-V. 32), the priests and temples that serve (cater to) and admit all (Brahmin, Kshatriya, Vaishya, Shudra including the disadvantaged or Dalit) should be accorded the greatest respect and support.

Illustration of the Rise of Sub-castes within Castes: As humans continued to create and adopt new occupations, move to new places and territories, or encounter unfamiliar surroundings and situations, the four primary vocations (castes: Brahmin, Kshatriya, Vaishya and Shudra) developed or transformed into several secondary sub-castes characterized by peoples' tasks etc. For example, vocationally speaking, if a person-while trying to become a Brahmin-learnt two Vedas, he would be called a Dwivedi, whereas the learner of three Vedas would be known as a Trivedi. It shows that titles (or sub-castes) as Dwivedi and Trivedi basically correspond to certain specific Brahminic pursuits.

Similarly, a Vaishya engaged in forming objects from loha (iron) would be called the Lohar, whereas, the maker of articles from sona (gold) would be called the Sonar. Moreover, if a Sonar's son pursued his father's occupation (business) and was followed by his son, and so on, it would give rise to a sub-caste (lineage) called Sonars within the Vaishya caste. Note that such preference or tradition for family business would occur for several reasons. First, the parents generally found it easy and safe to guide their young towards a familiar and time assured vocation. Second, the familiarity with parents' job made it easy for children to learn and practice that occupation. Third, it might probably help in attaining the familial stability and lead to an easy transfer of accumulated knowledge and expertise between generations.

The influence of migration on sub-castes can be similarly explored. Consider the following example. At some point in history, a certain inhabited area was to be inundated under a new dam and the people had to move and live elsewhere. As they settled in a new area, the locals there would address them as the Damiya (meaning-from the dam). Some of the newcomers might even prefer this new title to that they had before moving to the new place. Moreover, when, for example, a newcomer (migrant or Shudra) started working as Mistree (mason), he would be called a Damiya-Mistree (a Vaishya-usually a person in non-priestly or non-administrative occupation). Similarly, if the person worked as a priest, he would be known as the Damiya-Brahmin. This indicates that the title 'Damiya' had suddenly acquired the status as a sub-caste. More importantly, note that two principal castes (Brahmin and Vaishya) had gained sub-castes with the same name (Damiya) with reference to totally different tasks (as priests and masons).

The above examples illustrate the manner in which the sub-castes are created and the way they relate to the principal castes. Note also that, depending on the circumstances, the newly created sub-castes may either co-exist with the original sub-castes, or replace some or all of the latter. This surely can lead to drastic fluctuations in their numbers. As this process of creating and retaining of sub-castes occurs time and again over vast places and cultures, their numbers remain uncertain and alter frequently making it difficult to keep track of them. Nonetheless, the sub-castes are functional in character and subject to easy transformations.

Vedic/Hindu Tenets: The ancients were in favour of progressive ideas (*e.g.*, about the environment, philosophy / religion and life style) and appear to have conducted their affairs reasonably and democratically. They either shunned or actively opposed the stagnant, blind and baseless practices (rituals) and the intolerant / autocratic persons and beliefs (faiths). The rituals for invocations of the physical, imagery (tales / myths) and the mundane were deemed less rewarding than the meditation of the spiritual, the source (truth / logic) and the divine; (meditation is explained in Ch. 6 of the Gita). Note that the reality expressed in terms of various physical (artistic) forms or through poetry can have different interpretations. For example, in some of the ancient texts, a viman may just be a cart or chariot and not necessarily an airplane or sky-craft.

While considering chatur as four (and bhuj meaning arm, and mukh meaning face or mouth), chatur-bhuj and chatur-mukh are shown as four-armed and four-faced idols. In stead, consider for example, chatur as the skilled one: chatur-bhuj and chatur-mukh will then represent, anthropomorphically (like a human with a face and two arms), a god (deva: friendly and blissful, superior being) who is skilled-armed (or ambidextrous: probably in all the occupations) and skilled-orator (*i.e.*, a fine instructor).

Thus, chatur-bhuj and chatur-mukh are, respectively, symbols of the omnipotence and the omniscience of One God, or reflect His excellence in enterprise (as Vishnu) and instruction (as Brahma). God is One: Braham or Brahman (not the Brahmin caste). When He (as Atman) enters the body (or as spirit unites with nature), life begins, and He is called Brahma. As long as He stays in the body, the life continues, and He is seen as preserving it and is called Vishnu. Once He leaves the body, life ends (or body expires); and His departure is seen as if He has worked as Rudra in bringing an end to life. But, throughout, He remains One: Brahma, Vishnu and Rudra are only His aspects of creation, preservation and termination.

Thus, in regard to man-made symbols for displaying various Divine attributes for the purposes of worship and meditation etc., there should be some correspondence between the attribute and the symbol. For example, if omnipotent God is to be represented 'as meaning Vishnu' in human form, it is sufficient and logical to interpret chatur (in chatur-bhuj) as skilled (even as ambidextrous) in all the tasks. Similarly, if omniscient God is to be represented 'as meaning Brahma' in human form, it is sufficient and logical to interpret chatur (in chatur-mukh) as skilled in oratory and knowledge.

Thus, there is no need to interpret chatur as four in chatur-bhuj or chatur-mukh; and hence it is unnecessary to assume or create various four-headed and four-armed religious symbols for representing God anthropomorphically. Incidentally, note also in Ch. 11 of the Gita, Arjuna-after having realized vision of the Omnipresent encompassing all Creation-wishes (verse 46) to see the lord (mentor) in chatur-bhuj form (holding scepter and circle), which seems to refer only to latter's dexterity. And Arjuna's wish is soon fulfilled (Ch. 11-V. 50) as he is able to see Krishan as a regular (normal looking) person, and there is no suggestion anywhere that the former had an encounter with anyone bearing four arms.

Metaphorically speaking, Shiv-Linga (or Shiv-Lingam) refers only to Shiva-the remover of destruction, *i.e.*, same as the preserver (Vishnu or God), and it necessarily is not a certain special symbol (*e.g.*, shown often in pollex or index form); because in Linga (or Lingam), the word Li (which in second or Object case singular form becomes Lim or Lin with nasal sound ending) means loss or destruction, and ga (or gam) implies removing or going away. Thus, Shiv-Linga (or Shiv-Lingam) symbolizes God's power (attribute) to extricate from destruction or loss.

Note also that the symbol (such as, the pollex, ling or phallus looking), portrayed in various religious rituals (Hindu and elsewhere), has probably the origins in the ancient fire (Agni) sacrifice or worship to God. It appears to be a solid image of jwala (flame) from a yajna (sacrificial fire) and was perhaps introduced long ago as a duplicate for the sacrificial fire. Because creating and lighting of a yajna used to be a very difficult and time-consuming process (as indicated in some of the Vedic hymns also), this image made the worship possible anywhere anytime (*i.e.*, by using it in place of live fire and pouring oblations upon it).

Note that the smearing of the solid symbol with ash also points to a close association with fire worship. Similarly, when this fire (Agni) solid (symbol) is placed under a pitcher from which the libation slowly and continuously flows over it, it appears to give the impression of an unending and uninterrupted active worship even during the absence of worshippers. There, the solid symbol represents the live fire in a yajna and the pitcher (with dripping libation) symbolizes the worshipper pouring oblations into the fire. In addition, it is worth noting that some of the practices in present-day worships appear to relate closely to the original fire sacrifice: the lighting of lamps or candles represents the actual or original fire (flame), and the burning of incense recreates the aroma that would be given off by the oblations (soma etc.) into the live fire.

In this regard, the symbols dedicated to Agni (or Shiv, God) should also correspond to logic and not just to myth or fiction. The identification of Agni symbol (*i.e.*, jwala, or Agni-ling: ling meaning symbol) as a phallus is perhaps due to the confusion that their shapes are similar. Note that the early humans were praying and worshipping for everything. They also prayed to God for children (heroes, sons). In this regard, religiously and psychologically, the Agni symbol 'looking like phallus' became the favourite idol. Unfortunately, over time, people forgot about its association with Agni, and identified it only in terms of biology and procreation. (Note: Since Shiva refers also to the auspicious flame or Agni-jwala, Agni-ling or a similar looking object probably was referred to as Shiv-ling.)

Note, Agni is a manifestation of BRAHMAN or Iswara. Agni in the male aspect is Shiva, and as female is Shakti. The Agni-jwala (flame) is called Shiva. The common symbols (*e.g.*, long or stubby ling or symbol) for Shiva and Shakti are just solid images of Agni (Yajna fire). Incidentally, Shiva and Shakti always appear together--perhaps due to their common association with Agni. Moreover, Agni is also probably the biggest destroyer. Thus the connection between Agni and Shiva as the destroyers can be seen. On the other hand, Shankra is the greatest among Rudras; and Rudras are destroyers. Thus Shiva (through a connection with Agni as the greatest destroyer) probably, in His destructive aspect at least, is also identified with Shankra (the greatest Rudra destroyer). Note, Agni probably also is the origin of a number of other dark coloured gods (idols), where their colour corresponds to dark (black) coloured ash (associated with fire or yajna).

In references to Hanumat or Hanuman, the name appears simply to imply a strong-jawed (or a very strong) person and not necessarily a monkey or monkey-chief. Similarly, Ganesha or Ganapati may simply mean Lord (Isha, Pati) of the people (Gana) and not just an elephant-headed figure (ganika meaning a female elephant).

Thus, it seems that there is a tendency to express and endorse a certain specific divine trait as a whole (entire) phenomenon through recognizable art (shapes and forms) and stories (fictional accounts) to make it more appealing and understandable to the masses. Unfortunately, if such a message is not communicated properly or is lost over time, it will mislead and confuse people and may even wrongly imply that there is more than one real source of divinity. Note, as indicated also in Rigveda (Book 1: Hymn 164 # 46) and the Gita (Ch. 13: Verse 16), the Source basically is, locally and universally, the same and complete in essence and attributes.

Similarly, in the Rigveda, the division of Purusha (Being or Spirit) is indicated to have taken place at the beginning; the implication of which really is the transcendence of the (chaotic) old into the (stable) new in terms of evolution of the society. There, the emergence of Brahmin, Kshatriya, Vaishya and Shudra from the body of Purusha symbolically corresponds, respectively, to their occupations giving the society its voice (arising as if from Purusha's mouth), order (as if through Purusha's arms), form (as if on Purusha's thighs), and change or migration (as if via Purusha's feet).

Furthermore, in the three original (basic to Hinduism) Vedas (Rig, Yajur and Sam) referred to above, little mention or support is shown for astrology; and sorcery, witchcraft, magic and worthless worships are condemned (RV: Book 7, Hymn 104.20, 23-25; Book 10, Hymn 37.4). Similarly (RV: Book 7, Hymn 104.5,7, 13-16), civic or religious (for god or faith) deception (corruption, cheating and wickedness) and exploitation (including coercion, bondage, aggression and plundering) are forbidden and not to be tolerated.

Note, the Gita (Ch. 16) reiterates these precepts; and (Ch. 3-V. 26) favours advancing of religion/spirituality peacefully and by example.

Salvation, Karma, Reincarnation and Metamorphosis: It was realized long ago that, irrespective of one's background, attaining the immortality or overcoming the death (or the fear of it) is in understanding oneself (individual life or being)-the union between soul (spirit-real, sat or eternal) and body (matter-unreal, asat or transient)-as part of the Supreme (stated also in Ch. 2, 6, 7 & 9 of the Bhagawad Gita). Symbolically, therefore (as stated in Ch. 8 of the Gita), following the path (or going in the time) of clarity (as in the light of day or the sun) about the self is liberating (Ch. 6); whereas, following the path (or going in the time) of confusion (as in the darkness of night or the moon) about the self brings nothing but fear (morbidity). It is worth noting (the Gita: Ch. 6-verse 45) that, whatever a person's social status or civic duty, the spiritual gains derived from all efforts for achieving the union of one with the One are imminent and cumulative.

In this context, the Karmic principle (*i.e.*, a good or bad action leads to a good or bad outcome) is assumed to influence the course of events taking place during this life and, supposedly, afterwards. Accordingly, each experience or action by a person affects him in body* and soul in the next situation or future. Each experience itself is a life/Janma: its beginning and end symbolically being birth and death. Moreover, according to the Karmic principle, even when the body dies, the soul continues to live and may feel the residual effect of the preceding existence. The reincarnation therefore symbolically represents the extension of this principle during the hereafter.

It is, in other words, a new opportunity or promise to accrue spiritual gains on the basis of actions during previous life. Note also that reincarnation merely presents to a person a new possibility (opportunity) arising out of countless influences, and, depending upon the new surroundings (people, environment etc.) and the future actions by the individual himself, it may or may not fully materialize (the Gita: Ch. 18-verse 14). For example, as indicated above, even though Satyakama started as a Shudra (in a non-Brahmin vocation), he went on, through his own initiative and effort and with the help of his guru, to acquire new skills to become a Brahmin (the profession of choice for him).

Thus, reincarnation-being associated with the soul-appears to be unimportant with regards to the worldly pursuits such as involving vocations (castes) etc. Similarly, salvation (Moksha)-which also relates to the soul-is achievable by all (irrespective of their background), and can be easily attained by uniting (elevating) one's soul with God by practicing good deeds and penance etc. The Gita, to this end, states (in Ch. 2)-in response to a query in Ch. 1 (verse 42) regarding the rituals to ancestors-that God's grace and the good deeds by a person during his own lifetime are important to seek salvation.

The supposed metamorphoses of God as Ram and Krishan etc., heroes of the early civilizations (in epics Ramayana and Mahabharata etc.), should be taken in spiritual/moralistic/ philosophical context. The reverence (mainly ritualistic or for a reward) to them-dedicated according to their physical eminence and existence, and based primarily on the stories which appear to be skewed over time into myths/tales (Pauranic etc.)-thus needs to reduce. Note that God alone is deemed worthy of all worships (the Gita: Ch. 9-V. 24, Chs. 10 & 4) since all the eminence and creation--including even all the gods and goddesses associated with various places, times or events--are ultimately due to Him. Incidentally, when Krishna speaks in the Gita, he is not only speaking as a friend (well-wisher) and charioteer (worker and assistant) of Arjuna, but he is also advising Arjuna in the capacity of a guru. Above all, in essence, Krishna also is both BRAHMAN (Iswara) and Atman in the Gita.

Note also in this regard that the notion of a personal God sometimes results in a very informal devotee-deity relationship. The devotee often uses various preferred salutations, representations and rituals (worships and offerings) to express his unique love and reverence towards the 'kind and caring' deity. But, when many people engaging in this manner-in their own special ways of worships, etc., are viewed collectively, their society is seen to be overly ritualistic and following many gods, even though, in reality the ultimate object of reverence remains One. (Note, the Gita: Ch. 9-V. 26).

Conclusion: The vocational choice long ago was mainly need-based (personal and tribal) and circumstantial (in terms of the availability of labour at a place or time, natural disasters and battles among tribes). It inspired that the societal tasks and responsibilities be dispensed solely in terms of a person's nature or qualification (Guna) and his active undertaking or assignment (Karma). It was a great vision at work that is referred to also in the Bhagawad Gita (as in the original Sanskrit verse 13 of Ch. 4, where the reference is made only to Guna-nature/qualification, and it does not mean born nature). Incidentally, the original vocations seem to have been similar to the present jobs that also require compatibility between the worker's qualifications and the potential assignment.

Inherently, the above system satisfied one and the all. The Gita (Ch. 18-verse 41) further elaborates that all occupations are important and correspond to various needs or segments of the society and are dispensed according to ability (svabhava) on the basis (prabhva) of qualification (guna; which does not mean born nature). The duties relating to each adopted vocation (as explained in the above Introduction: Brahmin, Kshatriya, Vaishya, Shudra) are also listed in the Gita (Ch. 18-verses 42, 43 & 44). It is also indicated in the Gita (Ch. 5-verse 4) that all spiritual paths are applicable and bring same results to people with different vocations.

The Gita (Ch. 16 & 18) stresses that, while it is of utmost importance to recognize and adhere to one's own responsibility or the task at hand, there is no other special advantage or basis (in terms of ritualism or one's heredity) for pursuing a particular undertaking. A socially necessary and useful activity for the physical well-being of person is as important as any worship/puja for his/her salvation (The Gita: Ch. 3-verse 8). The Gita (Ch. 3-verse 35) further notes that taking care of one's own responsibility (purpose/dharma) merits higher than venturing needlessly elsewhere, since keeping one's own obligation (even in a miniscule way) leads to satisfaction that outweighs the trappings, uncertainty and formidableness associated with another's task.

It is also stated in the Gita (Ch. 12, Ch. 18-verses 45 & 46) that, no matter what a person's duty or task (whether shubh-appealing, or ashubh-unappealing), he attains perfection or heavenly bliss if he is fully dedicated to it and performs it with pleasure and interest as if it were a service to the Lord (Transcendent or the Manifest). Lord, God or Hari (Saviour) is expressed (Ch. 17) divinely (in accordance with tattva) as OM TAT SAT (Creator, Master and the Righteous). (Creation seems to arise from OM during contemplation as the omniscient, TAT is what maintains it through omnipotence, and it has the noble and righteous end according to SAT.) Note also that God is one, yet He can manifest in more ways than one (Ch. 4 & 9); and He dwells in the heart of all (Ch. 18). He is One in all (stated above; the Gita: Ch. 13-verse 16). In addition, one need not be preoccupied about the hereafter (or the heaven and the hell) as long as he understands the good from the bad (Ch. 16 of the Gita) and the redemption (spiritual) through penance (monetarily free and as stated in the Gita: Ch. 9-verses 30 & 31).

Thus, the Vedic religion (Hinduism) is universal and progressive: the Hindu way of life is open to all, and without any discrimination on the basis of gender, race, heredity, beliefs, occupation, social status or background, and the place of origin. It is very logical (promotes knowledge and science / vigyan-the Gita: Ch. 6-verse 8), encourages reasoning (the Gita: Ch. 18-verses 63, 71 & 72), and is quite easy to understand and practice (as indicated in Ch. 3, 9 & 16 of the Gita). It is based on the fundamental principle of 'one to One relationship' or unity between a person and the universal God. In other words (*e.g.* the Gita: Ch. 9-v. 10 & 29), everyone abides identically to the supreme, is significant to the creation, and has the same right to seek and realize the divine. In conclusion and at the personal level, one easily attains perfection and heavenly bliss in any activity (duty) if he / she keeps anger, lust and greed in check (the Gita: Ch. 16); stays mindful of the Lord (the Gita: Ch. 8), such as in the sense of the mantra (sacred words) 'Hari OM TAT SAT' (the universal God is the means of salvation); and through that undertaking (activity) adores/serves Him and His creation (the Gita: Ch. 11 & 18).

Thus it is also clear from the above that one (of any caste or background) need not feel disadvantaged, discriminated, dispossessed or deprived of spirituality as a Hindu if he/she pursues God by own free will in a manner convenient or appropriate to him/her. Remember that everyone is entitled to the same inspiration (guidance) and bliss (love) from God, who (as the source of vision and benediction) is the ultimate (greatest) guru/prophet (the Gita: Ch. 11) and friend / benefactor (the Gita: Ch. 5).

Closing Comment: It is okay for a person-having no one to extend to him objective or satisfactory help and guidance in the matters relating to spiritual fulfilment, prayer and the place to pray-to choose a mode of worship suited to his needs and resources. Incidentally, worthless worships, myths / tales, hate-mongering and evil/corrupt deeds are detrimental to spirituality / faith.

It is also worth noting that all-men, women, believers, nonbelievers and others-have the same rights and freedoms and they all deserve equal protection and consideration under a law that is constantly evolving with time and according to the need of the society.

Thus, a contemporary civil legal code-progressive and reflective of the peoples and times-seems preferable to a law that may be perceived as antiquated, dictatorial, discriminatory, cultist or religious.

The notion that a group/nation run by decree will be foremost in freedoms and human rights is misguided. A diverse, pluralistic and progressive society subjected to an autocratic or religious law/ rule can quickly drift into a puritanical, singular and regressive system as the dissenting people either run away from it or totally succumb to the ruling dogma to ensure their own safety. Thus, the sectarian territorialization or vision of the world must cease, and any regime adverse to progressiveness should be shunned.

In addition, the practices of casteism (social stratification in terms of vocation or caste), animal abuse, child labour, gender discrimination, dowry, veil (*e.g.* the body and face covering apparel) etc. must stop. It is also in the interest of humanity to rise above various tenets and practices and, while not ignoring the local issues, tackle serious global problems: rapidly deteriorating environment, depleting natural resources, disappearing flora and fauna, and overpopulation-already indicating a population exceeding the reasonable limit of about five billion people worldwide..

Bibliography

Adikaram, E. W.: *Early History of Buddhism in Ceylon,* D. S. Puswella, Migoda, 1946.

Agrawala, V. S.: *Shiva Mahadeva: The Great God,* Veda Academy, Varanasi, 1966.

Ahmad, Imtiaz: *State and Foreign Policy: India's Role in South Asia,* Vikas, New Delhi, 1993.

Ahmad, Jamil-ud-din: *Some Recent Speeches and Writings of Mr. Jinnah,* Lahore, Ashraf, 1952.

Aiyar, R. Krishnaswami: *Outlines of Vedaanta,* Chetana, Bombay, 1978.

Archer, W. G.: *The Kama Sutra,* Unwin Hyman, London, 1990.

Ashton, S.R. : *British Policy Towards the Indian States, 1905-1939,* London, Curzon, 1982.

Aurobindo, Sri: *Vyasa and Valmiki,* Acharya Press, Pondicherry, 1956.

Avalon, Arthur and Ellen: *Hymns to the Goddess,* Ganesh and Co., Madras, 1964.

Aziz, Ashraf: *Light of the Universe: Essays on Hindustani Film Music,* Three Essays Collective, New Delhi, 2003.

Bagchi, P. C.: *Studies in Dharmashastra,* University of Calcutta Press, Calcutta, 1939.

Bahadur, K.P.: *The Wisdom of Vedaanta,* Sterling Publishers Private Limited, New Delhi, 1996.

Banerjea, J. N.: *Pauranic and Vedanta Religion,* University of Calcutta, Calcutta, 1996.

Bankimchandra, C.: *Essentials of Dharma,* Sanskrit Book Depot, Calcutta 1979.

Basu, Manoranjan: *Dharmashastra: A General Study,* Shrimati Mira Basu, Calcutta, 1976.

Beaumont, Roger : *Sword of the Raj: The British Army in India, 1747-1947*, Indianapolis, Bobbs-Merrill, 1977.

Benjamin, Joseph : *Scheduled Castes in Indian Politics and Society*, New Delhi, Ess Ess Publications, 1989.

Bhattacharyya, B.: *Nispannayogavali of Mahapandita Abhyakara Gupta*, Oriental Institute, Baroda, 1949.

Borchert, Bruno: *Mysticism: Its History and Challenge*, Samuel Wiser, York Beach, 1994.

Bose, D. N.: *Dharmashaṣtra: Their Philosophy and Occult Secrets*, Kali Press, Calcutta, 1965.

Bowle, John: *The Imperial Achievement: The Rise and Transformation of the British Empire*, Little, Brown, 1974.

Brockington, J. L.: *Righteous Rama: The Evolution of an Epic*, Oxford, London, 1984.

Bromley, D.: *Krishna Consciousness in the West*, Bucknell University Press, Lewisburg, 1989.

Brooks, E.: *The Original Analects: Sayings of Confucius and His Successors*. Columbia University Press, New York, 1988.

Bruhn, Klaus: *The Jina-Images of Deogarh*, MacMillan, Leiden, 1969.

Burke, Mary Louise: *Swami Vivekananda in America: New Discoveries*, Advaita Ashrama, Calcutta, 1966.

Chaudhary, M.: *Partition and the Curse of Rehabilitation*, Calcutta, Bengal Rehabilitation Organization, 1964.

Chaudhuri, Nirad: *Thy Hand, Great Anarch! India: 1921-1952*, London, Chatto & Windus, 1987.

Coomeraswamy, Ananda K.: *Buddha and the Gospel of Buddhism*, MacMillan, London, 1928.

Crawford, Cromwell S.: *Ram Mohan Roy: His Era and Ethics*, Acharya Press, New Delhi, 1984.

Dalton, Dennis : *Gandhi's Power : Nonviolence in Action*, New Delhi, OUP, 2001.

Danielou, Alain: *The Complete Kama Sutra*, Park Street Press, Rochester, 2000.

Dasgupta, Shahana: *Rani Lakshmibai: The Indian Heroine*, Rupa & Company, Calcutta, 2002.

Datta, V.N.: *Sati: Widow Burning in India*, Manohar, New Delhi, 1990.

David, M. D.: *John Wilson and his Institutions*, Mumbai, 1957.

De Bary: *Self and Society in Ming Thought*, Columbia University Press, New York, 1970.

De, Sushil Kumar: *Ancient Indian Erotics and Erotic Literature*, Firma K. L. Mukhopadhyay, Calcutta, 1959.

Deak, Istvan: *The Lawful Revolution: Louis Kossuth and the Hungarians 1848-1849*, Columbia University Press, 1979.

Dhar, Niranjan: *Vedanta and Bengal Renaissance*, Minerva Associates, Calcutta, 1977.

Dikshit, D.P. *Political History of the Chalukyas of Badami*. New Delhi: Abhinav, 1980.

Donat, K.: *Meditate the Tantric Yoga Way*, George Allen and Unwin, London, 1973.

Doniger, W.: *The Rig Veda: An Anthology*, Penguin, New York, 1981.

Duboi, Abbe: *Hindu Manners, Customs and Ceremonies*, Fifth Indian Impression, CUP, 1985.

Dwivedi, M.: *The Principal Upanishads*, Adyar Library, Madras, 1931.

Eaton, Richard M.: *Sufis of Bijapur, 1300-1700: Social Roles of Sufis in Medieval India*, Princeton University Press, Princeton, 1978.

Edwardes, Michael: *Battles of the Indian Mutiny*, London; B. T. Batsford Ltd., 1963.

Erickson, Erik H.: *Gandhi's Truth: On the Origins of Militant Nonviolence*, Norton, New York, 1970.

Farquhar, J.N.: *Modern Religious Movements in India*, Munshiram, New Delhi, 1967.

Fay, Peter Ward: *The Opium War, 1840-42*, University of North Carolina Press, 1975.

Fisher, Michael H.: *The Politics of British Annexation of India - 1757-1857*, Oxford, 1996.

Frauwallner, E..: *History of Indian Philosophy*, Motilal, Delhi, 1973.

Gambhirananda, S.: *Brahma Sutra Shamkar Bhasya*, Adavita Ashrama, Calcutta, 1977.

Gambhirananda, Swami: *Brahma Sutra Shamkar Bhasya*, Adavita Ashrama, Calcutta, 1977.

Gandhi, M. K.: *The Story of My Experiment With Trust*, Washington, Public Affairs Press, 1948.

Keith, Arthur Berriedale: *The Religion and Philosophy of the Veda and Upanishads*, MacMillan, Delhi, 1925.

Kishwar, Madhu : *Religion at the Service of Nationalism, and Other Essays*, OUP, Delhi, 1998.

Klaus, K.: *A Survey of Hinduism,* State University of New York Press, Albany, 1989.

Knipe, M.: *Hinduism: Experiments in the Sacred,* Harper, San Francisco, 1991.

Knott, K.: *Hinduism, A Very Short Introduction,* Oxford University Press, New York, 1998.

Kosambi, D. D. : *The Culture and Civilisation of Ancient India in Historical Outline,* London, Routledge and Kegan Paul, 1956.

Kottackal, Jacob: *Religion and Ethics in Advaita,* C.M.S. Press, Kottayam, 1982.

Kuiper, F.B.J. : *Aryans in the Rigveda,* Rodopi, Amsterdam, 1991.

Kuppuswamy, Sastri S.: *Compromises in the History of Advaitic Thought,* Kalyani Press, Madras, 1940.

Louis, Fischer: *Essential Gandhi: An Anthology of His Writings,* Vintage, New York, 1983.

Low, D. A. and Brasted, Howard: *Freedom, Trauma, Continuities: Northern India and Independence,* New Delhi, Sage Publications, 1998.

Maheshwari, Shriram: *Rural Development in India: A Public Policy Approach,* New Delhi, Sage, 1995.

Makhan, L.: *The Ramayana of Valmiki,* Munshiram Manoharlal, New Delhi, 1978.

Mathew, Arnold: *Culture and Anarchy,* The University Press, Cambridge, 1935.

Mayer, A. : *Caste in an Indian Village: Change and Continuity 1954-1992,* Delhi, OUP, 1996.

Mazumder, Sukhendu : *Politico-Economic Ideas of Mahatma Gandhi: Their Relevance in the Present Day,* New Delhi, Concept Pub., 2004.

Mearns, David J.: *Shiva's Other Children: Religion and Social Identity amongst Overseas Indians,* Sage, Walnut Creek, 1995.

Mearns, J.: *Shiva's Other Children: Religion and Social Identity amongst Overseas Indians,* Sage, Walnut Creek, 1995.

Mehra, Parshotam: *A Dictionary of Modern Indian History, 1707-1947*, New Delhi, Oxford University Press, 1985.

Metcalf, Thomas R.: *The Aftermath of the Revolt: India, 1857-1870*, Princeton, Princeton University, 1964.

Mohan, K.: *The Mahabharata*, Munshiram Manoharlal, Delhi 1997.

Mookerjee, Ajit: *Kali The Feminine Force*, Thames and Hudson, London, 1988.

Mookerji, Satkari: *Modern Polity and Vedanta*, Sanskrit College, Calcutta, 1972.

Moon, Penderel: *The British Conquest and Dominion of India*, London, Duckworth, 1989.

Morris-Jones, W.H.: *The Government and Politics of India*, London, Hutchinson, 1971.

Nanda, B. R. : *Gandhi and His Critics*, Oxford University Press, Delhi, 1993.

Neale, Walter C.: *Economic Change in Rural India: Land Tenure and Reform in the United Provinces, 1800-1955*, New Haven, 1962.

Nevile, P.: *Lahore: A Sentimental Journey*, New Delhi, Penguin, 1993.

Oddie, G.A. : *Hindu and Christian in South-East India*, London, Curzon Press, 1991.

Pathak, Dr S.P.: *Jhansi during the British Rule*, Ramanand Vidya Bhawan, Delhi, 1987.

Preston, Diana: *The Boxer Rebellion*, Berkley Books, 2000.

Raimundo Panikkar: *The Vedic Experience: Mantramanjari*, Longman Todd, London, 1977.

Raja, C. Kunhan : *The Taittiriya Sarvanukramani of Yaska*, Madras, 1931.

Ramamurti, A.: *Advaitic Mysticism of Sankara*, Visvabharati, Santiniketan, 1974.

Ranajit Guha: *A Construction of Humanism in Colonial India*, CASA, Amsterdam, 1993.

Renou, Louis: *The Nature of Dharmashastra*, Walker and Co., New York, 1997.

Robson, Brian: *Sir Hugh Rose and the Central India Campaign*, Sutton Publishing Ltd for the Army Records Society, UK, 2000.

Satyapal Verma: *Role of Reason in Sankara Vedanta*, Parimal Publication, Delhi, 1992.

Savarkar, Vinayak Damodar : *The Indian War of Independence* 1857 Rajdhani Granthagar, Delhi, 1988.

Scheftelowitz, Isidor : *Die Kasmirische Rezension von Katyayanas Sarvanukramani,* Zeitschrift fur Indologie und Iranistik, 1922.

Shukla, D. N.: *Vastu-Shastra,* Motilal Banarsidass, Delhi, 1966.

Singh, Birendra Kumar: *Early Chalukyas of Vatapi, circa A.D. 500 to 757*, Delhi, Eastern Book Linkers, 1991.

Smith, Col. J. T. : *Silver and the India Exchanges,* Effingham Wilson, London, 1876.

Strauss, L.: *Political Philosophy,* The Bobbs Merrill Co., New York, 1975.

Swami Vishnu Tirtha: *Devatma Shakti,* Swami Shivom Tirth, Rishikesh, 1962.

Talageri, Shrikant : *Aryan Invasion Theory and Indian Nationalism,* Voice of India, Delhi, 1993.

Tejomayananda, Swami: *Hindu Culture: An Introduction,* Chinmaya Publications, Piercy, 1993.

Thapar, Romila : *Ashoka and the Decline of the Mauryas,* London, Oxford University Press, 1961.

Thompson, Edward: *The Making of the Indian Princes,* Oxford University Press, London, 1943.

Trautmann, Thomas R.: *Kautilya and the Arthasastra: A Statistical Study,* Leiden, Brill, 1971.

Trimingham, J.: *Sufi Orders in Islam,* Oxford University Press, New York, 1998.

Utpat, V.N.: *Riddles of Buddha and Ambedkar,* Itihas Patrika Prakashan, Thane 1988.

Vable, D.: *The Arya Samaj. Hindu without Hinduism.* Vikas Publ., Delhi, 1983.

Vedalankar, Pandit Nardev : *Basic Teachings of Hinduism,* Veda Niketan, Durban, 1978.

Visvantha, K.: *Essentials of Hinduism,* Narosa Pub. House, New Delhi, 1989.

Wendy Doniger: *Siva: The Erotic Ascetic,* Oxford University Press, Delhi, 1998.

Zaidi, A. Moin: *Evolution of Muslim political Thought in India,* New Delhi: S. Chand, 1975.

Index

T

U

V

W

Y

Z

□□□